SUN
KING

SUN
KING

The Life and Times of
SAM PHILLIPS,
the Man Behind
SUN RECORDS

KEVIN AND TANJA CROUCH

piatkus

PIATKUS

First published in Great Britain in 2008 by Piatkus
This paperback edition published in 2009 by Piatkus
Reprinted 2011, 2012, 2013, 2014

A CIP catalogue record for this book
is available from the British Library.

ISBN 978-0-7499-2946-6

Typeset in Stone Serif by Palimpsest Book Production Limited,
Grangemouth, Stirlingshire
Printed and bound in Great Britain by
Clays Ltd, St Ives plc

Papers used by Piatkus are from well-managed forests
and other responsible sources.

MIX
Paper from
responsible sources
FSC® C104740
www.fsc.org

Piatkus
An imprint of
Little, Brown Book Group
100 Victoria Embankment
London EC4Y 0DY

An Hachette UK Company
www.hachette.co.uk

www.piatkus.co.uk

Contents

Introduction

ALTHOUGH THE CITY'S official slogan, 'The Home of the Blues and the Birthplace of Rock and Roll', is of fairly recent origin, Memphis has a long musical tradition. Geographically situated both at the crossroads of the region and at the gateway to the Mississippi Delta, Memphis, Tennessee had long been a place where cultures rubbed elbows and new ideas took root. With no city of comparable size for over a hundred miles in any direction, Memphis became the centre of regional commerce and entertainment. All of this contributed to the city's unique blending of black and white, rural and urban, Northern and Southern influences.

Memphis was also home to a thriving black community, focused on Beale Street. Established in the 1880s, this vibrant city within a city came alive at night, with jazz and ragtime music spilling into the street from the bars and brothels that lined its sidewalks. The arrival of early blues pioneer W.C. Handy at the beginning of the twentieth century made the city the centre of the nation's blues scene, as the music progressed from rural juke joints to Beale Street nightclubs. In the still strictly segregated South, Beale Street was one of the very few public places where black people could relax and socialise away from the scrutiny of the white populace. As such, it became the weekend destination of choice for many black residents of the small towns throughout the area.

Beale Street remained segregated until the 1940s, when whites were first allowed to visit its clubs during designated hours. It soon attracted a small share of adventurous whites – primarily young – that were drawn to the music and the energy it generated. It was likely the only opportunity most urban white people had to hear black musicians play blues music in its true form, rather than diluted to make it acceptable to white ears. Beale Street was also one of the few places where black culture was on display unedited for white eyes. The area thus had an exotic allure for some whites, though it was avoided like the plague by most others.

A 1939 family road trip provided 16-year-old Samuel Cornelius Phillips with his first introduction to Memphis and its vibrant centre of black culture. He had long dreamed of having the opportunity to visit the city. 'I had wanted to all my life,' he later explained, 'because W.C. Handy was born in the same town that I was born and raised in – Florence, Alabama – but, man, we never had enough money to do anything.' The family arrived in an old Dodge coupe, stopping on their way to Dallas, Texas to hear a renowned Baptist preacher. 'We finally got enough money to go all the way to Dallas, and as we came through Memphis, Beale Street was the first thing I wanted to see.' What Sam Phillips saw was unlike anything he had previously encountered. 'So Beale Street, it just blew me away. We got there at 4 o'clock on a Saturday morning. It was pouring down rain. We were in a little coupe with five of us boys, and the top was down and it was raining. And at 4, 5 o'clock in the morning, the street was full of people, because they'd saved their money for two years to get to spend the weekend in Memphis on Beale Street. Black folks, mainly.'[1]

Riding in the family car, Phillips excitedly soaked up the intoxicating sights and sounds. It was not just the music that he responded to, but the energy with which black singers and musicians infused it. In black music he encountered an element that touched him in a manner that other musical styles did not.

That elusive sound flowing through Phillips' young mind had its origins in the cotton fields of his childhood: unaccompanied vocalisations that helped ease the tedium of long, backbreaking hours of toil; that provided a cadence for work and helped to make bearable the oppressive humidity of scorching Southern summers. It was the 'race' music – blues and gospel – sung by black field labourers, and the 'hillbilly' country music of white sharecroppers. Songs of heartache and despair, of love and loss, songs of loneliness, of longing for home and the elusive hope of better times to come – all melded together in Phillips' brain to create a sound that only he could hear. In many ways it was the music of life, raw and real – at least life as Phillips saw it in his hardscrabble corner of the rural South.

But Phillips' passion for music was frustrated by his inability either to sing or competently play an instrument. Searching for another avenue of expression, he spent his late teens and early twenties at various radio stations in the mid-South, developing his on-air abilities as a producer and announcer. Along the way, he listened to every record in each station's studio library, becoming knowledgeable in jazz, blues and pop music.

Initial recognition came as host of the innocuously named *Saturday Afternoon Tea Dance* at WREC in Memphis, where Phillips took advantage of the opportunity to introduce his listeners to all the various forms of music he loved. For many white Southern teens, this was their first formal exposure to 'race' music. They enthusiastically demanded more, in direct proportion to the vehemence with which their parents denounced it. Still, none of the recordings he played echoed what he heard in his head. Phillips was soon in search of another form of musical expression.

Memphis Recording Service opened its doors for business in January 1950, and for the next two years Phillips barely scratched out a living recording weddings, funerals and the occasional bar mitzvah. He started up the Sun Records label in 1952, although his motivation is a source of speculation. Much of the way of life that Phillips had grown up with was being modernised out of existence in the years following the Second World War. Whether it was the immediate need to provide for a young and growing family that prompted him to branch out or, as he later claimed, the prescient desire to preserve a musical heritage that was rapidly disappearing remains a matter for debate. But there is no dispute that the fledgling talents of B.B. King, Ike Turner and Chester 'Howlin' Wolf' Burnett were all captured for posterity under Phillips' hand.

Despite high hopes, Phillips struggled to keep his infant record label financially viable. Late in 1953, a painfully shy, pimply-faced 19-year-old walked through the doors of Memphis Recording Service to cut a $3.98 recording of syrupy ballads as a gift for his mother. Phillips remembered the boy's voice the following year when the singer of a country and western combo he was working with unexpectedly walked out. Within a year, Elvis Presley was a national sensation, having stayed just long enough at Sun Records to cut five singles before moving on to explode to icon status.

Elvis was the first in a dream lineup of future legends that got their start at Sun Records. Then came gifted guitarist Carl Perkins, the man who might actually have had Elvis' career, had he not been sidelined by a car crash at the critical moment. Next in line was the lugubrious Johnny Cash, who deeply resented Phillips' efforts to mould him into an Elvis replacement. Cash was followed by lonely balladeer Roy Orbison, who endured Phillips' misguided attempts to fashion him into a 'Rockabilly Cat'. He was followed by the volatile Jerry Lee Lewis, a genuine rocker whose meteoric career imploded in notoriety at the very brink of stardom. Finally, there was Charlie Rich, who met with limited success recording boozy, jazz-infused blues at Phillips' insistence, but later hit pay-dirt in Nashville as a top-grossing country singer.

Phillips evidently recognised true talent when he heard it, but it is equally evident that he often did not know how to develop its potential. That music he heard in the back of his head always seemed to get in the way. Even if he had known how to success-fully exploit the impressive array of talent that miraculously found its way to his door, as the owner of an independent regional label, Phillips had neither the financial clout nor the distribution connections to get his recordings national airplay. Perennially short of cash, the outrageous royalty deals he struck with his artists garnered him the bulk of copyright revenues, while virtually guaranteeing the artists' later resentment and angry departure at the first opportunity. Always a shrewd businessman, perhaps Phillips recognised that his label's limited resources required him to make the most of his narrow window of financial opportunity with each artist. He made sure that he was compensated for each of his discoveries, then left it to the major labels to whisk them away and cash in.

Once Phillips achieved relative financial success, he was able to move to larger facilities that boasted all the modern sound technology he had once only been able to imitate. But by that time the days of all-night jam sessions, where the tape recorder was left to run for hours in the hopes of capturing spontaneous magic, were a thing of the past. The business of music had also changed. The recording industry was now dominated by a few corporate labels; the day when an independent regional label like Sun Records could hope to capture market share had largely passed. Public tastes increasingly drifted towards more sophisticated production styles until the Brit-ification of the American music scene, which began with the Beatles phenomenon in the mid-1960s, struck the final blow.

Sun Records finally closed its doors in 1969. By that time, most of the former Sun artists who had gone on to greatness were embarrassed by their recordings for the label, and had little good to say about either Phillips or his 'Sun Sound'. That attitude continued into the late 1970s, until music historians began looking back fondly at the infant years of rock 'n' roll. As the roots of rock 'n' roll were uncovered, Phillips' pivotal role in the development of this musical genre began to be recognised and appreciated. A few of Phillips' former artists continued to grumble when interviewed about those early days, but in the golden glow of remembrance ushered in by the establishment of the Rock and Roll Hall of Fame in the following decade, even they were willing to admit a grudging admiration.

Superficially, Phillips' legendary Sun Sound might appear to be no more than imaginative cross-wiring and on-the-fly improvisations, rather than the result of conscious creative intent. In reality, spontaneous improvisation is as much evidence of genius as the same effects produced by a battery of expensive sound equipment. Perhaps even more so, given that this signature sound was the artistic product of one man, achieved in a one-room storefront recording studio with only the barest minimum of primitive equipment, at a time when only he believed in what he was doing.

Notes on Sources

THE AUTHORS' FIRST introduction to Sam Phillips occurred in the mid-1990s, as witnesses to an extensive live interview he gave for a proposed documentary. At the time, the authors were employed by the estate of singer Roy Orbison: Tanja as vice president and Kevin as archivist. Although the documentary never materialised, elements of Phillips' story continually cropped up during research for subsequent Orbison projects, offering random glimpses of Phillips' life and influence as it touched the careers of some of the greatest names in early rock 'n' roll history. Thus began a personal project to place these accumulated bits and pieces of information into a meaningful order and context. Much later, as additional accounts were found and fitted together, a timeline began to take shape, which eventually became the framework of this book.

A continual source of frustration in the authors' research of Phillips' history was the lack of actual dates for many of the stories connected with his earliest recording sessions. From 1950 to 1955, Memphis Recording Service and Sun Records was essentially a two-person operation. Sam Phillips operated the recording and transcription equipment in the control room, and handled on-the-road promotion. Marion Keisker ran the day-to-day business and nearly everything else. The early operation's only historical documentation consists of the notebook in which Keisker wrote important dates and events; Phillips was notorious for his lack of record keeping.

In the absence of written documentation, most of the story

comes from the personal recollections of Phillips, Keisker and some of the artists who recorded at the studio. Those recollections vary in numerous instances – depending upon who told the story, and when it was told – and conflict on several key points. In such cases, preference is given to the version recounted closest to the time of the actual event, or by the person deemed least prone to distortion of the facts. Some rarely told a story the same way twice; others rarely varied in the telling, no matter how much time passed. Where a bone of contention still exists, conflicting versions are both presented.

Part I

I Followed Music

'There is nothing in this world that has contributed to the everlasting understanding of the people of the world like the music that originated right here, called rock and roll.'[1]

Chapter One

Hard Times, Sweet Sounds

SAM PHILLIPS' FATHER was not a wealthy man; he did not own the land he worked. Rather, he was a tenant farmer, growing primarily cotton in 300 acres of rich soil near the small rural community of Florence, Alabama, bordering the states of Tennessee and Mississippi. Charles and wife Madge were the parents of eight children. Their youngest child, born 5 January 1923, was christened Samuel Cornelius Phillips. Despite having little in the way of material possessions, life was relatively comfortable for the Phillips family in Sam's early years.

That all changed in the wake of the Crash of 1929. Many of the nation's local banking institutions folded, wiping out their depositors' life savings. Like scores of their neighbours, the Phillips family suffered severe financial losses. 'My daddy lost everything that he'd lived for and worked for,' Phillips recalled.[1] 'One day my father had money. The next thing he knew, it was gone. A few hundred dollars left maybe.'[2]

The Depression hit the South hard, and its effects lasted longest there. Many white families that had lived in genteel poverty prior to the Crash found themselves in desperate situations afterwards. 'That kind of thing could break you,' Sam explained, 'but my father had courage and determination and refused to give up.'[3] Sam ascribed his own strong work ethic and drive to succeed to the example set by his father. From him, Sam learned 'that you have to believe in yourself and what you can do'.[4]

The elder Phillips children shouldered much of the responsibility for tending and harvesting the cotton crop. Picking cotton is difficult and tedious work, made worse by the blazing heat and suffocating humidity of late summer. Although he was not physically robust, Sam also worked in the fields, dragging a heavy canvas sack between the rows and filling it with fibres plucked from the dried and prickly plants. This experience was probably the first close contact he had with the black people of his community. 'In Florence,' Phillips later remembered, 'white and black people picked cotton together, plowed together, did everything except "socialize".'[5] In marked contrast to the prevailing attitude of the time, the Phillips family did not consider themselves superior to their black neighbours. 'I was right in the middle of people that worked hard, black and white,' Phillips recalled. 'And even though I lived in the South, we didn't see the color line like a lot of people. We weren't better than anybody.'[6]

While it is unlikely that Phillips understood the complex racial inequalities that played out around him at this young age, he was sensitive to the social inequity between the 'haves' and the 'have-nots' and the intrinsic unfairness of it all. For those at the bottom of the pile, it was a pain often soothed by music. 'There were two types of downtrodden people back then,' Phillips observed. 'There were the black field hands and the white sharecroppers. It was impossible in those days not to hear and grow to love all the music of oppression and the music that uplifted people – blues, country, gospel, all of it.'[7] 'I learned so much from those days,' he explained, 'because it was one of those times when people . . . The only hope they had was to sing the blues and to sing religious songs, and to hope and pray that times would be better. I picked up on it, and it made a great impression on me.'[8]

Local white musical tastes tended to look northwards to Nashville and the hillbilly sound of the *Grand Ole Opry*, the legendary weekly country music radio programme. 'I was raised on the *Grand Ole Opry*,' Phillips stated, 'because I could get it just like the local station, although I was 119 miles away from their transmitter site in Nashville.'[9] But black musical tastes looked south, to the rich legacy of Delta blues. It was during long days spent in the fields that Phillips first heard the music of black field hands: gospel, blues and working songs called 'field hollers'. 'I worked in the fields when I was this high,' said Phillips, indicating his height as a young child. 'A day didn't go by when I didn't hear black folks singing in the cotton fields. Did I feel sorry for them? In a way I did. But they could do things I couldn't do. They could out-pick me. They could sing on pitch.'[10]

Phillips was particularly impressed with the depth of emotion and human experience – the loneliness, hardship and oppression – that could be conveyed within the deceptive simplicity of blues music: 'The black man gave up so many things that were import-ant to him just to survive and to please. But think about the complexity, yet simplicity of music we have gained from hard times – from the sky, the wind and the earth. If you don't have a foundation, you don't know what the hell I'm talking about.'[11] Significantly, he recognised the difference between the way that black musicians tailored their music for white audiences, and the way it was sung and played among their own. 'You see,' he explained, 'we've forgotten how much they have sacrificed to please the white man. For years white people have denied what the old black man with four strings on his guitar could do, just saying, "OK, let's hear this nigger play." A black man playing for white folks was "fun", but that was all.'[12]

To those black field hands can be traced the beginnings of Phillips' musical education. 'One man in particular,' Phillips remembered, 'Uncle Silas Payne, an old black man, taught music to me. Not musical notes or reading, you understand, but real intuitive music.'[13] Phillips was drawn to the raw emotion of the sound, moved by its ability to touch something spiritual within the hearer: 'Now we've learned so much from some of these people we thought were ignorant, who never had any responsi-bility other than chopping cotton, feeding the mules or making sorghum molasses. When people come back to this music in a hundred years, they'll see these were master painters. They may be illiterate. They can't write a book about it. But they can make a song, and in three verses you'll hear the greatest damn story you'll ever hear in your life.'[14]

Growing up in the rural South, where church is an integral part of community social life, Phillips would also have been strongly influenced by the religious music he heard at weekly meetings. But it was to the black expression of that music that he felt a connection. 'They had a little church down from our church – Howard Baptist – a Methodist church on the corner just a half a block away. We would get out of church on Sunday – nobody had air conditioning in those days – their windows were open and their choir was just getting going good after we'd been through the choir bit and the sermon and everything.'[15]

As a child, Phillips seemed to be tuned in to music wherever he encountered it: 'So many things influenced me to love music and know that it was a great potential forum for communication, way beyond the idea of black or white or rich or poor.'[16] He obviously enjoyed the sound of the music he heard, whether in church or on the radio or in the fields, but as he grew older he seemed to appreciate another element in it: that music could give voice to feelings that were otherwise difficult to express. 'So my music was always there,' he observed, 'but more so, it was what humans were all about, and what they had to say. Most of us can't talk and tell it, but I found out during my lifetime that a lot of people can tell you an awful lot about themselves and their experiences, good and bad, if they can just have a guitar or pat their foot and sing it to you.'[17]

Phillips first expressed his love of music by playing in the school band, although he was admittedly not a very good musician. 'I followed music,' he explained. 'I was in the band in high school and junior high, and played the sousaphone and a little trombone and drums, and was the leader of the 72-piece marching band that we had.'[18] On becoming band captain in high school,

Phillips discovered that he had a gift for conducting. 'I could always see the people that did have talent,' he observed, 'and get it out of them. And they would *know* that I was getting it out of them.'[19] As time went on, Phillips came to understand that his own musical talent was not in playing the music himself, but in recognising that ability in others, and in enabling them to articulate it.

Chapter Two

On the Air

IN 1940, AGED 17, Sam acted as MC and conductor of a band concert for the local chapter of the American Legion. The concert was broadcast on the radio by station WLAY. Station manager Jim Connally was sufficiently impressed to offer Phillips a job as an announcer. 'I was just a Southern boy that never thought anyone would listen, or even hire me,' he explained. 'It was a part-time thing. I was still in high school when I started at a little 250-watt station, the only one in the Muscle Shoals area.' Phillips was put in charge of a 30-minute gospel programme called *Hymn Time*. 'They put me on a program of religious songs,' he remembered. 'And I loved that, because I enjoyed quartet music. White quartet music; and I enjoyed black quartets and trios, and black choirs.'[1]

Sam's entry into radio may have come through his older brother Jud, who was a manager at WLAY and sang in the station's gospel quartet. As a youth, Sam felt himself to be very much in Jud's shadow. Jud was a gregarious boy with an easy laugh and an enormous personality, whom people found to be intrinsically likeable. In contrast, Sam was quiet and reserved, and described himself as being somewhat prickly: 'I was the greenest persimmon on the tree. If you took a bite of me, you didn't like me too much.'[2]

Phillips' passion for music was equalled at the time only by his dream of becoming a lawyer. He had long spoken of his desire to become a criminal defence lawyer who, like Clarence Darrow, would represent the poor and downtrodden. As a child, Phillips liked to listen to the attorneys argue their cases during the Circuit Court hearings at the local courthouse: 'To me, they were kind of evangelical in their approach. A lot of times it didn't matter what the facts were – all you had to do was sway the jury.' Even then, Phillips recognised that life, and the law, discriminated between races and classes of people: 'There was a lawyer in the white cases, if the [defendants] had any property . . . The blacks were usually not represented by anyone. I saw both blacks and whites get sentences because they didn't have the money to be represented like they were supposed to . . .'[3]

The death of his father in January 1942 was particularly hard for Phillips, effectively ending his dream of going to law school. With a legal career now out of the question, he reluctantly dropped out of high school during his senior year and found a job at a grocery store in order to supplement family finances. To spare his mother's feelings, he told her that he had lost interest in a law career and wanted to go into radio instead. Phillips was now responsible for the support of his mother and a deaf-mute aunt who resided with the family, which probably exempted him from being drafted into the military as the nation entered the war. A later job with an undertaker proved invaluable in teaching Phillips people skills: 'I was very sensitive to the things I heard, saw and felt around me. Those times working with the country mortician made me very aware of how to handle people and their problems later on.'[4]

In addition to working and his duties at WLAY, Phillips began taking correspondence courses in engineering and science from Alabama Polytechnic Institute. His work at the radio station further fuelled his fascination with black music: 'back in the 1930s all the music of the country peoples – black blues, hillbilly and spirituals – all influenced me, and in radio I saw a medium where I could do something with the music I loved'.[5]

Phillips married diminutive Rebecca Irene Burns from nearby Sheffield, Alabama in 1942. The two had met as teenagers when both were working part time at WLAY. Soon after the wedding, Phillips upgraded his employment to an engineer position at station WMSL in Decatur, Alabama. 'I was mediocre,' is how he assessed his on-air vocal quality at the time. 'I got a lot of South in my mouth.'[6] The couple's first son, Knox, was born during their stay in Decatur.

★ ★ ★

Phillips travelled to Nashville, Tennessee in December 1943 to audition at station WSM, home of the *Grand Ole Opry*. While there, he heard about a job opportunity across town at WLAC, where announcer John Richbourg had been called up for military service. Phillips landed the job, which gave him his first big-city radio experience.

After nearly 18 months at WLAC, he felt ready for a new challenge. 'Well, my boss told me about a job in Memphis,' Phillips recalled. 'I walked into the WREC studio in the Peabody Hotel, and just down the block was Beale Street, and I thought, "Wow."'[7] An additional draw was the fact that his older brother, Jud, also worked at the station as a singer with the Jolly Boys Quartet. Phillips moved his family to Memphis in June 1945. 'I had in my mind that I wanted to live in Memphis,' he said. 'Something led me. Something guided me beyond my conscious efforts. To get that opportunity was like a door opening for me.'[7] The move was not greeted with universal enthusiasm. 'When I decided to move there,' Phillips remembered, 'some people back home asked me, "Do you really want to go where there are so many niggers?"'[8]

Phillips' first assignment at WREC was as a 'spotter' for a nightly big band concert, broadcast live from the Peabody Hotel's opulent Skyway Ballroom. It was his job to relay technical information via telephone from the ballroom to the engineer in the WREC control room, who used the information to produce a show that went out on the CBS network. 'I was working like, fifteen to eighteen hours a day,' Phillips explained, 'because I did all the big band broadcasts. Two and a half years before that I never imagined I would ever *see* a big band.'[9] He later recalled his reaction to landing the job: 'Here I am in the Peabody Hotel, and the finest studios in Memphis, which WREC had in the basement of the Peabody. And I was taking care of all the PA systems in the Continental Ballroom and the Skyway. Hell, what more could a 22-year-old kid want?'[10]

The job evolved to include several additional duties. As the station's assistant transcription manager, Phillips pre-recorded station programming on to 16-inch acetate discs for later replay. He got his first on-air break under the soubriquet 'Pardner' as host of the daily 4 pm *Songs of the West* show. 'After I got into radio,' Phillips explained, 'I worked hard at becoming an announcer – there were no DJs as such then – but I really wasn't a talented announcer in the strictest terms, although I had to be good just to hold my job in those days.' Radio provided a job with a future, but Phillips did not find the work particularly fulfilling. 'I looked at it as a serious job through the later part of the 1940s,' he continued, 'because I had to make enough money to live and raise a family.'[11] A family that now included second son Jerry.

Phillips also acted as the station's sound effects man, as well as doing whatever else needed to be done. 'One of my first jobs was to go to the Home of the Blues record store and buy up any records that WREC weren't getting shipped to them,' he remembered. 'I would listen to a lot of what was current, and I would also go play a lot of the older records they had accumulated.'[12] Phillips eventually put his eclectic musical tastes to good use in hosting the deceptively tame-sounding *Saturday Afternoon Tea Dance*, where in addition to the staid fare that the programme's name implied, he also played and discussed some of the blues, jazz and pop records that he loved. As in the past, Phillips found himself drawn to recordings that were often overlooked by other announcers: recordings with an edgier sound than was currently popular.

Chapter Three

We Record Anything – Anywhere – Anytime

THE DREAM OF opening a recording studio had been in the back of Phillips' mind for some time, but he began to consider it seriously around 1949. 'I may not know much,' he said, 'but I do know sound. And here I am thinking about opening a little recording studio – for one reason: I wanted to record black people, those folks who never had the opportunity to record. My unconscious mind was just saying I should do it.'[1]

Unlike a number of cities that had established black communities, like St Louis, Chicago and New York, Memphis had no local black recording industry. Not for lack of talent, but for the simple reason that there was nowhere blacks could record. 'I can tell you that the opportunity to do music from Memphis wasn't really here until I opened my studio,' he observed. 'On the local basis, the little bands, jug bands and everything else, that was very conducive to an interesting facet of people, and how badly they wanted to make music and make contact.' Phillips recognised the great, untapped musical potential that existed in Memphis: 'I knew that if it could be found, it would come from this area more abundantly than from anywhere else.'[2]

It was not altogether an original idea. Royal Recording had opened in 1948 and closed down a year later. The quick demise of that operation prompted Phillips' employers at WREC to warn him about trying to open his own. But Phillips had a dream, and with his wife's support he signed the lease on a property in October

1949. 'I took that studio and I was so proud to get this little old storefront building,' he recalled. 'I walked in there and you would have thought God had delivered heaven to me.'[3]

Located at the corner of Union and Marshall Avenues on the edge of the downtown district, Memphis Recording Service opened for business on 1 January 1950. The studio was initially intended to be a part-time venture, operated in Phillips' free time away from his radio career, as a source of extra income. 'I also knew that when I opened it up we'd record anywhere, anything, anytime,' he explained. 'I meant that, but I had to have some kind of idea how I was going to pay the rent and everything, and not impose on my salary from WREC. I often was asked at that time, "What in the world are you all building a recording studio [for] and who you going to record?" and so forth and so on. I said, "Well, man, I'm going to record anything I can."'[4]

Phillips' unofficial business partner was Marion Keisker, a co-worker from WREC who had begun her radio career there at the age of 12, and had gone on to become a popular talk show host and on-air personality. Well educated and gracious, it was to her that Phillips often spoke of his dream 'to have a facility where black people could come and play their own music', Keisker recalled, 'a place where they would feel free and relaxed to do it'.[5]

In January 1950, at the age of 33, Keisker was a busy career woman and the divorced mother of a nine-year-old son. She also harboured a hopeless, unrequited crush on Phillips that even decades later, she was at a loss to explain. 'I knew nothing about the music, and I didn't care a bit . . . my participation was based totally on my personal relationship with Sam in a way that is totally unbelievable to me now. All I wanted to do was to make it possible for him to fulfill his vision . . .'[6] The depth of Keisker's affection for Phillips can be guessed at from the words she chose to describe his appearance at the time of their first association: 'He was a beautiful young man. Beautiful beyond belief, but still that country touch, that country rawness. He was slim and had those incredible eyes,' she remembered. 'He was very, very particular about his appearance with touches of real elegance, beautifully groomed, terrible about his hair.'[7] Two things that people consistently remarked on at the time were the piercing intensity of Phillips' eyes – 'swirling pools of insanity' as one associate described them – and his full head of reddish hair, which he exerted great effort in keeping meticulously coiffed.

Keisker helped Phillips raise the capital for his venture. Once the location was secured – a bland storefront at 706 Union Avenue, next door to Mrs Dell Taylor's restaurant – the two did much of the renovation work themselves, with a budget of $1,000. 'I knew how much work it was going to require,' Phillips explained, 'and I knew I didn't have any money and all that stuff, but anyway, in less than a week, I was working. And I didn't have the money to hire a contractor or, really, any carpenters. I did hire one carpenter part-time – I had to have *some* help on – but I did that and built the studio like it is now.'[8] The space was partitioned to create a shallow reception area across the front, with a control room and a 20 by 35 foot studio directly behind. Phillips and Keisker laid floor tiles, painted acoustic boards and hung wide Venetian blinds in the windows fronting the street. Thanks to a two-year loan from another WREC co-worker, Phillips installed what little equipment he could afford. Once the neon signs were installed in the windows flanking the entrance door, Memphis Recording Service was ready for business.

From a vantage point many years later, Phillips stated that his reason for opening Memphis Recording Service was to record local singers and musicians who performed blues music, both country blues and rhythm blues. 'I always felt that the people who played this type of music had not been given the opportunity to reach an audience,' he explained. 'My aim was to try and record the blues and the music I liked and to prove whether I was right or wrong about this music. I knew, or I *felt* I knew, that there was a bigger audience for the blues than just the black man of the mid-South. There were city markets to be reached, and I knew that whites listened to blues surreptitiously.'[9]

Much of the impetus that propelled Phillips to record black artists appears to have come from a strong desire to prove a point, if only to himself: 'The only thing I wanted to do is to see if I was right or wrong. I wanted to record it, get it on the market, and see if the people would accept it or reject it.'[10]

More importantly, Phillips believed that he was the man to take on the challenge. 'I just thought that black music should be exposed in the right forum, and somebody that purveyed it should not be ashamed of it. As a child, there was a real awakening of my spirit because I had spent so much time around black people. I saw the unbelievable talent these people had.'[11] As he explained elsewhere: 'I knew what they were going through; they were people laboring under very difficult personal circumstances physically, but most especially emotionally. And not because they were beaten as slaves every day or anything like that; but that they, over all the years, were having to live their lives within themselves to such a degree. I felt that these people must have something to say.'[12]

Contrary to the rhetoric, Phillips did not see himself as part of a social or political movement, nor did he attempt to speak for the black community. For him, it was all about the music, and the music spoke for itself. 'I wasn't out to change the world or anything like that,' he clarified. 'I was out for these people to be heard.'[13] However lofty the goal, it would have to wait for a while. Bills had to be paid.

Phillips' first paying job came from country singer Buck 'Snuffy' Turner, the WREC co-worker who had lent him money for studio equipment. Phillips recorded Turner and his band performing 15-minute programmes for the Arkansas Rural Electrification Corporation, and cut 16-inch acetate disc transcriptions for distribution to about 20 mid-South radio stations. Other jobs were more prosaic: he recorded bar mitzvahs, civic club functions, weddings, funerals and political speeches. He bid for and was awarded concessions to operate the PA systems at the Peabody Hotel and the local baseball stadium. Most of Phillips' early jobs lived up to the Memphis Recording Service motto: 'We Record Anything – Anywhere – Anytime'.

★   ★   ★

By today's standards, the recording equipment Phillips installed in his studio's control booth was incredibly basic; it seems almost impossible that he was able to cut a record at all. It is a testament to Phillips' skill as a sound engineer that he was able to accomplish what he did with such simple tools.

Phillips was nevertheless immensely proud of the equipment he originally purchased for his studio: 'I had a little Presto five-input mixer board. It was portable and sat on a hall table. The mixer had four microphone ports, and the fifth port had a multi-selector switch where you could flip it one way and get a mic, and flip it another to play your recordings back. That was my console.'[14]

Prior to getting a professional model, he made do with two reel-to-reel tape recorders manufactured for home use: 'I had a Presto portable tape recorder, a PT 900, companion piece to the mixer . . . I was real proud to get the Presto. Man, that was big-time for me!'[15]

Magnetic tape was a fairly new recording medium at the time, and its durability was as yet unproven. For this reason, Phillips relied on acetate discs: 'In the very beginning, I recorded a lot onto those sixteen-inch discs, which I cut at 78 rpm. Normally you wouldn't do that. You recorded at 33 rpm on transcriptions, but in order to improve the sound, I recorded at 78 rpm and would make an acetate master from there. For making acetates, I had the Presto 6-N lathe, which was connected to a Presto turntable. That's how I cut most of my early music.'[16] Sometime late in 1951, Phillips switched from the cumbersome acetate discs to magnetic tape.

Tape had the advantage of being reusable, a decided advantage given the way he conducted recording sessions.

It is significant that Phillips' first pieces of equipment were portable. The budget did not allow for duplicates, so he had to use the same pieces for off-site jobs and for studio sessions. Several years later, as finances allowed, Phillips replaced his portable tape recorder with two Ampex 350 models, and his portable mixer board with an RCA 76-D radio console, which he modified for recording. 'I saw an ad in one of the trade papers that there was an RCA 70D board, used,' he recalled, 'so I called the engineer up there and I said, "How much do you want for it?" and he said, "Five hundred dollars." Well, of course, that was a lot of money too, but I got that damn thing down here and all the electrolytic capacitors for the amps for the program amplifier and the alternate program amplifier monitor, they were just *cooked*, really. Well, I had that thing up and running in a week's time and that damn thing, it was just so perfect for what I needed.'¹⁷ From about 1954, this was the equipment Phillips used.

Part of Phillips' genius as a sound engineer was his ability to wrest an identifiable, signature style from such minimal equipment. The famous Sun Records sound relied on the use of echo. Echo lends depth and texture to a recording, producing a fuller, richer sound. It can 'fatten' sound, allowing a few instruments to produce the effect of many. Most recording studios of the time preferred a 'dead' sound, employing various means to muffle the natural echo produced by sound waves reverberating off the walls. Phillips preferred the 'live' sound produced by throwing a lot of volume into a small space. To achieve it, he devised an artificial echo effect which he called *slap-back*, manipulating sound through the heads of his reel-to-reel tape recorder during the recording process. 'Then I came up with this little slap-back: delayed tape,' he explained. 'You have an erase, a record and a playback head . . . instead of putting my output on record I'd put it . . . it sounds so simple that it's ridiculous to even mention the fact . . . I would put it on playback and play it back on record just slightly delayed.'[18]

This innovation meant that the sound transferred on to the master tape was a simultaneous mixture of the musical notes that the musicians were playing live in the studio, and the same notes delayed by a split second. The delay was created by running the sound from the record head, through the playback head, then back through the record head and on to the tape. The fixed distance between the mixer board's playback and record heads ensured that the length of the delay remained consistent. The depth of the effect could be modified by controlling how much of the echo signal was returned from each of the microphones. Because the echo effect was produced within the mixer board, the musicians in the studio never heard it as they performed.

Tight financing had allowed for only the simplest operation with the most basic equipment, but Phillips was justifiably proud of what he had been able to accomplish. Becky Phillips commemorated the new venture with an addition to the family scrapbook. She attached a snapshot of her husband standing in front of his new studio, writing underneath it the caption: 'A Man's Dream Fulfilled – What Next?' [19]

Chapter Four

The Hottest Thing in the Country

ABOUT SIX MONTHS passed before Phillips began to recruit and record artists, thinking to lease or sell the masters to independent regional labels that specialised in the music markets ignored by larger labels. 'When I opened the studio I had already talked to record labels, but I didn't have any deals lined up,' he recalled. 'I felt I had to please myself first with the music and then go out and sell it.'[1] Although Phillips chose the cuts that he thought were most marketable, and worked with artists to get the best performance from them, he did not usually dictate what material an artist should play or how they should interpret that material. 'My feeling was that there was more talent, innately natural, in the people I wanted to work with – Southern black, Southern country white – than there was in the people who wrote down arrangements.'[2]

In the beginning, Phillips actively recruited talent from among the artists he had come to know through his work in radio. Many of these were regular performers on local radio broadcasts who were popular in the Memphis area, but unknown outside it. Once word got around of what he was trying to do, and recordings were made and sold, artists began to show up at the studio, asking for auditions. Eventually, enough quality talent found its way to Phillips' door that he no longer had to go out in search of it.

Phillips sold his first recording to 4-Star Records, a West Coast label owned by Bill McCall, a businessman whom he had known for some time. 'Boogie for Me Baby', by blind South Memphis piano player John Hunter, was described by a *Billboard* reviewer as 'crude boogie blues' suitable for Southern juke joints. Later 4-Star purchased some country numbers by Slim Rhodes' Mountaineers as well.

Inspired by what indie labels like 4-Star were doing, Phillips made a bold decision. In partnership with Memphis DJ Dewey Phillips, he would release recordings on his own label.

Dewey Phillips was the host of an immensely popular nightly radio show called *Red, Hot and Blue* on station WHBQ in Memphis. On air, he was a sort of one-man train wreck: imagine a hillbilly Robin Williams hopped up on amphetamines. 'His style was pure country. He was an irreverent squawker with a stream of consciousness speed rap that never quit – even when the record was playing. From the midst of trained, deep and resonant voices that filled the airwaves, came this countrified rapid-fire drawl with an indefinable vocabulary.'[3]

For two and a half hours, from Monday to Saturday, listeners tuned in to hear Daddy-O-Dewey play whatever music took his fancy: blues, hillbilly, pop – played it multiple times if he liked it, or raked the needle through the grooves and broke the disc if he did not. Because of his eclectic musical tastes, Memphis radio listeners were exposed to recordings that were probably heard nowhere else in the South. Dewey's maniacal antics made him a favourite with younger listeners, but understandably provoked the ire of the more sedate members of the population. 'There are two kinds of people in Memphis: those who are amused and fascinated by Dewey, and those who, when they accidentally tune in, jump as though stung by a wasp and hurriedly switch to something nice and cultural, like Guy Lombardo.'[4]

Dewey always referred to Sam as his half-brother, despite there being no family connection. They were so close that it made Marion Keisker jealous: she considered Dewey to be a bad influence (which he was) and could not stand to be in the same room when the two men were together. Although they frequently argued like brothers, Sam respected and appreciated Dewey's abilities and often sought out his musical opinion.

Temperamentally, as well as in manner and personal presentation, Dewey and Sam were direct opposites. Dewey said and did whatever sparked in his brain, whereas Sam's every word and action seemed carefully considered. Dewey's spontaneous, fly-by-the-seat-of-your-pants attitude towards life was a relaxing influence on tightly wound Sam. Despite the many differences, their shared love of the music produced by black artists proved to be a binding connection. Both men were willing to cross the musical colour line at a time when doing so was neither safe nor fashionable. Both felt impelled to make that music more widely available, Sam by recording it and Dewey by broadcasting it.

'Dewey and I were together quite a bit,' Sam remembered. 'We figured that if we had a record out we could feel out the record business on a local basis and that would help both of us . . . It was partly a lark for both of us to see how far it would go, but Dewey was a hot DJ in town, and I knew that we had a good chance to get some recordings played.'[5] Thus was born the Phillips label. 'The Hottest Thing in the Country', one of Dewey's many on-air catchphrases, was co-opted to serve as the new label's motto.

Phillips was working with a number of artists at the time, including a gospel group, jazz pianist Phineas Newborn Jr, Memphis Jug Band player Charlie Burse, and a one-man-band street performer named Joe Hill Louis. Joe Hill had landed in town as a 14-year-old runaway in 1936. Following a fight with a local bully, the triumphant Hill was dubbed 'Joe Hill Louis' in tribute to famed heavyweight boxer Joe Louis. Hill developed his act on the streets of Memphis, simultaneously playing the harmonica, electric guitar and a full drum kit. Along the way, he gave himself the moniker 'The Be-Bop Boy' and eventually became a regular performer at radio station WDIA. He had recorded unsuccessfully for Columbia Records in Nashville before Phillips found him.

Phillips recorded Burse performing the novelty number 'Shorty the Barber' in July, borrowing an actual pair of barber's shears in order to get the proper sound effect. A frustrating month-long series of letters followed, in which Phillips requested various agencies for permission to license the song for release. Such was his inexperience that he did not know the music publisher's permission was unnecessary. In the end, Phillips selected for the Phillips label's first release two original Joe Hill Louis songs that had been intended for sale to another label. An order for 300 copies of 'Gotta Let You Go'/'Boogie in the Park' was placed on 30 August, at a cost of $51.00. It was the label's only release. Poor sales failed to recoup the investment, and the enterprise was quickly abandoned.

★ ★ ★

Although Phillips was by now a proficient sound engineer, he really knew very little else about the recording industry. The learning curve was steep during his first years in the business, and much of the knowledge he gained came from trial and error. What Phillips had going for him was a tenacious drive that sustained him long after most people would have given up in despair. Not only did he have to overcome his inexperience, but also the racism that posed a continual threat to the achievement of his vision. And that racism cut both ways, from whites who despised black music and from untrusting black musicians who had been cheated in the past. Phillips walked a fine line in seeking to establish a rapport with both camps.

When Phillips first began making commercial recordings, he was auditioning talent that in many cases had been performing for years, but had never been inside a recording studio. For some, it was a last chance at a dream they had almost given up on. 'Having worked in radio,' Phillips explained, 'I knew the toughest thing in the world to do is an audition. I knew what they were going through. They were so damn proud, and the toughest thing is: "Lord, I never thought I'd get this opportunity, now I can't blow it." Well that just makes it more difficult.'[6]

The Memphis Recording Service studio was fairly small, but it could be intimidating. The control booth that housed the recording equipment was separated from the studio by a large pane of glass set into one wall. Phillips sat at the recording console, waiting, his intense eyes seeming to bore holes through the glass. With the weight of hopes and expectations riding on this one chance, and all hinging on the decision of one man, it might be difficult to pull off a stellar performance. '[Try to imagine] a black musician trying to play,' Phillips said, 'looking at some white dude behind a window, and they've been kicked around all their life.'[7]

What Phillips instinctively understood from the beginning was that any artist who was accustomed to feeding off the energy and approval of a live audience was unlikely to perform to the best of his ability when isolated in a recording studio. And a black artist, in particular, was likely to tone down the intensity of his performance when instructed to play on cue by a white man. Phillips recognised the necessity of setting an artist at ease. He knew that his artists needed to feel comfortable in their surroundings: 'I had to get their confidence up. You can't record anybody when their damn throat is in their stomach.'[8]

Beyond establishing a rapport through his own demeanour, Phillips also understood the importance of downplaying the performance anxiety that many artists experience when they know they are being recorded. 'And sometimes you can be too cocky around people who are insecure and just intimidate them,' Phillips explained. 'I mean, as far as actually saying, "Hey, man, don't be scared," I've never told anybody in my life not to be scared of the microphone – don't go calling attention to the thing you know they are already scared of.'[9]

In the early days of Memphis Recording Service, when Phillips was working solely with black artists to record black music, he faced a lot of resistance from the white community. The majority of white Memphians disdained black music and avoided any exposure to it. Their contempt often extended to Phillips himself, because of his association with black musicians. Even within the black community, musical tastes had shifted away from the country blues that he favoured to the more urban R&B. For these reasons, Phillips must have known that his records had limited market appeal. Still, he hoped to educate people's musical tastes, to increase their awareness and appreciation. Perhaps all of this worked together to make him less concerned about current commercial appeal than he might otherwise have been.

Phillips auditioned many musicians, selecting to record those whose unique quality caught his notice. Sometimes it was a matter of personal taste; sometimes there was broader appeal. Still, Phillips had a talent for spotting potential in artists that they might not yet see in themselves, then bringing that potential to fruition: 'I saw my role as being the facilitator, the man who listened to an artist for his native abilities, then tried to encourage and channel the artist into what would be a proper outlet for his abilities. I wasn't interested in just a good singer. There had to be something distinctive there for me to want to spend time with an artist.'[10]

Accomplishing that goal necessitated having a strong sense of purpose. 'I had a mental picture,' said Phillips, 'as sure as God is on his throne I had a mental picture of what I wanted to hear; certainly not note for note, but I knew the essence of what we were trying to do. But I also knew that the worst thing I could do was to be impatient, to try to force the issue – sometimes you can make a suggestion just [to change] one bar and you kill the whole song.'[11]

Although Phillips claimed to know in advance what it was he wanted to hear, each artist was free to interpret the music in his own way. Particularly for black artists, this meant overcoming their preconceived notions of the style of music they thought he wanted from them. 'When [Sun] first started,' Phillips explained, 'every black artist played nothing but gutbucket blues. When they came in they saw this white man behind the glass; well, they just knew that I wanted another Count Basie or whatever. We established in a hurry that if they didn't give me some of what *they loved*, then they weren't gonna get any time of mine.'[12] Phillips valued that artistic honesty: 'So many black people started out trying to play something to "please" the white man behind the glass, thinking, "He don't want to hear what I do out on the back porch." But that was exactly what I was after. I don't care about making a hit record. That's what I used to tell them. I only care about making a good record.'[13]

Each recording Phillips produced had a consistent and identifiable sound, the result of his individual production talents. However, he insisted that each artist perform according to their own personal style. 'By no means – that is, by *no* remote stretch of the imagination – was he one of those producers who like to impose their own "style" on artists who come into their studio,' recalled Johnny Cash. 'Sam's basic approach was to get you in there and say, "Just show me what you've got. Just sing me some songs, and show me what you'd like to do."'[14]

Phillips did the best he could to ensure that the sound quality of each recording was as perfect as he could make it, but he was less exacting when it came to the perfection of a performance. Because he was not a musician himself, he could respond to the feeling of a performance rather than its precision. Spontaneity and energy were often more important to him than technical proficiency. 'We both felt that if the performance was really there at the heart of the song, it didn't matter much if there were some little musical error or a glitch in the track somewhere,' Cash explained. 'There are mistakes on several of my Sun records – Luther fumbling a guitar line, Marshall going off the beat, me singing sharp – and we all knew it. Sam just didn't care that much: he'd much rather have soul, fire and heart than technical perfection.'[15]

In certain instances, Phillips *was* willing to settle for less than perfection, but he never gave up trying to achieve it. He was willing to exhaust both himself and others in the attempt to capture that magic moment on tape. 'I still remember the times when everyone would be so tired, and then some little funny thing would set us off,' Marion Keisker remembered. 'It was a great spirit of – I don't know, everyone was trying hard to hang very loose through the whole thing. [Sometimes] Elvis would do something absolutely extraordinary and somebody would hit a clinker or something would go wrong before the tape was completed, Sam would say, "Well, let's go back, and you hold on to what you did there. I want that." And Elvis would say, "What did I do? What did I do?" Because it was all so instinctive that he simply didn't know.'[16]

Today, a musician frequently sits alone in a recording booth, adding his instrumentation to previously recorded tracks that he hears only through headphones, never interacting with the other musicians that contribute to the number. In the early days of Phillips' studio, the musicians and vocalist all crowded into one room and recorded the number together in one take. A mistake by any individual meant that the entire recording had to be scrapped and another one made from the beginning. The immediacy that comes across in this approach was one of the characteristics Phillips most valued, and which he felt was lost due to later technical innovations. 'Too many people go into a studio depending on overdubbing and covering up,' he declared. 'There's too many musicians doing too damn much. I don't go for it. I understand all the techniques and the bullshit, but I just don't see the spontaneity . . . The result may be a little prettier, the tonal quality may be good, but an awful lot of the essence is gone.'[17]

Even when an artist was at ease in a studio setting, the pressure to deliver a perfect performance inevitably created tension and frustration. Phillips saw it as his purpose to minimise the tension and to inspire confidence, but he took a low-key approach. 'I was never a real forward person,' he said, 'because I didn't give a damn about jumping out in front to be seen, but I tried to envelop them in my feelings of security.'[18]

Sometimes, despite Phillips' best efforts, a recording session was slow to get going. Hours might go by that produced no usable result. Elvis Presley commonly arrived for a session anxious and over-energised, requiring several hours to settle in and focus before he hit on the proper mood and direction. 'Atmosphere is so important,' Phillips maintained. 'There is so much psychology in dealing with artists. If you don't know what you are doing with people and don't care about them individually – their strong and weak points – both psychologically and musically, you are bound to not get the best from them.'[19] Carl Perkins, who was musically confident enough to write lyrics and compose arrangements on the spot, needed frequent sips of Early Times whiskey to loosen his nerves to the point where he felt ready to record. In such instances, Phillips showed his adaptability to the needs of individual artists. 'I would often take less than their capabilities would provide,' he recalled, 'and I didn't want that; I wanted the best they could provide. I'm real selfish. But it was up to me to set the stage for them, where it looked appetizing. Even if I didn't get what I wanted, they got to the point where they felt like they were maybe not doing it in their garage at home, but close to it.'[20]

Phillips built that sense of security by 'Letting you do your thing,' said Perkins. 'He'd just sit back there, and when you'd hit something he'd punch a button and say, "You're getting close." He had a knack of knowing when we had it pretty well together, and he'd say, "We oughta start taping some of them now." And that's how he'd do it. But he'd let you take all the time you wanted. Let the bass player try different things, guitar player, singer; he never rushed us. That was one cool, good thing about Sun Records. That clock wasn't on that wall and there wasn't no red light that come on and scared you.'[21]

Phillips could also be a cheerleader, if that was what was required. 'I liked working with him in the studio,' Cash said. 'He was very smart, with great instincts, and he had real enthusiasm; he was excitable, not at all laidback. When he'd put something on tape he liked, he'd come bursting out of the control room into the studio, laughing and clapping his hands, yelling and hollering. "That was great! That was wonderful!" he'd say. "That's a rolling stone!" (by which he meant it was a hit). His enthusiasm was fun. It fired us up.'[22] In a newspaper article for the Memphis *Press Scimitar*, journalist Edwin Howard reported his own in-studio experience: 'Sam was totally involved in what he was doing. He was very enthusiastic. He played that control board like a musical instrument and talked a lot back and forth between the control room and the studio. He'd do a take, talk about it, do another, talk about it. Over and over and over.'[23]

Part of what makes Phillips' studio technique interesting is that it is so contradictory. One artist's experience implies that Phillips did nothing more than sit in the control booth and roll tape in the expectation that eventually *something* would be worthy of release. Another's account suggests that the sessions were extremely collaborative, that Phillips took an active role in the development and direction of the music. 'I'm a hell of a taskmaster,' he said, 'but there's times that you use that and there's times that you use something else.'[24] Perhaps Phillips was a chameleon, instinctively making as much or as little of his presence felt as each artist and situation required. Or perhaps his presence was so intense that it drove the session to a degree that some artists were unaware of. Phillips' own account varies as well, but suggests that the sessions he produced were more thought out and calculated than might readily be apparent. 'I wanted simplicity,' he said, 'where we could look at what we were hearing mentally and say, "Man, this guy has just got it." But I wanted some biting bullshit, too. Everything had to be a stinger. To me, every one of those sessions was like I was filming *Gone With the Wind*.'[25]

Of course, part of what makes a film director great is his ability to extract a performance from his actors, one that goes beyond what they think they are capable of. The same is true of a great record producer. 'Sam had an uncanny knack of pulling stuff out of you,' said guitarist Scotty Moore. 'Once you got a direction, he'd work you so hard you'd work your butt off. He'd make you so mad you'd want to kill him, but he wouldn't let go until he'd got that little something extra sometimes you didn't even know you had.'[26] Phillips explained it a bit differently, stating that he had a 'talent for seeing in people things that, a lot of times, I don't think they knew they had themselves. Now, that sounds like a profound statement, and it is. God gave me the best set of ears, I believe . . . and I just had different ideas.'[27]

Phillips liked interacting with his artists: 'I didn't have a talk-back mic in the control room. Didn't want one. I wanted to stay close to the performers in the room.'[28] Nor did he sit around the control booth dispensing advice or waiting for inspiration to strike. In addition to propelling the session along, he had work of his own to do. While the musicians worked up their numbers, he was busy setting up microphones, adjusting sound levels, and arranging the musicians so that the session reflected as closely as possible the way the artist performed live. 'I love to move mics around,' Phillips stated. 'I don't like a standard setup. I mean, onstage they always played loud. I said, "I don't want you to play studio volume. I want to be able to let you play as close to what sounds natural to y'all."'[29]

Phillips also had a talent for manipulating sound within his cramped studio. 'I am a sound freak,' he once said. 'I could play around with sound forever. I know that was part of my success.'[30] Phillips was known to use wooden crates as baffles to deflect sound reverberation, and wads of paper to alter the tone of equipment. He even occasionally co-opted the studio restroom to act as a primitive echo chamber. The effects were simple, as are all magic tricks once they are explained, and were used judiciously to enhance production value.

The simplicity that Phillips sought is deceptive, however, and derived from an innate ability to clear away all extraneous elements. The result can be heard in the instrumental backing of any of the recordings he produced. Phillips employed only the barest minimum number of instruments necessary to carry the music along, where the addition of a single instrument would weaken the emotional power of the whole. This is particularly evident in the hauntingly spare backing used on his recordings of Johnny Cash. '[Phillips] really did have a genius for the commercial touch,' Cash related, 'the right way to twist or turn a song so that it really got across to people. He did have strong ideas. Sometimes I didn't like it much when I felt that his mind was closed to something I wanted to do – he had a way of ruling out ideas, seemingly without even thinking about them, but ultimately I never had a real problem with that. I don't think it ever caused us to lose any good work, and anyway, he listened to me most of the time.'[31]

Phillips was indefatigable once the creative spark was ignited. 'The sessions would go on and on,' Marion Keisker recalled, 'each record was sweated out. Sam showed patience beyond belief – in a personality that's not really given to patience.'[32] Carl Perkins also remembered the long hours: 'It was always dark when we got through. I don't ever remember going in there and not doing from six to sixteen hours. I have been in there all day and all night and half the next day. Yes, sir. And got some good stuff at two or three o'clock in the morning.'[33]

Recording sessions would generally end with Phillips inserting a slip of paper into the master reel to indicate the beginning of the take he had selected for release. Most times there was a consensus about which take was best, but sometimes artist and producer disagreed. One such instance was the Johnny Cash classic 'I Walk the Line'. Cash had initially conceived the song as a slow ballad, and had insisted on recording it that way in the studio. Phillips was not satisfied. He asked Cash to try another take at an increased tempo, just as an experiment. Unbeknown to Cash, Phillips released the faster version. 'I was in Florida when I first heard "I Walk the Line" on the radio,' Cash remembered, 'and I called Phillips and begged him not to send any more copies out. I thought it was so bad. I thought it was a horrible record. And he said, "Let's give it a chance and see," but I didn't want to. I wanted it stopped right then. I got upset with him over it; I thought it sounded so bad. Still sounds bad – the arrangement – and I didn't like the sound, the modulation and all. But that's what turned out to be the most commercial part of it. Sam was right about it.'[34]

Not every artist Phillips worked with appreciated his approach to producing a recording session, or agreed with the music as he heard it in his head. Roy Orbison felt stifled by Phillips' insistence on casting him as an up-tempo novelty singer. He was confused when Phillips instructed him to sing in a blues style. Orbison was from Texas and had no affinity with such a style. 'When we were recording "Ooby Dooby",' he explained, 'Sam Phillips brought me out a set of thick 78 records and said, "Now, this is the way I want you to sing." And he played "That's All Right" by Arthur Crudup. I sort of took a little notice and he said, "Sing like that . . . and like this." And he put on a song called "Mystery Train" by Junior Parker. And I couldn't believe it . . . And I said, "Now Sam, I want to sing ballads, I'm a ballad singer." And he said, "No, you're gonna sing what I want you to sing. You're doing fine. Elvis was wanting to sing like the Ink Spots or Bing Crosby." And he did the same thing for him; did the same thing for Carl Perkins.'[35]

It seems unlikely that Phillips mistook Orbison for a blues singer. More likely, he was attempting to elicit the same kind of intensity and emotion from Orbison's studio performance as was heard on those blues records. The problem evidently lay in communication rather than ability; Phillips never managed to tap into the soaring emotionalism that would become the key feature of Orbison's later recordings. In this instance, it was probably a case of conflicting visions: each man following a very different beat playing inside his own head.

Orbison's account of his in-studio experience with Phillips differs markedly from that of most other artists. The majority found his direction neither intrusive nor dictatorial. They comment on his patient willingness to allow their numbers to evolve organically in their own time and direction. He would offer suggestions when the work appeared to be stalling, or when the artist was in danger of losing something Phillips thought was good, but he rarely imposed his own will. What he was not willing to compromise, however, was the integrity or validity of the music he produced. '[Phillips] did care when something I did challenged his notions of good and bad music, though,' Cash explained. 'Then he was quite frank. "That's awful," he'd tell me. "Don't do that." I'd say, "All right, I won't," unless I disagreed strongly. Then we'd work it out between us.'[36]

For Phillips, the disagreements, frustrations, cajoling, and continual give and take were all a part of the creative process. 'I could tolerate anything,' he stated. 'We could have tensions as long as I knew that we all had confidence in what we were trying to do, and I could get everybody relaxed to the point where they could hear and react to something without that threshold of apprehension where you almost get to a point where you can't do anything right. Every time we did a number I wanted to make sure to the best of my ability that everybody *enjoyed* it.'[37]

Phillips did not believe in rushing the recording process. He understood that it took time to establish the necessary rapport between himself and the artist in order to achieve the best results. 'We had a great time,' he recalled. 'I don't mean we didn't work our ass off, but we had an awful lot of what I call absolute confidence in each other, once we got to know each other. I said, "If I don't get to know you and you don't get to know me, chances are we're not going to do a whole hell of a lot together."' Once artists understood what Phillips was after, the session was able to progress to a different level: 'After a while, you'd be surprised at the psychological effect it had on people being able to deliver what they felt. Not trying to please some dude behind the glass that they thought might have some money.'[38]

Unusually – miraculously, even, given the times – Phillips saw much more commonality than difference between himself and many of the musicians he recorded. 'We were poor folks,' he affirmed. 'Black and white poor folks, including myself. Sometimes we learn more from the extreme circumstances that we find ourselves in. And I have found that so many ways, in country music, and black music, and gospel music – both black and white gospel music . . . I have said it so often, but there has never been an elixir that is so freeing, to the people that need freedom the most, as music. And I'm not just talking about the color of skin. I'm talking about people who never thought they'd have a damn opportunity for anybody to listen to them.' Phillips seems to have counted himself among those longing to be heard. He had found a way to get people to listen, but he recognised that the opportunity did not exist for everyone, and likely would not unless he provided it. 'They didn't know how,' Phillips said of the many talented musicians in Memphis who wanted to record, 'or couldn't get to New York or Chicago or Nashville. And [those cities] were loaded down with so many people that they couldn't take them all. I'm not saying anything against these people. I'm just saying that, godawmighty, I came in to help myself, but I came in to help them, too.'[39]

Chapter Five

Pursuing the Dream

THE FINANCIAL FAILURE and discontinuance of the short-lived Phillips label had been a disappointment, but by mid 1950 Phillips had found a new opportunity with Modern Records. Based in Los Angeles and owned by the three Bihari brothers, Modern was a successful independent label that was searching out 'race' material for their new subsidiary, RPM Records. Phillips sent samples of some of the artists he was working with, and the result was an assignment to record RPM's newest artist acquisition.

Riley Ben King was a guitar player who had arrived in Memphis in 1947, where he was able to turn a one-night gig at a local nightspot into a live daily show on WDIA, the nation's first black-oriented radio station. First nicknamed Bee-Bee, then B.B. (short for either 'Blues Boy' or 'Singing Black Boy' – take your pick), King's popularity with radio audiences led to a contract with Nashville-based Bullet Records, which yielded two singles in the latter half of 1949. When the contract expired, Jules Bihari scooped up King and assigned him to Phillips, who recorded King under Bihari's direction until June 1951.

RPM Records released five singles from the sessions Phillips produced with King, each of which adhered to what would become the standard Phillips formula of pairing an up-tempo number with a slow one. The recordings reveal King at the beginning of his career, before his guitar style had fully developed and matured. Phillips' production technique was also in a nascent stage, but his rendition of 'She's Dynamite' exhibits the explosive energy and experimentation that would later become his trademark.

As a result of his relationship with Jules Bihari, Phillips was able to get Joe Hill Louis a contract with RPM Records. Louis was exactly the type of artist Phillips had envisioned when he initially thought of opening Memphis Recording Service: primitive, raw, home grown – different. He played harmonica, drums and electric guitar, none of them exceptionally well, but with the driving beat and forcefulness that always appealed to Phillips.

Even with opportunities like these, keeping Memphis Recording Service afloat demanded long hours of work. The $150 monthly rent and the $25 he paid to Marion Keisker each week did not amount to much, but Phillips was often hard pressed to come up with it during those first years. 'I didn't dare try and borrow a hundred dollars on a little rent payment,' he explained. 'I didn't want to make a damn fool of myself, because no one would invest in this wild idea that I had. Not that I was smart, but they damned sure didn't think I was smart.'[1] As usual, Phillips' first big break came just when the situation seemed darkest.

Word of what Phillips was doing in Memphis spread through the black music community. B.B. King passed the word to Ike Turner, a DJ at WROX in Clarksdale, Mississippi. Turner styled himself 'The King of the Piano' as the leader of a six-piece band that featured a young singer named Jackie Brentson. For their audition with Phillips the group put together 'Rocket 88', an energetic R&B number named after a supercharged Oldsmobile coupe. On 5 March 1951, Turner and his band made the drive to Memphis. Along the way, the guitarist's amplifier fell from the roof of the car, damaging the speaker cone. 'We had no way of getting it fixed,' Phillips recalled, 'so we started playing around with the damn thing, stuffed a little paper in there and it sounded good. It sounded like a saxophone.'[2] Phillips turned up the volume on the sound produced by the rigged amp, allowing guitarist Willie Kizart to provide the beat that drove the instrumentation.

While it is difficult to pinpoint the beginning of a new movement within any evolving art form, most music historians now acknowledge 'Rocket 88' as the first recording of what would come to be known as rock 'n' roll. The song's boisterous energy and driving beat mark it as being different from anything that had come before, and the precursor of what was to follow. When later asked if he knew 'Rocket 88' was destined to be a hit when he recorded it, Phillips responded, 'Yes, I did.' But he was quick to qualify the statement. 'Well, I mean there ain't nobody going to say, "You know you got a hit." You can say one thing and never know a damn thing about music, and you can look back down, especially at this time, and say this was a hit, or that was a hit. But I never looked like that.'[3]

Phillips sent acetate copies of 'Rocket 88' to Chess Records. Brothers Phil and Leonard Chess were Chicago nightclub owners who had broken into the record business in the late 1940s and had recently opened their own label. The Chess brothers had much in common with Phillips in their appreciation of blues music, although they preferred the urban sound of R&B and jump blues. The decision to do business with Chess was made after confirming with local record distributors that the label reliably paid its bills. Phillips sent special 16-inch acetate discs: 'I wanted all the little nuances to be conveyed for them to listen to,' he explained.[4] Unfortunately, the Chess equipment could not play the outsized discs, so Phillips had to recopy the material on to standard 12-inch discs.

The Chess brothers snapped up 'Rocket 88' and several other numbers. Released in April, 'Rocket 88' made its first appearance on the R&B charts in May, and climbed to no. 1 in June, eventually becoming the number two selling R&B record for the year. Its huge success marked a turning point for Phillips. It gave him access to a wider market, as well as providing a much-needed boost of encouragement. It was evidence that the long hours he had poured into Memphis Recording Service were beginning to pay off.

From January 1950 until the middle of 1951, Phillips continued to work his regular schedule at WREC as well as recording sessions for the RPM and Chess labels, and the other jobs he took on in support of Memphis Recording Service. He typically worked an 18-hour day, putting in eight hours at the radio station before his shift ended at 3.30 in the afternoon, getting in five or six hours at the studio, then heading over to the Peabody for the 10.30 nightly big band broadcast. Many of his co-workers at the radio station were less than sympathetic. It was common knowledge that Phillips was associating with black musicians, which elicited bigoted remarks from the WREC staff. The grinding pace, plus the worries of a struggling business and a young family to support, began to take their toll. Phillips suffered a nervous breakdown and was twice hospitalised at Gartly-Ramsay Hospital, where he received electro-shock treatments. When station owner Hoyt Wooten made a snide comment about his absences, it was the last straw. Phillips resigned from WREC in June.

The decision to approach Chess Records with 'Rocket 88' proved a mixed blessing. On one hand, it brought Phillips to the notice of the larger music industry, and gave him the courage to devote himself to developing his recording business full time. On the other, it ended his relationship with RPM Records and the Bihari brothers, who thought the hit should have been given to them. There 'wasn't any great split,' Phillips remembered, 'I just wanted to see what kind of an association I could build with Leonard and Phil.'[5] Unfortunately, the falling out also meant the end of Phillips' recording work with B.B. King.

Chess Records now provided the only outlet for Phillips' product. He worked on a speculative basis, as he would for some time to come – auditioning the talent, producing the sessions and recording the songs. When he thought he had viable material, he made an acetate copy and sent it to a label. Neither he nor the musicians were paid unless a label leased or purchased a recording for release. There were no contracts; Phillips operated solely on a handshake basis. No bank would extend a loan to cover costs under such a precarious arrangement, so Phillips was forced to cover them himself out of the proceeds from previous sales.

★ ★ ★

The phenomenal success of 'Rocket 88' had Chess Records clamouring for a follow-up. The problem was that the very success of the record had torn the band apart. Bandleader Ike Turner was jealous that singer Jackie Brentson had got all the credit and adulation, while Turner had been pushed into the background – it was *his* band, after all. To Phillips, it was simple. No matter how good a musician Turner was, he could not sing. Brentson, on the other hand, had a powerful voice, and it was the voice that sold the song. Turner took the band and went to work for the Bihari brothers as their A&R representative in Memphis. Brentson too went elsewhere in search of a new band.

Left in the lurch and with Chess breathing down his neck, Phillips recruited a local singer and piano player named Billy 'Red' Love and undertook a questionable bit of subterfuge. 'Juiced', performed by Love, was issued under the name of Jackie Brentson as the follow-up to 'Rocket 88'. Record buyers may have been fooled, but sales figures failed to match those of Brentson's single. Phillips' subsequent recordings of Love were released under the artist's own name. The real Brentson came back to the studio with a new band following the release of 'Juiced', but his next records proved unable to recapture the momentum of his previous hit, and he eventually returned to Turner's band.

Desperate for talent, Phillips began to press into service artists whom he had previously recorded for RPM, such as Joe Hill Louis and pianist Roscoe Gordon Jr. Phillips had acquired a song titled 'Booted' (a slang term for intoxicated), and he had Gordon perform it in a rolling, drunken manner. Released by Chess near the end of 1951, 'Booted' reached no. 1 in the R&B charts. The Bihari brothers were angry at being shut out a second time, and they quickly got Ike Turner to record Gordon singing the same song for the RPM label.

Reliance on verbal agreement is a common mistake of the in-experienced, and in learning the business as he went along this was one of the many mistakes Phillips made. The lack of a written contract with the Bihari brothers created all sorts of problems: rights over artists were never spelled out, so the brothers claimed first right of refusal to the product of any artist Phillips had ever submitted to them. Phillips meanwhile viewed each recording as a separate entity. In the case of another artist he recorded for Chess, this was to cost him plenty.

Chester Burnett was a giant of a man: 'six foot six, with the biggest feet I've ever seen on a human being', Phillips recalled.[6] He was a 40-year-old farmer from Mississippi, who daily sang his unique brand of Delta blues on black-oriented Memphis radio station KWEM. His nickname, 'Howlin' Wolf', was reflective of the raw, primitive, animalistic quality of his voice. 'When I heard him,' Phillips cryptically stated, 'I said, "This is for me. This is where the soul of man never dies."'[7]

Phillips' first session with Burnett probably took place in May 1951, yielding 'How Many More Years' and 'Baby Ride With Me'. Copies were sent off to RPM at the same time as his split with the Bihari brothers over 'Rocket 88'. Phillips switched Burnett to Chess and returned to the studio to record a second version of 'How Many More Years' and 'Moanin' at Midnight', which became the singer's first release. Once again, the Bihari brothers got Ike Turner to record Burnett singing the same songs (although mysteri-ously renamed 'Morning at Midnight') for the RPM label. The release landed on the national R&B charts in September.

Chess and RPM resolved their dispute in February 1952: Chess took Burnett, and RPM took Roscoe Gordon. However, another problem had been brewing between Phillips and Chess. Sales of follow-up records were disappointing, and continued to decline with each new single. Chess blamed Phillips for the situation, while Phillips felt he had not been paid what he understood was his due. 'Confusion arose between Leonard Chess and me about what I was supposed to be paid,' Phillips asserted. The relationship deteriorated as the year continued, due largely to Phillips' naïve reliance on verbal agreements. Because the terms of the business arrangement between the two parties had never been spelled out, it was impossible to resolve the inevitable disagreements that arose. 'Len and Phil [Chess] were not being honest with me,' Phillips continued. 'I have to say that. I was not being greedy. I'd have stayed with them, but I was working my ass off and I couldn't afford not to get what was due to me.'[8] He said elsewhere: 'I'm not saying they were bad people, but they stood for things I didn't stand for.'[9]

A further source of frustration was Phillips' lack of interest in the commercial aspects of his craft. 'If I'd had my way,' he explained, 'I'd rather have done only the creative end and left the business to other people, but once you set up in business you have to carry it through.'[10]

Perhaps even more galling was the proliferation of record labels in town since Memphis Recording Service opened in 1950. With various rivals now vying for the same talent, Phillips was faced with the unwanted prospect of having to form his own label. 'I truly did not want to open a record label,' he stated, 'but I was forced into it by those other labels either coming to Memphis to record or taking my artists elsewhere.'[11] This was not a totally new idea; Phillips had probably recognised its inevitability at the time of his aborted experiment with the Phillips label. In early spring of 1952, as his relationship with Chess deteriorated, he reconciled himself to taking on the additional responsibilities of ownership.

Phillips sold masters of Rufus Thomas and Bobby 'Blue' Bland to Chess, and continued to record Chester 'Howlin' Wolf' Burnett for the label, until October 1952. The final split was provoked by disagreement over who was to pay the costs of a Jackie Brentson promotional tour. In the ensuing scramble for assets, both Phillips and Chess laid claim to the artists Phillips had recorded. Not wanting a repeat of the RPM incident, Leonard Chess convinced Burnett to move to Chicago, where he was out of Phillips' reach. In the years that followed, Chess frequently joked that 'if I hadn't messed up, I could have had Elvis and Jerry Lee Lewis.' To which Phillips would half-seriously reply, 'Yes, you could have.'[12]

Of all the important artists he would ever record, Phillips counted Burnett as his greatest discovery, and the one with whose talents he felt the most affinity: 'Wolf was, and still is, probably *the* most exciting person to record in the studio of any person I ever recorded, black or white.'[13] He recalled, 'the greatest sight you could see today would be Chester Burnett doing one of those sessions in my studio. God, what it would be worth to see the fervor in that man's face when he sang. His eyes would light up, you'd see the veins in his neck and, buddy, there was nothing on his mind but that song. He sang with his damn soul.'[14] 'He had no voice in the sense of a pretty voice,' Phillips explained, 'but he had command of every word he spoke. When the beat got going in the studio he would sit there and sing, hypnotizing himself. Wolf was one of those raw people. Dedicated. Natural.'[15]

Phillips' love of black music, and his belief that it could help bridge the divide between the races, were often criticised in the crudest terms. It was not uncommon for white acquaintances to comment that the smell of the black artists he worked with clung to him. 'I didn't know the reaction I was going to have,' Phillips stated, looking back on the resistance he met with. 'It's hard, unless you lived back then . . . The racial situation across the nation, especially in the South, wasn't good . . . And for a long time, people didn't understand what I was doing out there with the "niggers". It was really kind of a tough thing.'[16]

'I knew the way whites felt about blacks,' Phillips explained. 'I didn't feel that way, yet I didn't condemn the other people because I knew that to a degree they had no control over generation after generation of prejudice. These things I had to deal with, the social situations.' Although a man of strong opinions, Phillips was not overtly confrontational. 'I'm not a shrinking violet,' he continued, 'but I never would have made it had I gone out and tried to challenge. I really found this out when I started Sun – how deep the resistance was. I just did my thing and tried to do it in the manner in which it would have been the most effective for our causes. I say *our* causes because I knew it would involve mostly black people.'[17]

Two years had passed since the opening of the Memphis Recording Service. The business still struggled, but in that time Phillips had achieved sufficient artistic success to bolster his courage. He had also encountered enough hassle from the record companies he supplied to know that he did not want to continue his relationship with them indefinitely. Phillips felt ready for something new, ready to further advance his dream of bringing attention to black music. As he weighed his options, the timing seemed right for Phillips to make another attempt at launching his own record label.

Chapter Six

A New Day

THE STORY BEHIND the Sun Records name and logo is fairly simple. 'I had chosen the name Sun right at the beginning of 1952,' Phillips recalled, 'when I had determined to try to start issuing my own recordings. The sun to me – even as a kid back on the farm – was a universal kind of thing. A new day, a new opportunity.'[1]

'My first step was to sketch out a label design and take it to Memphis Engraving on North Second Street. A man named Parker I had known and played with in the high school band was there. He drew several designs from my sketch and I decided on the one with the sunrays and the rooster. I can honestly say that I know what it's like to have a baby. That's what Sun Records was to me.'[2]

The story of the first Sun single is less straightforward. When Walter Horton was not working at his job delivering blocks of ice, he was playing harmonica on the street in Memphis. Phillips first heard him play in Handy Park in February 1952. Several days later he saw Horton passing by on the street and invited him into the studio. 'Blues in My Condition' and 'Sellin' My Stuff' (later retitled 'Sellin' My Whiskey') were recorded with Horton and jug band musician Jack Kelly (a.k.a. Jackie Boy and Little Walter) on 25 February 1952. On 1 March, Phillips recorded 'Drivin' Slow', an improvised composition by 16-year-old saxophone player Johnny London. Copies of this and a second London number, 'Flat Tire', were given to Dewey Phillips for trial broadcast on his radio show that same night. Copies of all four recordings were made on 5 March and offered to Chess for release, but were rejected.

Believing that Chess was wrong to turn down the material, Phillips rerecorded 'Drivin' Slow' on 8 March and sent out copies of it and 'Blues in My Condition' for airplay on local radio stations, in announcement of his new label. Positive audience response encouraged him to assign issue numbers to both releases, and to place an order on 10 March to have metal pressing plates cut for record production. However, while waiting for the plates to be delivered, Phillips reconsidered, deciding that only London's tunes were strong enough to launch the label. 'Blues in My Condition'/ 'Sellin' My Whiskey', Sun Records no. 174, was never manufactured. 'Drivin' Slow'/'Flat Tire', Sun Records no. 175, was pressed on 27 March and released in April 1952.

There was trouble almost from the beginning. Within weeks of his label's first release, Phillips was served a cease and desist order from a recording company in Albuquerque, New Mexico, laying prior claim to the Sun name. Worse, 'Drivin' Slow' did not deliver the hit that Phillips had hoped for. It appeared briefly on a few local charts, but failed to pay off in any significant way. Still, Phillips proudly hung a copy of his label's first single on the wall of his studio and awaited the results of his second release that month. Sun Records no. 176, a middling pair of blues numbers by a Forrest City, Arkansas DJ named Walter Bradford, was an even bigger disappointment. It failed to make any impression at all.

Phillips realised that his lack of business experience and inadequate financing were liabilities he needed to address straight away. Rival labels Duke, Meteor and RPM were all scoring major hits, while his was on the brink of foundering. The constant struggle to eke out a living was taking its toll on Phillips, and he often became depressed. 'It was a frightening experience for me,' he recalled. 'I had a heavy workload already, and now here I was with lack of time, lack of know-how, and lack of liquidity.'[3] More than once Marion Keisker put her own money in the cash drawer in order to hide the truth about the studio's dismal financial situation. Looking back on those troubled times from the distance of several decades, Phillips ascribed his ability to endure the hardships to his determination to fulfil what he increasingly believed to be his purpose in life: 'If you only knew how deficient we were in funds . . . Whatever we did was from hard work and giving people the opportunity and showing them that they could deliver, quote unquote, the sermon they had in mind. They couldn't do it any other way.'[4]

Aid came in the form of a business partnership with Jim Bulleit, one of the founding fathers of the Nashville recording industry. Bulleit's training as a classical vocalist had landed him an announcing job at station WSM, home of the *Grand Ole Opry*. He made the segue from radio announcer to booking agent for several Opry performers, which in turn led to the formation of Bullet Records in 1946.

Although he originally recorded hillbilly and gospel music, Bulleit soon discovered that R&B records were more profitable. For a time, black music accounted for the bulk of the label's output, but the fluke success in 1947 of a pop song titled 'Near You' by white Big Band leader Francis Craig gave both Bullet and Nashville the first recording to sell over one million copies. As a result, the label shifted its emphasis to pop records, but the inability to recapture the success of 'Near You' caused a rift among the label's partners. Bulleit left Bullet Records in 1949 and formed a succession of independent labels, but found he could not compete for quality talent once the major East Coast record companies realised Nashville's money-making potential. As a result, he was available to bring his hard-won expertise to Sun Records at just the moment Phillips most needed it. 'Jim'd had hits that were real door-openers for independent labels,' Phillips explained. 'He really helped me an awful lot as much as understanding what the problems were and could be, and he gave me most of the early insight into what I was confronted with – and that was frightening.'[5] Bulleit orchestrated the label's distribution deals, and managed its copyrights through his own publishing company.

The legal wrangling with the New Mexico recording company was eventually resolved, and Phillips was granted sole rights to the Sun name. With Bulleit's guidance, Phillips marked the re-introduction of Sun Records in January 1953 with the release of three new singles. It was an inauspicious beginning; none of the three made an impact on the charts. In retrospect, it is evident why Phillips' first half-dozen recordings for his own label failed to find an audience. Record buyers of the time were accustomed to the sophisticated, urban sound produced by the major record companies. By comparison, Phillips' recordings were raw, primi-tive, primal, compelling. It was a personal taste that would later come to be appreciated but at the time lacked commercial appeal. 'I was recording the *feel* I found in the blues,' Phillips explained. 'I wanted to get that gut feeling onto record. I realized that it was going to be much more difficult to merchandise than what Atlantic or Specialty, for example, were doing, but I was willing to go with it.'[6] Until he found the ability – or the desire – to marry his vision to marketability, success would elude Phillips. His next three releases proved the point.

Walter Horton was back in the studio exactly a year after his first effort nearly became Sun Records' first release. This time he brought along drummer Houston Stokes and guitar player Jimmy DeBerry. Phillips recorded three numbers on 25 February, one of which was Horton's variation on the 1950 Ivory Joe Hunter hit 'I Almost Lost My Mind', which Horton named 'Easy'. Another number was DeBerry's 'Before Long'. The two were paired for release in March.

Studio records indicate just how little these early artists earned for their efforts. DeBerry was paid $2. Phillips gave Horton $1 to purchase a harmonica and paid him $3 for the session. Stokes received $5, plus 75 cents to transport his drum kit home in a cab. Phillips did little better. Profit margin on record sales was minimal and collecting even that small amount was difficult, as distributors were notoriously slow to pay. The little profit that came his way was reinvested in manufacturing and promoting the next round of releases. Until Sun Records could produce a hit, the income stream would remain a trickle.

It was radio DJ Rufus Thomas who cut the single that finally turned things around for Sun Records, although the result proved to be a mixed blessing. Phillips had first recorded Thomas in 1951, leasing three singles to Chess Records. Thomas was summoned back to the studio on 8 March to record 'Bear Cat', a novelty song Phillips had hurriedly composed as a male answer to Big Mama Thornton's current hit 'Hound Dog', which had been issued two weeks previously. Released near the end of March, 'Bear Cat' appeared on the national R&B charts on 18 April, peaking at no. 3.

Up to this point, much of Phillips' time had been spent in the arduous task of promoting his label's records. This entailed long days of driving from distributor to distributor, from city to city, within a 500-mile radius of Memphis, stopping in at every radio station he passed along the way to talk to the DJs and hand-deliver a sample disc. The revenue from 'Bear Cat' finally made it possible for Phillips to hire some extra help. Older brother Jud came on board to take over the promotional duties, and his gregarious nature and larger-than-life personality made him an excellent representative. More importantly, the addition of Jud freed Sam to concentrate his time and attention on the studio.

Although it was the label's first hit record, 'Bear Cat' was not without problems. Phillips' general lack of industry procedure once again got him into trouble. His composition had supplied original lyrics but had 'borrowed' the tune used in 'Hound Dog'. 'I should have known better,' he later commented. 'The melody was exactly the same as theirs.'[7] Phillips was named in a copyright infringement lawsuit brought by Don Robey at Peacock Records/Lion Music, who was awarded two cents royalty from each record sold, plus court costs, when the case went to trial in July.

Phillips and Joe Hill Louis co-wrote Thomas' follow-up single,

'Tiger Man'. In what was now a predictable pattern, it flopped. Subsequent events made Thomas bitter about his relationship with Phillips. 'I sold a hundred thousand records for him,' Thomas later complained, 'and all the time he was looking for a white boy. Sam never mentions that I was the first to make money for Sun Records either.'[8]

'Tiger Man' was to be Thomas' last recording at Sun. He later had hits with 'Walkin' the Dog' and 'Funky Chicken' on the Stax label in the early 1960s. 'Tiger Man' was released on 8 July, the same day that Phillips' newest discovery released his debut single. Little Junior Parker and his band, the Blue Flames, had originally auditioned for Phillips earlier in the year, but he had decided their sophisticated R&B sound was too polished for his label. Still, he was impressed by their musicianship, asking them to come up with something in a more primitive blues vein. The group later returned with a tune called 'Feelin' Good', which was more to Phillips' liking. The song slowly climbed the local charts before entering the national R&B charts on 3 October and peaking at no. 5. It was the second-best showing on the label to date.

Parker's follow-up was one of those songs overlooked in its own time, but which assumes greater importance when it is finally recognised later on. 'Mystery Train' would achieve legendary status almost two years after its 1 November release, for the part it played in inspiring the first rock 'n' roll superstar. However, at the end of 1953, the song only served to irritate Parker. He felt no affinity for the blues music Phillips requested of him, and was eager to move on to a label that would allow him to play in his favoured R&B style. Don Robey at Duke Records offered Parker that opportunity. When Phillips found out, he brought a suit against Robey. At trial, Sun Records was ultimately awarded a $17,500 judgment. More importantly, Phillips gained half the publishing rights to 'Mystery Train'.

★ ★ ★

The weeks leading up to the summer of 1953 were busy ones for Phillips. The constant pressure to audition and develop new acts for his label placed great demands upon his time and energy. In addition to his records with Thomas and Parker, Phillips issued five other singles in June and July. Two of those July releases were by an unlikely black vocal group called the Prisonaires.

The group came to Phillips' notice through Jim Bulleit, who had been given a demo tape by Nashville music publisher Red Wortham. The Prisonaires were under the direction of lead singer Johnny Bragg, who formed the group soon after being incarcerated in the Tennessee State Penitentiary in Nashville in 1943. By the early 1950s, they were regularly featured on two local radio stations, one of which had made the tape that found its way into Phillips' hands. The group's close-harmony style was not to Phillips' usual taste, but he recognised their commercial appeal and the unique marketing angle.

One song on the tape, 'Just Walkin' in the Rain', particularly caught his attention. Following a mountain of red tape and the governor's intercession, the Prisonaires were transported to Memphis under armed guard for an all-day recording session on 1 June. Bragg recalled that the session did not go well: he had problems phrasing some of the words, and Phillips was ready to give up on the song. 'I was getting disgusted,' he later explained, 'because Sam didn't like "Just Walkin' in the Rain" and I knew it could amount to something.' After getting some help with his diction, the session continued and 'we got it on the first cut'.[9] Released two weeks later, the song had sold about 50,000 copies by November. Sales would have undoubtedly been higher had the group been able to perform publicly in support of the record.

Predictably, response to the Prisonaires' follow-up singles in July and November was disappointing. The material chosen was weak, but Phillips' lack of affinity for spiritual music was also partly responsible. Despite the range of talent available to him, Phillips was reluctant to record gospel music. It was a difficult product to market, requiring time and interest that he probably felt were better invested elsewhere. 'There's no telling what I could and should have done in gospel music from the Memphis area,' he explained. 'I'm ashamed to say I barely touched the surface. It was a whole different area to merchandise, and you run out of time after working eighteen hours a day.'[10]

Jud had been on the road throughout the summer and autumn, by which time he had developed a clear picture of the regional distribution network. More importantly, he had uncovered some of the questionable deals Jim Bulleit had worked with individual distributors on Sun's behalf. In order to cover losses from his own labels, Bulleit had promised some distributors free Sun Records product, taking a serious bite out of Sun's already small profits. For this and other reasons, by the end of the year Sam was anxious to terminate the partnership with Bulleit, and began to pressurise him to sell out. In February 1954, an agreement was reached for Jud to purchase Bulleit's share of Sun Records for $1,200, the buyout price being covered by a loan. The separation was complete when the label set up its own publishing company, Hi-Lo Music, to handle its copyrights.

★ ★ ★

Almost from the very beginning Phillips issued records in groups of three or four, presumably hoping that at least one might be a hit. During the seven months from December 1953 to the middle of July 1954, Sun Records released an astonishing 16 singles, an average of one every two weeks. Unfortunately, none proved more than locally successful.

Musical tastes were changing. The gritty country blues that was so integral to the Sun Records repertoire had fallen from favour, replaced by a taste for R&B with pop leanings. Phillips was momentarily caught out. He knew that he needed to broaden his market base but was not sure how. 'Keep in mind,' he later explained, 'there were a number of very good R&B labels. The base wasn't broad enough because of racial prejudice. It wasn't broad enough to get the amount of commercial play and general acceptance overall – not just in the South.'[11]

Phillips had spent a lot of time on the road, working with distributors, talking to jukebox operators, listening to retail vendors. They all appeared to be concerned about the same thing – that black music was ruining white children. Obviously Phillips did not agree, but it was not his style to be confrontational: 'When I'd hear [a racial comment] I didn't get into a big argument with them. I listened and learned their feelings. Just leaning on the counter, talking. We just didn't talk about "You ought to have a different attitude . . ." I was going to let the product deliver itself.' Part of the reason for Phillips' forbearance may have been an understanding of just how unpopular his position was: 'I didn't need to make any damn enemies. There were enough already there.'[12]

Phillips knew from a lifetime of experience that the racial divide ran too deep to be bridged by any argument he could offer. Instead, he turned his mind to solving the question of how to make black music – or rather, the *feel* of black music – palatable to white audiences. Until the answer came, Phillips went on the only way he knew how: he sought out and recorded the music he loved. During this period, Sun Records was to become a virtual incubator for emerging talent.

Most of the early Sun artists were locals who performed at Beale Street nightspots or on one of the city's black-oriented radio stations. Several had got their start as teenage street performers. Some, like Big Memphis Marainey, D.A. Hunt and Raymond Hill, disappeared into oblivion after their Sun Records debut. Many others found that success eluded them in Memphis, but went on to become fixtures in the post-war Chicago blues scene. Significantly, Phillips was equally drawn to the vocal abilities *and* the musicianship of the blues artists he recorded for his own label.

1953 began with the release of 'Baker Shop Boogie' by Willie Nix, 'The Memphis Blues Boy'. Nix was a drummer who got his start on Beale Street as a tap dancer, later turning to singing and songwriting. He probably attracted Phillips' notice playing drums on earlier sessions Phillips recorded with Joe Hill Louis, B.B. King and Junior Parker for Chess Records. Nix followed the latter two performers to Chicago, where he recorded for the Chance label.

Phillips first recorded Doctor Ross 'The Harmonica Boss' on 29 November 1951. Ross was a singing one-man band who played harmonica and guitar, although Phillips brought in back-up musicians for the sessions, Two cuts were leased to Chess, 'Country Clown' and 'Dr. Ross Boogie', for release in March 1952. Ross was next in the studio on 3 October 1953 to record his debut Sun single, which was released in December. Another session late in 1954 produced Ross's second and final single for the label. Neither record sold well outside Memphis. At the end of 1954, Phillips had 23 unreleased Doctor Ross songs on tape. The fact that they were kept, rather than recorded over as usual, is a testimony to the esteem Phillips had for Ross's work. Ross retired from music in 1955 and became an auto factory worker in the Detroit area.

Milton Campbell (dubbed 'Little' Milton to differentiate him from his father, rather than denoting youth or height) came to Phillips' attention in 1953 through the talent scouting activities of Ike Turner. Campbell was a songwriter and a proficient guitar player who could capably perform any style of blues. However, it was his passionately dramatic delivery that most impressed Phillips. The first of Campbell's three Sun singles was released in December 1953. He moved on in 1955 to further develop his distinctive vocal style on the Chess and Stax labels.

Phillips first encountered James Cotton when he was brought into the studio as a backing musician for a Howlin' Wolf session. Cotton was a singer and harmonica player who went on to land his own show on Memphis radio station KWEM in 1952. The four sides he cut for Sun in 1954 were rural blues that sold well in the local market, but not enough to keep him in town. He moved on to Chicago to work with Muddy Waters, and to record for the Chess and Verve labels.

Frank Prestage Floyd was a white blues singer who played harmonica and guitar. Never formally named, and known only as 'Shank' for the first 14 years of his life, he named himself and adopted the moniker 'Harmonica Frank' in the early 1920s as a medicine show entertainer. He played primitive country blues in an antiquated style that Phillips loved, but which was not commercially viable. Phillips first heard him on station WMC in Memphis in 1951 and recorded him soon after. Material for two singles was leased to Chess for release in August 1951 and January 1952. Floyd made one record for Sun in July 1954 and probably would have been forgotten, if not for the revival of interest in folk music in the early 1970s.

Billy 'The Kid' Emerson was a songwriter and pianist, another of the artists scouted for Phillips by Ike Turner. Emerson got his nickname from the cowboy stage clothes he had once been required to wear as part of a band playing in St Petersburg, Florida. Phillips produced sessions with Emerson in January, April and October 1954 and May 1955, resulting in five singles. Emerson's talent for songwriting was his greatest contribution to the Sun label: a cover version of 'Red Hot' became a rockabilly anthem in 1957 and was periodically revived into the 1970s. He left Sun in 1955 to record in Chicago for Vee-Jay and Chess.

Phillips expressed admiration for some of the great R&B records being produced in the early 1950s by bigger labels, featuring artists like Big Joe Turner, Wynonie Harris and Johnny Otis. He thought he could have achieved similar results, but he felt impelled in a different direction: 'I wasn't interested in having music as great as all those labels like Atlantic and Specialty and Imperial. I could have made some R&B records in the tradition of some of these labels that were making fantastic music. I just had to do it different. I had no idea. The only thing I knew was that if I could get the opportunity to expose it to the people, and if I could just hang on long enough . . . . Because I know ain't nobody going to invest in what I'm doing. There ain't nobody that stupid. If I could hang on long enough, the people would tell us whether I was right or wrong in giving these people something we could enjoy.'13

★   ★   ★

Sun Records quickly gained a reputation for producing authentic blues recordings, but between the beginning of 1953 and the middle of 1954 Phillips also recorded several country artists. Some attracted him because of the pure and honest emotion conveyed in their untrained voices. Others he recorded solely for their ability to sell records. Unlike the blues artists he recorded during the same period, Phillips was primarily interested in country artists' voices rather than their instrumental talents.

Sidney 'Hardrock' Gunter, Jr. earned his nickname when an incident involving the hood of a car provoked comment that his head was hard as a rock. He had previously scored one hit record on the Bama label and released several singles for Decca, and was working as a DJ in Birmingham, Alabama when he first came to Phillips' attention. Gunter's recordings demonstrate an early amalgam of western swing and R&B that would later find fulfilment in Carl Perkins. Significantly, neither of Gunter's two Sun singles were produced or recorded by Phillips; the masters were merely leased and edited by Phillips for release on the Sun label.

Earl Peterson, 'Michigan's Singing Cowboy', was a regular radio performer in his native state before coming to Memphis expressly to audition for Phillips. His 1954 country boogie Sun release 'Boogie Blues' sold about 2,700 copies. Peterson reprised his Sun recording for the Columbia label in 1955, before returning north.

As front man for the Starlite Wranglers, Doug Poindexter performed at a Memphis honky-tonk named the Bon Air. His sole Sun release, 'No She Cares No More for Me'/'My Kind of Carryin'

On', was sung in a nasal backwoods hillbilly style and sold only 330 copies. He dropped out of the band to sell insurance soon after. Poindexter's biggest claim to fame is that two musicians from his band became Elvis Presley's first backing musicians.

Local bandleader Ethmer Cletus 'Slim' Rhodes had been a fixture on Memphis radio station WMCT since 1944. Phillips first recorded his band in 1950 and leased sides to 4-Star Records. Slim Rhodes and his Mountaineers performed in whichever style of country music was currently in vogue, as their widely varied recordings for Sun attest. Vocalist Dusty Brooks (a.k.a. Ronnie Hesselbein) was a vanilla Elvis soundalike who recorded for Phillips both with the band and as a solo performer. Phillips was not overly impressed with the band's style, but could count on its local popularity to sell records.

Howard Seratt was a crippled hillbilly gospel singer from Arkansas. Phillips loved the honest simplicity of Seratt's voice, and would have liked to continue recording him, but Seratt's insistence on recording only spiritual material made further sessions impossible. The Sun single 'Troublesome Waters'/'I Must Be Saved' is Seratt's only known recording.

None of Sun Records' country releases from this period achieved more than minor local success, and many of the artists were never heard from again. Phillips' forays into true country music were few, probably due to his lack of interest in then popular orchestrated style of material that Nashville was producing. 'I wanted gut bucket white and black,' he said of his musical preferences, 'but I didn't want country, as such, because the *Grand Ole Opry* was doing great. Of course, it would have been a hell of a lot easier, as I look back upon it, because I knew I could make some damn good country records.'[14]

★ ★ ★

Although Sun Records occasionally produced a single that reached the national charts, it was primarily a regional label serving a regional market, the bulk of whose songs – if they charted at all – found recognition only in the Memphis charts. There were hundreds of small record companies like Sun in the 1950s, independently owned and serving the market in which they were located. These indie labels had the advantage of knowing the musical preferences of their record-buying audience, and could frequently respond to emerging trends quicker than one of the major labels. They were also more willing to take a chance on new talent and on locally known artists. The disadvantage was that indie labels had little promotional capital and limited distribution systems. Even if a single was believed to have national hit potential, there was little these labels could do to push it in distant markets.

The charts by which a single's success was measured were compiled and published by trade magazines – the most respected of these were *Billboard* and *Cashbox* – and were divided into national, territorial and regional sections. *Billboard* magazine's C&W Territorial Best Sellers listed regional sales rankings for cities like Birmingham, Charlotte, Dallas-Ft Worth, Houston, Memphis, Nashville, New Orleans, Richmond and St Louis. This would have been the chart of primary importance to Phillips, since it was the most likely chart for his label's offerings to register on. Chart numbers reflected record sales rather than radio airplay. Popular disc jockeys might be able to boost sales by putting a single into heavy rotation, but their influence extended only as far as the reach of the radio station's signal. This distinction would have been lost on most of the public; they would have assumed that a song receiving regular airplay in their city was receiving the same attention nationwide. Likewise, placement in one region's chart was an indication of its tastes, and might not translate to success in other regions.

In the early days of his operation, Phillips personally dealt with over 40 independent record distributors, each of whom did his own promoting and selling of records within his territory. Local distributors received lists of new releases from which they could place orders. The leading radio stations in each of the major cities of the Southern territory were mailed copies of each new single, along with promo sheets plugging the label's recent product. Influential disc jockeys received personal phone calls to enquire about audience response. Phillips purchased advertising in the trade publications for releases he believed in, with the expectation that the single might be reviewed. A single that became a hit in the major Southern or Midwestern regions would get a promotional push on the East Coast, then the West Coast, then nationwide.

Still, with limited resources, only a few singles received the promotional backing of the label. Consequently, many Sun Records artists had to do their own promotional work. Both Carl Perkins and Johnny Cash recount in their autobiographies how Phillips taught them to approach outlying radio station disc jockeys. On the long drives between gigs, Phillips coached his artists to watch for radio antennae on the horizon and to stop in at every little station they passed. They were to be polite, thank the DJ for playing their record (which he may or may not have done), give him a copy if he did not have one, and not take up too much of his time. Phillips knew from his own experience at local radio stations how much this personal contact could accomplish. If the encounter was successful, an artist might be rewarded by hearing his record announced and played as he drove away.

Part II

The Rising

Chapter Seven

Starlight

THE FIRST HALF of 1953 was frustrating for Phillips. On the one hand, his recording of 'Bear Cat' by Rufus Thomas had become a regional hit, giving the fledgling Sun Records some much-needed name recognition. Later in the year 'Just Walkin' in the Rain' by the Prisonaires and 'Feelin' Good' by Little Junior Parker would continue the trend. But the relationship with business partner Jim Bulleit was already strained, and the constant financial struggle to keep the studio afloat was taking its toll. There were frequent quarrels about money and everyone connected to the operation felt on edge. It was at this period that Phillips unknowingly got the biggest break of his life.

What happened that summer – probably in August, probably on a Saturday – is the stuff of legend. Yet, ironically, the pivotal event in the history of Sam Phillips and Sun Records, if not the whole of rock 'n' roll music, passed by with Phillips barely taking notice of it. Indeed, due to a chronic absence of record keeping, the moment existed only in recollections pieced together for promotional purposes months after the actual event took place. Details varied depending on who was telling the story and when it was told. Only later, when the historical significance of the moment became apparent, did the story become codified.

In reality, the day was no different from any other, when a shy 18-year-old named Elvis Presley walked through the door of Memphis Recording Service. He carried a beat-up guitar and mumbled to Marion Keisker that he wanted to make a recording as a surprise for his mother. Keisker told him the price – $3.98

plus tax for a two-song acetate – and asked him to take a seat while he waited his turn in the recording studio. Presley himself was little different from the dozens of others who had previously walked in the door and made the same request, except in his appearance. Those who knew him at the time varied in their estimations of his talent, but the one thing they all agreed on was that Presley looked different. From his long, greasy hair, to his predilection for pink and black colour combinations, to his flamboyant Beale Street clothing, Elvis Presley looked like nobody else. The dissonance between his sartorial bravado and his self-conscious, twitchy manner is probably what captured Keisker's attention enough to start a conversation. It was one she rehearsed to reporters many times in the following years.

Presley: 'If you know anyone that needs a singer . . .'
Keisker: 'What kind of a singer are you?'
Presley: 'I sing all kinds.'
Keisker: 'Who do you sound like?'
Presley: 'I don't sound like nobody.'
Keisker: 'What do you sing, hillbilly?'
Presley: 'I sing hillbilly.'
Keisker: 'Well, who do you sound like in hillbilly?'
Presley: 'I don't sound like nobody.'[1]

As we all now know, Presley did *not* sound like anybody other than himself. But by the same token, he did not yet sound like Elvis Presley either, at least not the Elvis Presley we think of today. That Elvis did not appear until about a year later. The songs he recorded that summer day in 1953 were a 1948 pop hit called 'My Happiness' and the 1941 ballad 'That's When Your Heartaches Begin', which concluded abruptly with Presley speaking the words, 'That's the end.' Each was sung with earnest emotion, neither hinting at what was to come. Phillips later described the singer he met at that first session as being 'the most introverted person that ever came into that studio . . . He tried not to show it, but he felt so inferior.'[2] 'He reminded me of a black man in that way,' Phillips explained. 'His insecurity was so markedly like that of a black person.'[3]

Phillips wound up the session with the comment that he thought Presley was an 'interesting' singer, that 'We might give you a call sometime.' Before setting up to record the next client, he instructed Keisker to take the singer's name. Whether Phillips actually meant what he said, or whether this was simply his polite, standard send-off is unknown. Keisker, however, did note Presley's name (which she misspelled), adding the postscript, 'Good ballad singer. Hold.' She then typed the song title and singer's name on to blank labels, fixed them to the acetate and handed it to the waiting Presley. He made a few painful stabs at conversation, hoping that Phillips might come out of the control booth, hoping to get a chance to speak with him, but ultimately left, record in hand, to wait for the call that never came. The entire episode was over in less than half an hour.

Presley stopped in at Memphis Recording Service frequently over the next ten months; not often enough to be an irritation, but enough that Phillips got to know him by sight. 'Here's ol' Elvis,' Phillips later reported saying, 'coming to see what kind of star we can make of him today.'[4] The ostensible reason for the visits was to enquire whether Keisker had heard of a band in need of a singer. Just like the black artists that Phillips worked with at the time, Elvis was either too wary or too inexperienced to ask directly for an audition. 'I had the hardest time in the world convincing them that the audition was for free,' Phillips recalled, 'that they weren't going to be charged for it on the way out the door. Elvis was the same way: so shy about it that he wasn't going to ask.'[5] Keisker was always polite in her responses to Presley's enquiries, always remembered him – who could forget anyone with such a distinctive appearance? He later recalled Keisker fondly, expressing gratitude for her kindness and encouragement.

Sometimes Phillips would pass through the reception area, sometimes they would exchange a few words. Most times he was too busy to stop. Presley always walked away unsatisfied, but unknown to him, he had made an impression. While in Nashville in May 1954, Phillips acquired a demo recording of a song titled 'Without You'. 'I was going to the maximum security prison in Nashville to record the Prisonaires,' Phillips explained. 'I had been told there was a prisoner that was a pretty good writer, that he had some songs he wanted me to hear while I was there recording the Prisonaires. There was one song I was impressed with . . . And I told Elvis when he made the demo if I ran across some material I would give him a call.'[6] Phillips played the recording again and again, attracted by the song's simplicity and the rawness of its production. There was a yearning quality about the voice that reminded Phillips of another young singer he had recorded nearly a year before: that funny-looking shy kid – the one with the greasy blond hair and wild clothes – who kept hanging around the studio. When he returned to Memphis, Phillips asked Keisker to give the kid a call. She telephoned immediately, requesting Presley to come in at three that afternoon. Both Presley and Keisker stated that he was at the studio almost before the receiver hit the cradle.

The resulting demo session began to look like a failure, as Presley struggled unsuccessfully to find his way through 'Without You'. 'I listened to him sing it and played the demo on it,' Phillips remembered. 'After I listened for a while, absolutely I could not go with him and do what I wanted to do doing a slow ballad, although he sounded pretty damn good on the song, even though it wasn't as strong as I thought it was going to be. I still would not have recorded him on a ballad.'[7] When attempt after attempt came to nothing, Phillips stopped the tape and asked Presley to sing whatever he knew. For about three hours, he sang every song he could think of, every snatch of lyric he could remember. When it was over, Phillips had nothing to show for his time except the belief that this raw kid just might have something he could work with. 'I could not define it,' Phillips stated years later. 'I could only tell then as I tell you now that I knew when I had an exciting feeling that black people seemed to get into their songs, even if they're ballads, that a lot of white people don't. I've known that all my life. I don't know that I could define it, but I knew it had to have that energy. Because we had to have the young people on our side or we weren't going to make it.'[8] Whatever it was that he heard in Elvis' voice, Phillips wanted to hear more. 'I knew that he was a good singer,' he recalled. 'Certainly he was not polished. He never did have a band until we put out a record on him, when I got Scotty Moore and Bill Black to work with him.'[9]

Phillips had found a fellow soul in Scotty Moore, the manager and guitar player of local hillbilly band the Starlite Wranglers, which Phillips had recorded in May 1954. The two spent hours together, holed up in a booth at the restaurant next door to Memphis Recording Service, drinking coffee and scheming about the future. Both Phillips and Moore were ambitious. They were dreamers who knew that they wanted more out of life than what they had seen. Sensing that there was a change in the air, they wanted to be a part of it, though they did not know what it was or where to look for it. 'What there was a need for was a rhythm that had a very pronounced beat,' Phillips later observed, 'a joyous sound and a quality that young people in particular could iden- tify with.'[10]

On the surface, R&B music should have fitted the bill, but Phillips recognised that it had one insurmountable problem. 'It got so you could sell half a million copies of a rhythm and blues record,' he related in 1959. 'These records appealed to white youngsters just as Uncle Silas [Payne's] stories and songs used to appeal to me . . . But there was something in many of those youngsters that resisted buying this music. The Southern ones especially felt a resistance that even they probably didn't quite understand. They liked the music, but they weren't sure whether they ought to like it or not.'[11]

It was during these coffee-shop planning sessions that Moore first began to hear the name Elvis Presley. Phillips seemed convinced that the young singer had potential and Moore was eager to find out for himself. After several weeks of talk, Phillips finally suggested that Moore contact Presley and give him a listen.

A session was held the following day at Moore's apartment. It included Presley, Moore and Bill Black, who played bass in the Starlite Wranglers. Neither musician was impressed; neither thought the singer was anything special. Moore reported as much when he called Phillips afterwards. Still, Phillips believed. He wanted to hear what Presley sounded like on tape. He called the singer in for a second audition the following evening, inviting Moore and Black to come along and provide backing.

The audition began at 7 pm on a Monday in June. As usual, Phillips allowed everyone time to acclimatise themselves to the studio and each other. Finally, he turned to Presley and asked, 'Well, what do you want to sing?' It took some effort to find a song that they all knew, but eventually they launched into the Bing Crosby standard 'Harbor Lights'. A dozen takes of the country ballad 'I Love You Because' followed. Presley poured everything he had into every take, while Scotty and Bill trotted out every trick they knew, but nothing clicked. Phillips came out of the control booth now and again to adjust equipment or give the musicians an encouraging word, but the results grew more and more frustrating as the evening wore on. 'Elvis cut a ballad, which was just excellent,' Phillips recalled. 'I can tell you, both Elvis and Roy Orbison could tear a ballad to pieces. But I said to myself, "You can't do that, Sam." If I had released a ballad I don't think you would have heard of Elvis Presley.'[12] Finally, during a break, Presley relaxed a bit and started fooling around with an old blues tune he had heard many years before: Arthur 'Big Boy' Crudup's 'That's All Right (Mama)'. 'I was surprised Elvis even knew the song,' said Phillips.[13] Caught up in the bouncing energy of Presley's rendition, first Bill, then Scotty joined in. In the control room,

Phillips' ears perked up. He stuck his head out and asked, 'What are you doing?' The musicians replied, 'We don't know.' 'Well, back up,' Phillips replied. 'Try to find a place to start and do it again.'[14]

Scotty and Bill worked out the arrangement amid Phillips' continual urging to simplify. 'If we wanted Chet Atkins,' he laughed, 'we would have brought him up from Nashville and gotten him in the damn studio!'[15] Phillips employed a similar tactic with his inexperienced singer: 'I encouraged him to be real raw, because if he was artificial he wouldn't be able to keep it up.'[16] Presley quickly found his confidence, keeping his delivery fresh through a series of full and partial takes. When the final take was played back, everyone agreed that this sound was new and different and exciting, but no one quite knew what to make of it. It was unlike anything they had ever heard before.

Phillips may or may not have uttered the quote most often ascribed to him: 'If I could only find a white boy who could sing like a Negro, I could make me a million dollars.'[17] Marion Keisker maintained that he did; Phillips insisted that he did not. Still, the fact remains that others had tried that route before and failed, so there was obviously some other element to the equation. 'I was looking for something different,' Phillips stated, 'not necessarily a song, but a distinctive stylist you'd know the moment you heard him.'[18] Phillips probably recognised that a white boy who could capture the *feel* of black music stood a chance of succeeding with an audience that would never openly listen to the real thing. This was the element Phillips thought he saw in Presley.

Phillips arranged for additional sessions the next two nights, but neither recaptured the creative spark of the first. Having broken up the Wednesday session early, he called to ask Dewey Phillips to stop by the studio after signing off his nightly radio show and sat back to wait. Dewey arrived just after midnight. Phillips played the tape of Presley singing 'That's All Right (Mama)' over and over again as the two man sipped beer and whiskey long into the night.

Neither said much; neither knew what to say. It was just so different.

For once, the normally garrulous Dewey was at a loss for words. His boisterous on-air approval or disapproval alone could make a record a hit or a flop, but Phillips was in no hurry to get a response. '[Dewey] was reticent,' Phillips recalled, 'and I was glad that he was. If he hadn't been reticent, it would have scared me to death . . . What I was thinking was, where are you going to go with this; it's not black, it's not white, it's not pop, it's not country; and I think Dewey was the same way.'[19] The longer it took Dewey to process what he was hearing, the more Phillips began to be convinced that he was on to something big. The two men parted around two or three o'clock. Early the next morning, Phillips received a call from a sleepless Dewey, wanting two copies of the song that he could not get out of his head. He was going to play it on his radio show that night, though he told Phillips not to let anyone know.

Phillips made the acetate copies and dropped them off at the radio station. He called Presley after work to say that Dewey might play the record on his show that night. Presley tuned his parents' radio to the station and left for the cinema, too nervous to sit and listen. Around ten o'clock, Dewey announced that Sam Phillips had a new singer named Elvis Presley whose record was going to be a hit. Then – according to legend – he played the disc seven times in a row. 'He played that mother over and over and over,' Phillips recalled. 'And he would not have done that except for the response. No hype was done, absolutely. It was just more or less an experimental thing when Dewey played Elvis.'[20]

The switchboard lit up immediately. People called in from all over the city, asking about the singer and wanting to know where they could get a copy of his record. Dewey phoned the Presley home, looking for Elvis. When informed by Mrs Presley that her son was at the movies, Dewey told her to find Elvis and get him down to the station as fast as possible.

Elvis soon arrived in a panic, nervous and scared to death. Dewey told him to calm down, said he wanted to interview him on air, then cued up the next records and set them to play. After the caution, 'Just don't say nothin' dirty,'[21] and the promise to let the shaking novice know when the interview was ready to begin, Dewey launched into a conversation. He made a point of asking where Presley had attended high school, knowing that the answer would let the still segregated listening audience know that the singer was white. The conversation continued a little longer before Dewey thanked Elvis for coming in. 'Aren't you gone interview me?' the confused singer asked. 'I already have,' Dewey replied. 'The mic's been open the whole time.'[22]

Phillips sat alone at Memphis Recording Service with the radio tuned to Dewey's programme. Even before he was told about the favourable response to the recording, he had the feeling that it could be a hit. 'I knew we had to get young white people involved or it wasn't going to succeed,' Phillips observed. 'Jazz could have reached the young people as something they could have called their own, but it was taken and smothered by adults. The teenage years are the toughest years of your life. Take the child who has so much problem mixing and mingling with other people. Music can be the greatest educator in the world for helping such people.'[23]

The session Phillips scheduled for Friday night took on a sense of urgency, as the search began for a second side to complete the single release. The musicians went through every song they could think of over the course of three or four nights, but nothing matched the excitement of 'That's All Right (Mama)'. Once again, the right song came by accident. Bill Black began messing around with the old Bill Monroe bluegrass standard 'Blue Moon of Kentucky'. The others joined in, gradually upping the tempo over the course of several attempts, and it all came together. On a surviving bit of tape from the session Phillips is heard shouting, 'Hell, that's fine! That's different! That's a pop song now!'[24]

Much of the difficulty in finding the sound that Phillips was searching for lay in the fact that Elvis initially saw himself as a ballad singer. 'Oh, yeah,' Phillips explained. 'He liked not crooners, but people who really did know how to handle a ballad. Of course, he did some ballads – many of them – later on, but to introduce this young man at 18, 19 years old with that type of thing would have defeated the whole thing I had in mind: to find a white man that could give the expression that black people were giving through rhythm and blues. After we thought about [it], we did a lot of different things with Elvis before we hit upon "That's All Right (Mama)" and "Blue Moon of Kentucky."'[25]

Years later, Phillips speculated on the direction Presley's career might have taken if he had followed his original inclination: 'It's really hard to say, but I doubt if Elvis – and I really mean this – would have done anything other than wind up in a [gospel] quartet like the Blackwood Brothers . . . Now ultimately, he might have broke out of that and gone into the type of things we were doing, but I knew this: we just couldn't take this guy with this beautiful voice and say we're going to blow Nat King Cole and everybody out of the water. I knew better than that. We had to have a different approach. We had to have a beat. We had to have something the younger people could identify with and say, "By golly, I sure do like this."'[26]

Advance copies of the single were made for all the influential DJs in town, not just Dewey, who had had exclusive play on the record since debuting it on his show. Demand was such that there were already 6,000 local orders for the record when it was officially released on 19 July. 'God only knows that we didn't know it would have the response that it would have,' Phillips recalled. 'But I always knew that the rebellion of young people, which is as natural as breathing, would be a part of that breakthrough.'[27]

Just a week after the musicians had first met, Phillips made Moore the band's manager. Moore got 10 per cent of the proceeds off the top and the remainder was split 50-25-25, Elvis getting the bigger share. The plan made sense, as the original thought was for Elvis, Scotty and Bill to be a featured trio within the Starlite Wranglers. However, the rest of the group was quickly swept aside in the Elvis frenzy, and broke up within a few months.

Elvis first performed his two numbers in public two days before the record was released. Phillips drove him out to the popular Bon Air Club, a rough-around-the-edges hillbilly roadhouse, where he sang the two songs during one of the Starlite Wranglers' breaks. The audience response was tepid and Elvis felt he had failed, but the experience was significant for Phillips. Previous to this, he had viewed Elvis only in terms of his singing ability. He had never thought in terms of Elvis' impact as a performer, let alone as a personality. What Phillips saw that night was the reaction of the crowd. They liked the music, they just could not get past the appearance. The clothes, the colours, the greasy pompadour, the pimpled face, the general impression of being in need of a bath: it was more than most people could readily accept. But these were not negative aspects in Phillips' eyes. Not only did his new singer have a *sound* that no one could categorise; he had a *look* that no one could categorise either. The whole package was completely different, which was exactly what Phillips had been searching for.

Now the work of introducing this new act began. Phillips contacted local DJ Bob Neal, promoter of an upcoming package show that headlined hillbilly yodeller Slim Whitman, about getting Elvis on the bill. He did not tell Elvis about the booking straight away, as he hoped to stave off the inevitable jitters for as long as possible. When the big night came, Elvis was near panic. As he got closer to Overton Park and saw the size of the crowd, what little self-confidence he had quickly evaporated. Phillips arrived late, having had difficulty finding a place to park his car. Sizing up the situation, he adopted the role he always took with the singer: the reassuring, encouraging believer, always cool and in control. As for Elvis, he was so nervous waiting to go on stage that he was visibly trembling.

No one was prepared for what happened that night. Elvis went on stage to perform 'That's All Right' and as he later explained: 'I was scared stiff. It was my first big appearance in front of an audience . . . and everybody was hollering and I didn't know what they were hollering at.' The trio had loosened up a bit by the time they launched into 'Blue Moon of Kentucky', and the crowd response grew even louder. Elvis continued: 'I came offstage, and my manager told me that they were hollering because I was wiggling my legs. I went back out for an encore, and I did a little more, and the more I did, the wilder they went.'[28]

Since the trio still knew only two songs, Elvis did 'Blue Moon of Kentucky' a second time for an encore. The screaming crowd nearly drowned the singer out. Phillips took in the scene from where he was standing backstage. This was what he had been waiting for all his life.

Sun Records was essentially still a bare-bones operation. Marion Keisker kept the day-to-day operations going, but it was Phillips who found the talent, recorded the music and promoted the records. 'That's All Right' was an unqualified hit in Memphis, but someone had to get out and hustle the record if the company hoped to make sales. From August to October, Phillips spent most of his time on the road, driving across the Southern states from Texas to Georgia, trying to interest record distributors, jukebox suppliers and store owners in his newest release. '[Elvis] was an immediate hit in Memphis,' Phillips recalled, 'but on the road it drug my ass out.'[29]

'There wasn't any such name as "rock 'n' roll" then,' he explained. 'You should have gone with me and tried to talk to the country disc jockeys and to the few black disc jockeys that were available in the country. Just like in Shreveport with Fats Washington, who was a paraplegic black person, and he worked at KTNT with a night show from about 6 to 12 or 1 o'clock every night. A fantastic guy. He had played Little Junior Parker and the B.B. stuff I had cut, and "Rocket 88", but when I got down there with Elvis, he said, "I just can't play 'That's All Right Mama'."'

Even though the same song had been a hit for Arthur Crudup several years before, Washington stated that he could not play Presley's version because it was impossible to categorise. 'The same thing happened with a country jock down there that I knew very well, like I did Fats Washington,' Phillips continued. 'His name was Tommy Cutrer. And he was a wonderful, wonderful guy that I'd worked with at WREC here, and at that time he was at KCHA in Shreveport. And he said the same thing about "Blue Moon of Kentucky". He said, "I just can't play that."'[30]

Undeterred, Phillips stopped in at every radio station along his route, trying to charm the DJs into playing the single on air. Most gave the record a listen and most declined to play it; their typical response was that the music was just too raw. 'I recall one jockey telling me that Elvis Presley was so country he shouldn't be played after 5 a.m.,' said Phillips. 'And others said he was too black for them.'[31] Those DJs that did take a chance generally shared Phillips' progressive mind-set: that times had changed, music had changed, and radio airplay had to change along with it.

Elvis was still working as a truck driver for Precision Tool by day, but he often went to Memphis Recording Service in the late afternoon to answer the phone when Phillips was on the road. At the time, Elvis was dating Barbara Pittman, whom Phillips would soon sign to Sun Records as the label's sole female rocka-billy artist. She recalled how 'Elvis and I used to go down to the Sun Studio in the afternoons after he got off work. Sam had given him the key . . . Sam was never there, he and Marion were off somewhere . . . and Elvis used to answer the phone. There was really nothing going on there in the afternoons at that time. Everything was done at night. So Elvis and I were taking care of the studio. A lot of people were talking to Elvis on the phone at that time and never even knew it.'[32]

Meanwhile, in Phillips' absence, it fell to Scotty Moore to develop a stage act. He gathered the trio at his place after work each day to rehearse. There was a repertoire to build – they could not go on playing the same two songs for ever – and Elvis had to be coached on how to handle the microphone, his guitar and just about everything else. The Overton Park show had given Phillips a number of insights, the most important being that Elvis' key audience was too young to gain admittance to alcohol-serving joints like the Bon Air Club. Scotty began looking for school gymnasiums and civic clubs in the surrounding area who wanted to book a show. The group continued to play locally – often unpaid – at church halls and hospital wards, and as an opening act at local nightspots.

For all his apparent shyness, Elvis was extremely driven. Nothing was going to stop him achieving what he wanted, even though he lacked the words to express what that was. He seemed to come alive on stage, revealing an instinctive ability to respond to audiences' need in a way that egged them on to want more. The onstage wiggling and gyrating came naturally to him, yet he quickly learned to exploit whatever movements elicited the greatest audience response. Early descriptions have much in common – shy, tongue-tied, sincere, polite – yet also vary to an extent that suggests an ability to reflect back whatever it was the observer wanted to see. These are very complex skills, particularly from someone who was so frequently described at this time as being 'uncomplicated'.

By the end of August, the record was listed on the regional *Billboard* charts. Many in the industry began taking notice, although much of what they said was disparaging. Phillips did not care. As long as people were talking about the record, it was helping to build momentum. Resistance remained high, but as reports started circulating about the volume of sales the record was generating in some locations, money began to talk louder. Dollar signs in their eyes, distributors jumped on board despite their personal distaste.

Meanwhile, Phillips knew he had to get a second single out before losing the momentum of the first. Easier said than done, with Phillips frequently out on the road making sales calls, and the trio's weekend gigs and full-time jobs. The first few sessions yielded nothing usable. Phillips patiently oversaw the proceedings, prodding and cajoling when needed, driving the trio when he sensed they were getting close to inspiration, offering encouragement when confidence started to flag. Despite the seriousness of the work, he also made sure that the mood in the studio remained loose, that there was time for laughter and fooling around. And when the session finally gelled, Phillips instinctively knew the moment was right for magic to happen.

Near the middle of September the tide turned. From among a cluster of not-quite-right numbers emerged the final cuts: 'I Don't Care if the Sun Don't Shine', a winking version of an improbable song choice, and 'Good Rockin' Tonight', a rollicking version of an R&B classic. The single was released the week before a scheduled performance on the *Grand Ole Opry*. With 'Good Rockin' Tonight', Phillips had chanced upon a continuation of the sound accidentally created on Elvis' first release. Phillips had not yet discovered the formula, but he was on the right track.

Phillips had been campaigning to get Elvis booked on the *Opry* for weeks, but manager Jim Denny was reluctant. 'I knew Jim,' Phillips remembered, 'so I went over to play him the record. He said, "I've heard it, Sam. I just better not put him on right now because we might do something to the *Grand Ole Opry*, and it's so traditional." I told him I understood and then I went into this bit about younger people and I said, "These people that used to drive to town in a wagon – well, the world has changed: we got jet aeroplanes!" He said, "The door is not closed. I think it's an interesting record, but I don't wanna get sponsors cancelled."'[33] With the new release spinning on every radio station turntable and the first single still riding high in the charts in major metropolitan areas, even the staunchly conservative *Grand Ole Opry* could no longer resist Phillips' entreaties. Denny agreed – reluctantly – to allow Elvis to perform one song on the show's Hank Snow segment.

Despite the grudging acceptance, Phillips was thrilled. The chance to debut any new artist – particularly one whose entire career spanned just two months – on the *Opry* stage was a coup. Another prestigious venue, one that actually *wanted* Elvis, was the *Opry*'s more progressive cousin, *Louisiana Hayride*. Phillips booked the *Opry* show first, and the *Hayride* for two weeks later.

The 2 October *Grand Ole Opry* show proved exciting in anticipation, but disappointing in realisation. The crowd was polite, but that was all. Jim Denny met Elvis backstage after his performance to offer subdued congratulations, ending the conversation with the pointed suggestion that Elvis consider giving up singing and return to truck driving. 'Forget him,' Phillips said to Elvis as Denny walked away. 'That man threw Hank [Williams] off the *Opry*, too.'[34] There was undeniable prestige in performing on the *Opry* stage, but the tentative audience response and hesitant approval of *Opry* management left everyone feeling dispirited – except Phillips. The fact that anyone applauded at all, had *anything* positive to say, stoked his fire. For a man hell-bent on producing something new and different, full acceptance by the hidebound traditionalists of the *Opry* would have felt like condemnation.

Two weeks later, the *Louisiana Hayride* show did not start out much better. Elvis was so visibly shaken by nerves that Phillips, sitting in the audience, feared the singer might do himself damage. He sensed that the audience wanted to like Elvis, but that the singer's obvious discomfort onstage made them uncomfortable as well. Phillips took Elvis aside backstage between shows for a pep talk, which produced the desired effect. When Elvis hit the stage for the second show, his confidence was back and the response was totally different. The hall erupted as the audience leapt to its feet. One witness likened the effect to an explosion. Several big-name performers stood in the wings that night, criticising the singer's dirty neck and foolish stage antics, completely unaware that they were witnessing the coming demise of their own careers.

On the heels of the *Hayride* success, Phillips began negotiations to book his budding star on to the show as a regular performer. He also pulled in Bob Neal, the DJ who had promoted the Overton Park show, to take over the booking duties from Scotty Moore. Neal had been putting together package shows for a number of years, booking them in small towns throughout Mississippi, Arkansas and western Tennessee.

Bob Neal kept the trio working throughout the autumn of 1954, with Saturday nights reserved for *Hayride* appearances. The group managed to squeeze in rehearsal time and a recording session in early December. 'Milkcow Blues Boogie', an up-tempo version of the Bob Wills western swing classic, and 'You're a Heartbreaker', an original tune to which Phillips owned the publishing rights, became Elvis' third single. It was released on his twentieth birthday, 8 January 1955. Sales of the second single had fallen short of the first, and sales of the third sank lower still. None of the recordings managed to capture the charisma of Presley performing live. 'Milkcow Blues Boogie'/'You're a Heartbreaker' ranked last in sales of all Presley's Sun recordings.

Elvis officially signed with Bob Neal at the beginning of 1955, and afterwards toured almost non-stop. It was during a February booking at Ellis Auditorium in Memphis that he first met promoter Colonel Tom Parker. An illegal immigrant and one-time carnival barker who had appropriated to himself the title of 'Colonel', Parker was a respected if somewhat shady businessman. Between shows, Elvis went to a restaurant across the street from the auditorium for a meeting with Phillips, Bob Neal and Parker to discuss an upcoming tour in which Elvis would front for country singing star Hank Snow.

Parker and Snow were partners in Jamboree Attractions, the country and western booking agency that was promoting the tour. The meeting got off to a sour start when Parker voiced his opinion that Elvis would never amount to anything as long as he stayed with Sun Records; that Sun's lack of broad distribution would hinder his career growth. Phillips, who seemed to take an instant dislike to Parker, managed to keep his cool, but only because he reluctantly recognised the truth of what Parker said. In a very short time, Bob Neal had made Elvis into a regional attraction, but he lacked the contacts to take him national.

Similarly, Sun Records lacked the financial resources to fund the costs of increased promotion, production and distribution necessary to introduce a new artist to a national audience. In a January 1955 letter to brother Jud, who was pressing for repayment of the money he had put up to buy out the partnership with Jim Bulleit, Phillips responded that the label was on the verge of bankruptcy. Although he intended to repay every dollar owed, Phillips acknowledged that there was little hope Sun Records would ever turn a profit.

★　★　★

Stan Kesler was one of the musicians Phillips pulled in to play on the first post-'That's All Right' rockabilly sessions. Hearing that Phillips was looking for a B-side to Elvis' 'Baby, Let's Play House', Kesler wrote the country tune 'I'm Left, You're Right, She's Gone'. Sam liked it and the trio worked up the number at their December 1954 session, attempting to give it a slow blues feel. Phillips sensed that something was missing and brought in a local high school band drummer. For the first time a drum was used on an Elvis session; the beat lifted the melody, giving the song the tone Phillips thought it needed. By the final take, the song had been reworked into a mid-tempo hillbilly shuffle. The finished recording did not match the energy of Elvis' previous releases, but Phillips felt it was time to broaden Elvis' audience appeal. It was paired with 'Baby, Let's Play House' for the fourth single, released on 25 April 1955. In July, it became the first of Presley's singles to enter the national country charts. The record sold well enough that Phillips owed the writer of 'Baby, Let's Play House' a substantial $6,500 in royalties for the first pay period.

Near the end of the month, Bob Neal took the trio to New York

City. He had been saving up money and planning this trip for some weeks, hoping that an audition for the top-rated *Arthur Godfrey's Talent Scouts* television show would provide the vehicle for national exposure. The audition failed to impress, however, and the trip proved a wasted effort.

The boys were out on the road almost immediately, driving from show to show in Elvis' 1954 pink and white Cadillac. The grind of a show every night in a different town was wearing, but it provided Elvis the opportunity to hone his act and gain confidence. The shy kid who, only months earlier, had been incapable of anything beyond mumbled monosyllabic responses to interviewers was gone, replaced by a sneering – although still impeccably polite – performer who could masterfully drive an audience to hysterical frenzy. Even so, 'polished' was not a word anyone used to describe Elvis at the time: crude jokes, poor diction, belches into the microphone and chewing gum spat out on the stage were all regular features of his early stage performances. He was shocking, ferocious, wild, embarrassing and completely original. No one else moved the way he did, no one else sang the way he did, and the way he did both made every other artist he performed with seem pale and lifeless in comparison. Colonel Parker's own Jamboree Attractions promoted many of these shows, and while he never let on that he was interested in Elvis beyond the current tour dates, he was always around, watching and waiting.

Chapter Eight

Sold Out

THE MOMENTUM OF Presley's success also caught the attention of the major record companies. Columbia, Decca, Capitol, MGM, Mercury and RCA all expressed interest. Phillips hinted through intermediaries at being interested in a partnership deal, but always set the terms so as to ensure that he was turned down. In turn, each of the major labels declined Phillips' demands.

The rumour that Presley's contract with Sun Records might be available may have been a ruse Phillips employed to build industry interest – he was never genuinely interested in partnerships – but there was some truth there as well. Phillips was in serious financial straits. Presley's rapid rise to fame, with its attendant production and promotional costs, had drained the already struggling label. Phillips had to front all the money to pay the pressing plant, label printer, music publisher, and a host of related union and royalty fees just to get product manufactured. Afterwards, advertisements had to be placed in the trade papers to announce the release. In between, at least three months would pass before distributors began paying for the records they had ordered. Even then, a variety of markdowns and deductions were taken from those payments. Phillips assumed all the costs and risks, only making money if the records became hits.

Such was the downside of success. The upside, however, was the expectation that Presley's increasing popularity would propel Sun Records to national prominence. That hope gave Phillips determination to retain ownership of the contract. For the time being, he put on a brave face, but he recognised that if the financial demands did not abate soon, he would have no choice but to seriously negotiate a price for his label's only asset.

In the meantime, Colonel Parker made another move to cement his ties to Presley. At a meeting in Nashville early in June 1955, he and Bob Neal signed a deal whereby Parker would represent Presley in all business matters, while Neal would continue to act as personal manager.

Presley was back in the studio on 11 July, fitting in a recording session during a gap between tour dates. Phillips was adamant that the next release should include material to which he owned publishing rights. The fact that Presley did not write his own songs meant that royalties were continually being paid to outside entities, rather than enriching the label's own coffers. With finances in a shambles, Phillips had to employ every means possible to increase the income stream.

'I Forgot to Remember to Forget' was an original country number by Stan Kesler, the writer of 'I'm Left, You're Right, She's Gone'. Presley did not like the song at first, but Phillips saw its possibilities. He kept the country tempo, but gave it a kick with the addition of a drummer. In general, Phillips did not like using drums on recording sessions, not because he disliked the instrument, but because the sound overpowered the capabilities of his tiny recording studio. Western swing drummer Johnny Bernero, however, had a light touch that he could work with.

The second number that night was the result of an accident. While fooling around, someone played a phrase from 'Mystery Train', which Phillips had recorded two years earlier with Junior Parker. The rest of the trio caught hold of the phrase and began to play. Phillips, always watchful for the moment when magic was about to strike, switched on the tape. 'It was the greatest thing I ever did on Elvis,' he said. 'It was pure rhythm. And at the end, Elvis was laughing, because he didn't think it was a take, but I'm sorry, it was a fucking masterpiece!'¹ 'Mystery Train' proved to be Phillips' favourite out of all the songs he cut with Elvis: 'I recorded it. I helped Junior Parker to write it. It's a record that has got a beat that's extremely good and I guess I've played that thing probably 1,000 times. I surely enjoyed it.'[2]

The final cut of the evening was a second attempt at 'Trying to Get to You', a number which had been unsuccessful at a previous session. This time it came together. The introduction of drums and the musical cohesiveness born from months spent together on the road produced the natural flow of honest emotion that Phillips always sought for. Unlike earlier sessions, where he had had to prod and coax a performance from Presley, on this occasion the music just seemed to pour out of him. In the end, 'Mystery Train'/'I Forgot to Remember to Forget' became the fifth and final single that Presley recorded for the Sun label. Released on 1 August 1955, it went on to become the first of his records to reach no. 1 in the country charts.

Bob Neal quickly hired a drummer for the band and took the group back out on the road. Once a group of July tour dates in Florida were behind him, Elvis embarked on a package tour that included Phillips' newest discovery, Johnny Cash, among the list of performers.

Up to this point, Colonel Parker had been content to press his case in a roundabout way, offering professional advice and dangling promises in a friendly and easy-going manner. Elvis was already convinced and eager to sign with Parker, but as legal guardians of their underage son, it was Vernon and Gladys Presley who needed to be won over. Vernon seemed inclined enough, but Gladys was reluctant. She was sceptical of Parker's motives and slick ways, and fearful for her son's safety. Unnerved by the near-riots that now erupted whenever Elvis took the stage, she was frightened by the inflamed fans who more than once had torn the clothing from her son's body. With Elvis' fame on the rise, it was inevitable that the big-name management companies would soon come calling, and Parker wanted to get there first.

Parker now made a direct approach to Presley's parents, outlining the limitations of Bob Neal as a manager, and his own plans for promoting and building Elvis' career. Parker even had client and business partner Hank Snow, the great country singer, make personal phone calls to the Presleys to influence their decision. Impressed, Gladys finally gave her permission and on 15 August, a contract was signed with Colonel Thomas A. Parker as 'special advisor to Elvis Presley ("artist") and Bob Neal ("manager") for the period of one year'. The contract went on to grant Parker exclusive rights to produce and promote Elvis' appearances in nearly every major city in the United States, reimbursement for all related expenses, contract options, and the right 'to negotiate all renewals on existing contracts.'[3] Whether the parties involved understood it or not, Parker had gained effectual control over Elvis' immediate future.

Only Phillips was displeased. Even at this early date, he did not feel the move was in Elvis' best interests. But financial limitations tied Phillips' hands, preventing him from having any influence in the decision. At some level, Phillips must have recognised the probability that he would one day lose Presley to a bigger label. At least with Parker in charge of the negotiations, Phillips stood a better chance of profiting from the loss. Still, he was reluctant to let go, and put off making the decision until he was finally forced into it.

As soon as he had the contract in hand, Parker began moving to separate his new client from those who had influence over him: first manager Bob Neal, then musicians Scotty Moore and Bill Black. Everyone sensed that big changes were coming, but since no one knew exactly what those changes would mean, everyone's nerves were on edge. There was little Phillips could do; he had trouble of his own. He was simultaneously attempting to get a radio station up and running, trying to promote a crop of new recording artists, and pressing a lawsuit against Duke Records, charging owner Don Robey with poaching Sun Records artist Little Junior Walker.

As financial pressures threatened to bankrupt him, Phillips waited in dread. He desperately needed the infusion of cash that the sale of Presley's contract would bring in, yet at the same time he hated losing such a hot property. Elvis had given voice to Phillips' musical vision, and was taking that vision to an audience far beyond Phillips' field of influence. Phillips had to wonder if another voice would come along to continue his vision, or if he was watching the moment slip from his grasp.

There was a half-hearted attempt at a recording session in September, but with the mood of uncertainty that hung in the air, the session never really got going. During a break, Elvis and Phillips disappeared into the control room, and when Elvis emerged about 30 minutes later it was to announce that the session was over. Whatever was said, it was most likely at this moment that Phillips finally reconciled himself to Elvis' departure.

Keeping everyone involved off balance while he worked his deals was a favourite ploy of Parker's and he played the situation to his own advantage. Once word was leaked that Presley's contract was definitely up for grabs, Parker began fielding the offers that poured in. He pitted one label against another, ratcheting up the price, making sure that each label thought it was the only serious contender. RCA was the favourite, as Parker had a relationship with the label going back ten years with clients Eddy Arnold and Hank Snow, but executives there were by no means convinced. The musical movement that Elvis embodied still had no definite name at this point – each region seemed to have its own appellation – and few believed that it was anything more than a passing fad.

Parker believed. He believed in making money wherever the opportunity presented itself. Parker never understood the pandemonium that Elvis created, but he recognised its moneymaking potential. While attention was focused elsewhere, he staged his coup. In October, he arrived in New York City during a union stalemate that threatened the production of a film short in which

Elvis was scheduled to make a brief appearance. Parker produced a document signed by Elvis' parents, naming Parker as the singer's authorised representative. He ultimately used the document to oust Bob Neal, and to demand that Phillips immediately name a price for the release of Elvis from his Sun Records contract.

Phillips was furious. However, his reluctance to face the inevitable had helped fuel the uncertainty that now threatened Sun Records. Despite the recent rebound in the sales of Elvis' recordings, the rumours of troubles surrounding the label made record distributors wary of purchasing Sun product. The relationships with distributors that Phillips had so carefully cultivated and nurtured, and on which he was dependent for his livelihood, were being jeopardised. Anger finally provoked Phillips to action. He telephoned Parker in New York to confront him, brushing off the Colonel's pretended pleasantries to say that the situation had gone on long enough. When asked if he was interested in selling off Elvis' contract, Phillips replied that he had not thought about it but would let Parker know. Then he hung up. Phillips later stated that he thought about it for approximately 30 seconds before telephoning back to name a figure. The price was $35,000, plus $5,000 in back royalties owed to Elvis. As Phillips returned the receiver to the cradle, he was satisfied that the price he had named was so high that there was no chance of Parker's being able to meet it.

As if he did not already have enough on his mind, Phillips was in the midst of finalising arrangements to begin broadcasting from his first radio station. It was an idea he had played with since early on in his career as an announcer. The recent influx of funds from Presley's records gave him the encouragement to make this dream a reality. 'I actually had wanted to have an all-black station, but it was blocked. However, a 250-watt daytime station became available. At that time, women weren't in radio. So I got this wild-ass idea.'[4]

The idea did not come completely out of thin air. Both Phillips' wife and Marion Keisker had worked in radio. He was well placed to know first hand the injustices they had faced as women in a man's industry. Always the champion of the underdog, Phillips switched his focus: if he could not advance the cause of race, he would advance the cause of gender.

Female radio announcers were a rarity at the time. The few women that had managed to break into the business were largely relegated to token positions that carried little prestige. Phillips' station would be the first in the nation to feature an all-female talent roster. It would have an easy listening pop format ('sparkling, bright music'), and be housed in office space at a local Holiday Inn motor hotel. 'You're looking at a crazy man,' was Phillips' explanation for the venture. 'I wasn't trying to revolutionize the world.'[5]

The concept itself was simple enough. 'It wasn't all woman, it wasn't all female; it was all girl,' Phillips explained. 'I don't give a damn if they were fifty years old; they were all girls.' But making the dream a reality proved to be a different matter. Staffing presented the most immediate problem. Phillips initially turned to one of the few women he knew with any radio station experience. 'Becky, my wife, and I met in a little station back in Alabama. I said, "Becky, I've got a wild notion that women in radio could have some appeal. But how in hell are we gonna get anybody who can compete in this market?"'[6]

Part of the staffing problem was solved when Becky was persuaded to come on board as a DJ. Marion Keisker was the next to sign on. Keisker left her job at WREC, where she had been the popular talk show hostess of *Meet Kitty Kelly* since 1946, to join the staff at WHER. In truth, the relationship between Keisker and Phillips had slowly deteriorated as Sun Records' fortunes improved, and she may have seen this new venture as an opportunity to recapture the camaraderie the two had shared when they first opened Memphis Recording Service.

Phillips held auditions and made the hiring decisions. 'Every person at WHER was a girl, except I couldn't find a girl head engineer,' he said. Once staffing was in place, training became the next hurdle to cross. 'The people who came in to record for me [at Sun] had never seen a radio station, much less a recording studio. And I thought: these girls can be taught, too. Everybody had to work their own board, and [in the beginning] most of them didn't know what a turntable was. These girls were up to snuff in the shortest period of time.'[7] Phillips was especially careful about getting the on-air staff's vocal tone right, knowing that it was the quality the listening audience would connect with. 'The girls' voices were warm without being oozy,' he explained. 'They didn't try to be sexy or too sweet. It was just making contact with people – male, female, hermaphrodite.'[8]

Each woman interviewed assumed that she was being considered for a token female announcer spot, as was common at some radio stations of the time. It was not until the day before the station began broadcasting that they discovered that the entire on-air programming was to be handled by women, from playing the records and reporting the news to reading advertising copy and fielding questions on the city's first call-in talk show. The same was true behind the scenes: women ran the office, managed the station, wrote the copy and sold advertising. A local newspaper article described the station: 'The studio and offices have been feminized from front door to rear exit. The disc jockeys are called jockettes, the studio is known as the doll's den, the control rooms are called playrooms, the hallway is mirrored, the equipment room has been decorated in murals depicting the evolution of feminine clothing, the stationery is perfumed, the advertisers are listed in a date book, and the exit to the parking lot is lettered "Bye Bye Till Next Time."'[9]

Perhaps even more than breaking the colour line with his record label, Phillips was proud of what WHER represented: 'There will not be any experience greater than that. We broke another barrier, and that is: in the matter of five years there were women in radio everywhere.' And just like he had done in recording black artists, Phillips saw a bigger picture: '"1000 Beautiful Watts" was our slogan. But I never thought of it as a novelty. I really believe this little radio station transposed itself into markets all over the country. We started a second all-girl station in Lakewood, Florida: WLIZ. I hired girls who had no experience and it became the hottest thing in that market. It was easily 75 to 100 women who got their start at these stations.'[10] The station was to broadcast for 17 years before going off the air. WHER remained an all-girl operation for 11 of those years, until 1966, when the call letters were changed to WWEE and male announcers were added.

WHER – 'programming with glamour-sparkled spice' at 1430 on the AM dial – finally went on air on the morning of Saturday, 29 October 1955, several days later than originally planned.[11] The delay was caused by a series of equipment and transmitter malfunctions, which had necessitated Phillips spending three sleepless days and nights installing the ground system and checking the equipment. As a result, he was tired and easily provoked later that afternoon when it came time to negotiate the preliminary terms for the sale of Elvis' Sun Records contract.

Forty thousand dollars. Much has been made over the years of the selling price of Elvis Presley's Sun Records contract. Sam Phillips has been ridiculed for letting go of a star of Presley's magnitude and earning potential for such a paltry amount. What is forgotten is how audacious and shrewd a business deal it was at the time. Forty thousand dollars was a substantial sum in those days. Forty thousand dollars was significantly more than any record company had ever paid for an artist up to that time. Forty thousand dollars would not only clear all of Phillips' extensive debts, but would form the basis of the investments that would set him up for the rest of his life.

The deal was inevitable. Presley's contract was set to expire in a few months' time, and Colonel Tom Parker would undoubtedly place demands on the label that would make renewal impossible.

Remember, Elvis Presley was not a star at the time. He had only a regional following and was essentially unknown outside the Southern states. Forty thousand dollars was a record-breaking asking price, and once he had reconciled himself to its inevitability, Phillips never regretted making the deal. Or so he claimed at the time. Much later in life, he was not quite so sure. 'Oh, man,' he stated. 'We parted. I wouldn't have sold his contract, and he almost did not OK it. The man almost did not OK it. And if it hadn't been for the element with Mrs. Presley, that old Parker – Tom – put in, I'm here to tell you he would not have left Sun, and he would have been just as big or bigger.'[12]

Once the amount had been set, all that was left was to work out the terms. At a meeting in Memphis on 28 October, Phillips gave Parker two weeks' option to raise the necessary funds. Unbeknown to Phillips, RCA had already informed Parker that $25,000 was the extent of their interest, which included $15,000 kicked in by music publishers Hill & Range for a side deal. Parker set to work to find the remaining $10,000. On 15 November, the final day of the option period, the money was still not in place. In a last-ditch effort to pull the deal together, Parker reminded RCA singles division manager Bill Bullock that if the option expired, the price would likely increase, sweetening the deal with the promise of three national television appearances. Bullock wavered, but finally agreed to supply the full asking price. Parker sent a telegram to Phillips that afternoon, informing him that the deal was done.

Phillips had doubted all along that Parker could raise the funds, but now it was too late to back down. The deal was signed in Memphis on 21 November at the Sun Records studio, and was photographed for publicity purposes.

The association between Phillips and Presley did not end there. Presley's first RCA release, 'Heartbreak Hotel', was getting off to a slow start when Phillips released Carl Perkins' 'Blue Suede Shoes'. Watching Perkins' tune race up the charts, Presley's producer at

RCA began to question the decision to purchase Presley's contract. 'Steve Sholes called me,' Phillips remembered, 'and said, "Man, I don't know whether I bought the wrong person or not. That damn 'Blue Suede Shoes' is the hottest thing; it's breaking all over New York and everywhere I go." I told him he hadn't bought the wrong person. He asked if he could put "Blue Suede Shoes" out by Elvis because he couldn't get "Heartbreak Hotel" to do a damn thing.' Phillips did his best to discourage the idea, saying, 'Elvis has some momentum going. You know we talked about keeping things simple and not getting overly wrought and going too far country . . .'[13] In the end, 'Heartbreak Hotel' caught on and captured the no. 1 spot in the national charts, with Perkins' 'Blue Suede Shoes' behind it at no. 2.

The sale of Presley's contract was questioned in the media almost from the start. In a 1959 interview, Phillips established the public position that he maintained for the remainder of his life: that he had never second-guessed his decision. 'Selling that contract gave us the capital we desperately needed at the time for expansion,' he stated. 'To understand why I have never regretted the decision, you have to remember something. At that time, most of the experts thought that Elvis was a flash in the pan. Even RCA wasn't sure they had made a good deal.'[14] Later in life, his answer was more succinct: 'It worked out for everybody. We didn't do too bad.'[15]

From discovery to departure, Elvis Presley's tenure at Sun Records lasted barely 18 months. Although he would go on to record dozens of successful albums and singles, rarely was he able to convey the sense of unfettered fun captured on the Sun recordings. Many years later, Phillips was asked if he thought Presley had made a mistake in leaving Sun Records, if going into films had been a waste of his talent. 'I don't think it was a waste,' Phillips replied. 'Of course, the songs – most of them weren't up to par. "Jailhouse Rock" is an excellent song, movie or no movie, and a half-dozen others, but the rest of them were pure junk. Elvis knew that. He had an extrasensory perception for music, just like I've always felt

God gave me that, even if he didn't give me anything else. He had to do what he had to do. The young people loved those movies. The guy could have done anything if he'd had the opportunity. But that was convenient money and Tom Parker decided he was going to take advantage of it, and did.'[16]

Chapter Nine

A Different Country

WITH THE RELEASE of each new Elvis Presley single came another wave of artists claiming to perform in a similar style, all seeking to audition for Phillips. While he continued to personally rehearse and record the blues artists signed to Sun Records, late in 1954 Phillips turned some of the responsibilities for his country artists over to others. Even though he wanted to work with many of them, his time was so taken up with promoting Presley that there was little left over to devote to developing new talent. So he created the Flip label as a subsidiary to Sun Records, intending to channel all his country artists through the new label. He also hired additional producers to help these artists work up their material prior to recording sessions. In most cases, Phillips continued to audition country artists and often produced and engineered their recording sessions, but he delegated the rest of the responsibilities to Bill Cantrell and Quinton Claunch.

Phillips had known Cantrell and Claunch since their early days together in Alabama. Claunch played guitar and Cantrell was a fiddler. The pair had auditioned an original song for him earlier in 1954. He passed on the song, but it became a minor hit for Meteor Records and won its singer a contract with MGM Records. Not wishing to repeat the mistake, Phillips signed the pair to work with his country acts, securing first right of refusal to their future songwriting efforts. In October, Phillips assigned Cantrell and Claunch to rehearse newcomer Charlie Feathers.

Feathers was an artist who probably could have been a star –

possibly even *should* have been a star – but he never made it. The reason why depends on who is telling the story. In Feathers' version, it was a conspiracy – one in which he was sacrificed in favour of crowning Elvis Presley the King of Rock 'n' Roll. In Phillips' telling, it was Feathers' inability to take direction. 'Charlie was always a little difficult to work with,' Phillips charitably maintained, 'and that was why we never got the best out of him. He always felt he knew more than everyone else. He told his stories and got to the point where he believed them. That's too bad, because he was a damn talent . . . and Charlie's talent was in country music – the blues feeling he put into a hillbilly song.'[1]

The Flip label made its debut in February 1955 with the release of four singles by four new artists, including Perkins and Feathers. But Flip was shut down within weeks of its initial releases, the victim of a threatened lawsuit by Ed Wells, owner of a Los Angeles record label with the same name. Subsequent pressings of the Flip singles were released under the Sun Records name.

Phillips released two singles by Feathers, the first in February 1955 on the Flip label and the second in December 1955 on Sun. Both featured country numbers that Feathers had a hand in writing, and which were lyrically reminiscent of Hank Williams tunes. Unfortunately, both came out at times when Phillips was heavily pushing other acts, so they received little promotion. Feathers was back in the studio in January 1956, this time in a rockabilly mood, but the session failed to produce anything that sparked Phillips' interest. A final session produced a rockabilly version of the R&B classic 'Corrine, Corrina', which Phillips test-marketed locally with poor results. While Phillips wavered over releasing a third single, Feathers lost patience and defected to Meteor Records. Phillips was not sad to see him go.

The other acts that Cantrell and Claunch worked with were Bill Taylor and the Miller Sisters. Taylor was a trumpeter with Clyde Leoppard's Snearly Ranch Boys, a group from West Memphis, Arkansas. He and the band's steel guitar player, Stan Kesler, were working with Phillips at the end of 1954, writing songs for Elvis Presley. For a time, various members of the Snearly Ranch Boys formed Sun Records' unofficial country house band.

The Miller Sisters auditioned for Phillips in 1954 at the suggestion of a local DJ. The two women were actually sisters-in-law: Elsie Joy Wages was married to Mildred Miller's brother. Their initial singles, the first released on Flip in February 1955 and the second on Sun in January 1956, featured tight vocal harmony in a pure country vein. Neither single sold as well as Phillips expected, but he continued to believe in the Millers' potential. In consequence, Cantrell and Claunch sought a new direction. The Sisters' third single, released in August 1956, was a rock 'n' roll novelty number that failed to do justice to the beauty of the women's voices. A fourth session was held in 1957, which produced R&B material that Phillips decided not to release. The duo broke up soon afterwards.

The collaboration between Cantrell and Claunch and Sun Records did not last much longer either. Disappointed by meagre royalties from record sales, the two men left Phillips' employment in 1957 to help form Hi Records.

Phillips continued to dabble in country music for the next 12 years, although he rarely released more than one single by any of the country artists he recorded. While he appreciated the unique qualities of individual performers, he never had the passion – or perhaps the real understanding – for country music that he had for other musical styles. Then again, perhaps he simply had no interest in the type of country music that was then marketable. 'We had a pretty good country house band,' Phillips recalled, 'but I knew that cutting Nashville-style country music was not what I wanted. I knew I *could* cut it, but I knew it wasn't what I hoped to get.'[2]

The only pure country voice that Phillips recorded after 1954 was Ernie Chaffin. He is the only one of Phillips' country artists who stayed true to his country sound without veering into hillbilly, rockabilly or rock 'n' roll territory. Chaffin put out four singles for Sun between 1957 and 1959. While each was as good in its own way as anything Nashville produced at the time, none did well enough in the charts to capture broad attention.

In explaining why he failed to produce the country hits that his stable of talent had the potential for, Phillips hinted at two major reasons: his personal level of interest and his personal musical taste. 'I think I could have had a darn good country label,' he stated. 'Had I stayed in country music alone and dedicated myself to it, then I had the nucleus of several fine artists who could have made it – in particular Ernie Chaffin and Charlie Feathers. I just loved stylists; people you knew the minute you heard them on record. That's what it's all about. I had a different sound in country music, and I knew I would have had difficulty in orienting the taste of people and getting the radio play.'[3]

Before leaving on the Hank Snow tour, the trio returned to the studio to record their next single. Like each of the previous sessions, inspiration proved hard to come by. In the end, only a cover version of Arthur Gunter's self-penned current release, 'Baby, Let's Play House', hit the energy level that Phillips was searching for, but all agreed that it might be their strongest recording yet. The result exemplified the strong R&B influence that was beginning to creep into country music. It was a sound that the trade papers called by various names before eventually settling on 'rockabilly'.

★   ★   ★

While Phillips felt little affinity for traditional country artists, he was greatly interested in those performers whose beat-driven style of country music would come to be termed rockabilly. Rockabilly was not invented by Elvis Presley or Sun Records. It existed before Presley cut his first Sun recording and it continued after he left the label. Carl Perkins and his brothers had been playing it in local taverns around Jackson, Tennessee prior to hearing Presley's debut Sun single on the radio, and went on to record rockabilly's greatest anthem after Presley's Sun contract was sold. The music that Presley and Perkins played was not called rockabilly at the time; that came later. At first it was considered an aberration of country and western; only later, as its R&B influence grew more prominent, did it become known as rockabilly. As Carl Perkins explained: 'Rockabilly music, there ain't nothing to it. It's just a hopped up country song.'[4]

There is a little bit more to it than that, actually. Rockabilly was the intersecting of two musical forms that existed side by side in the South, but which rarely mingled. In general, white Southern audiences kept their radios tuned to the *Grand Ole Opry* and similar purveyors of country music. Black Southern audiences, with their heritage of gospel and Delta blues, increasingly favoured the R&B sound coming from the urban North. Where country and R&B influences did mingle was among poor Southern whites that, because of their economic status, had regular working interaction with the black population. This was the music often heard in the white working-class roadhouses that existed on the wrong side of the tracks in nearly every town throughout the South. It was rowdy and raucous, its lyrics littered with references to drinking, fighting and loving. In essence, rockabilly was a reflection of the volatile and sometimes violent life that played out within the honky-tonks.

The parameters defining rockabilly are fairly narrow. Musically, it is manically up-tempo, accented on the offbeat and driven by the rhythmic slapping of an upright bass. Drums and/or piano might provide added propulsion, but the traditional instrumentation is minimal and consists of rhythm guitar, lead guitar and standup bass. Its energy is high spirited, rebellious and chaotic, and very much derivative of Elvis Presley. Vocally, rockabilly relies on a variety of stylistic tics: hiccups, stutters, and spontaneous whoops and hollers. Lyrically, it tends to have little substance, with frequent references to children's rhymes, clothing trends and bebop nonsense lingo. Lastly, with very few exceptions, the classic rockabilly practitioners were predominantly male, which gave the music its sexually charged bravado and swagger.

Sam Phillips' contribution to rockabilly was his willingness to record and release it. The absence of rockabilly records prior to Elvis Presley suggests that Phillips was, if not *the* first, then among the first to see its potential. Even then, he was not sure. It was only after the positive wave of audience response to radio airplay that he finished and released Presley's first record. Given the inevitable racial backlash that rockabilly's obvious black influence was likely to provoke, the release of that first record was a huge risk for a struggling independent label to take. Phillips never reaped the full monetary reward, but the risk paid off in the stream of talent that made its way to his door in the aftermath of Presley's rising fame.

A number of singers and musicians throughout the South and Southwest recognised in Elvis' version of 'That's All Right' an unmistakable similarity to the music they were playing. Once 'That's All Right' became a hit, many of them were drawn to Memphis Recording Service, hoping that Phillips could do for them what he had done for Elvis. Although promoting Elvis consumed much of his time and energy, Phillips managed to record a few of these, such as 14-year-old Maggie Sue Wimberly, the Miller Sisters and rockabilly artist Charlie Feathers. Most were limited releases on Phillips' short-lived Flip label, and few got airplay outside the immediate area. Some, like Ray Harris, Hayden Thompson and Malcolm Yelvington, recorded a single or two for Phillips before returning to their country roots or dropping out of music altogether. Others, like Sonny Burgess, Billy Riley and Warren Smith, had at least one minor hit out of the handful of singles released by Sun Records, before moving on to other labels. None found the success they were seeking; most ended up bitter and disappointed. When their brief moment in the spotlight was through, all were left wondering why Elvis had made it and they had not. Largely it came down to truth and timing.

What all of these artists had going against them was that none of them was Elvis Presley. That sounds simplistic – and it is – but it is also true. None of them possessed his combination of talent, looks, style, charisma, timing, promotion, malleability and just plain luck. Just as importantly, none of them were the real thing. When Elvis performed, it was a release of the myriad influences and emotions bottled up inside him – it was sometimes raw, and late in his life it verged on becoming a train wreck, but it was real. And audiences responded to that. The artists who came after Elvis and did find success at Sun Records – Carl Perkins, Johnny Cash and Jerry Lee Lewis – achieved that success largely because the music they produced was an honest expression of their true selves. Others, like Roy Orbison and Charlie Rich, found success *after* their stints in the Sun stable for the same reason. The remainder, however convincing their performances and creditable their efforts might have been, were imitators. They came to Phillips as country artists – or in Burgess' case, R&B – and converted to rockabilly when Phillips said that was what he was looking for. When the rockabilly bubble burst, they returned to their musical roots.

Timing is a second consideration. Elvis Presley did not break nationally until after he left Sun Records and rockabilly behind, moving on to material that was heavily pop influenced. Carl Perkins too crossed over into the pop charts. By 1956, when the origins of Presley's success became widely known and the first wave of Presley aspirants came calling at Sun Records, the rockabilly trend had nearly peaked. Once Jerry Lee Lewis began pumping out his string of hits in 1957, excellent rockabilly singles that could have been successful just months earlier were consistently being trounced in the charts by rock 'n' roll tunes. Within another year, the raw rockabilly sound favoured by Phillips was too unpolished to appeal to audiences outside the South. By 1959, the rockabilly trend was essentially over and its practitioners had largely given up or moved on, but it is significant that from 1954 until then, few rockabilly artists outside of the Sun Records stable produced records that got noticed on the national charts.

Outside of Elvis Presley and Carl Perkins, none of the other Sun Records rockabillies achieved anything beyond regional celebrity. However, their collective stories provide insight into how Phillips assessed new talent and how the workings of his studio evolved over time.

Malcolm Yelvington's brush with fame extended little further than being the next artist to debut on Sun Records following the debut of Elvis Presley. Yelvington was the vocalist of a five-piece country band called the Star Rhythm Boys. The first of his two singles was country in much the same way that Elvis' singles could be classified as being country. Yelvington later recalled that it took six or more hours to get a take that Phillips could accept. The second single, released nearly two years later, was a rockabilly novelty number with distinctly hillbilly leanings. Neither single was commercially successful, although both were solid perform-ances. The problem was that what Yelvington did, Presley and Perkins did with far greater flair.

Nevertheless, Yelvington is interesting for his insight into Phillips' approach to auditioning new artists. 'We went down to see Sam,' Yelvington remembered. 'He asked us what type of music we played and we said, "Country." He said he wasn't interested, so I asked him what he wanted. He said, "I don't know, but I'll know when I hear it."'5 'That's the reason I listen to everyone that comes in,' Phillips explained. 'One of these days somebody's going to come in here and do something that I'm looking for.'6

Warren Smith was a singer who was briefly affiliated with the Snearly Ranch Boys, who sometimes stood in as studio musicians on Sun's country recordings. It was through them that he was introduced to Phillips, who was impressed with the purity of Smith's voice and wanted to hear more. His first single paired

'Rock and Roll Ruby', an atypical tune written by Johnny Cash, with the solid country number 'I'd Rather Be Safe Than Sorry'. At the time, rock 'n' roll was still considered to be a fad that might evaporate overnight, so Phillips possibly released the odd coupling with the thought of hedging his bets, the same as he had done with Carl Perkins. Phillips need not have worried. 'Rock and Roll Ruby' rose to no. 1 in the local charts within a month of its release, although it never cracked the national charts. Still, it sold more copies than Presley's, Perkins' or Cash's first records.

Sure that he was following in Presley's footsteps, Smith jettisoned the Snearly Ranch Boys and assembled his own band, causing hard feelings all around. His second single deservedly sold poorly, but it was followed up with 'So Long I'm Gone', a country-pop tune written by Roy Orbison, backed by the contagious rockabilly number, 'Miss Froggie', written by Smith himself. This third single should have been a hit. It even entered the Hot 100 charts, but it was quickly steamrollered by Jerry Lee Lewis' 'Whole Lotta Shakin' Going On'. Smith's fourth single, another rockabilly/country pairing, also should have been a hit, but was again shot down by Lewis, this time with 'Great Balls of Fire'. The ensuing jealousy and resentment would ultimately result in Smith's departure from Sun Records.

Smith must have been thrilled when Lewis' career imploded in scandal, thinking that he finally had a chance to get out from under his nemesis's shadow, but it was not to be. Despite glowing reviews, Smith's fifth and final Sun single languished from neglect as Phillips marshalled all his label's energy and attention to salvaging Lewis' deflated career. With his three-year contract almost expired, Smith left Sun Records for California, where he finally found chart success as a country artist with Liberty Records.

Phillips' later appraisal of Smith's abilities demonstrated his belief that the artist's true talent was for country music rather than rock 'n' roll: 'He had a pure country voice and an innate feel for a country ballad. With that music he was as good as anyone I've heard before or since.' Though Phillips' assessment of Smith's personality is in line with other accounts, it is notable for its blindness to the resentment that Smith and many Sun artists felt over Phillips' apparent preference for Lewis. 'Warren had a lot of emotional problems, though,' Phillips recalled. 'He needed recognition more than the average person . . . He was a difficult personality, but just interesting enough that I liked him a whole lot.'[7]

Billy Riley's first Sun single is an anomaly in that it was neither engineered by Phillips nor recorded at the Sun studio. The recording of 'Trouble Bound' was brought to Memphis Recording Service for mastering by musician and part-time record producer Jack Clement. Phillips was impressed enough to offer Riley a contract, and to hire Clement to take over some of his own engineering duties. The hiring of Clement marked another step in distancing Phillips from the day-to-day technical side of his operation as business demands began to consume his time.

Phillips did not care for Clement's choice for the single's B-side, so Riley came up with a rockabilly number titled 'Rock With Me Baby', which Clement recorded at a local radio station. Phillips bought the finished masters to both recordings from Clement and released the single in May 1956.

Riley could summon up an interestingly raspy quality to his voice, comparable to Little Richard. He also had a killer band, the Little Green Men, whose musicians were often put to use both in the studio and on the road to back other Sun artists. Which of the two – the voice or the band – Phillips found more intriguing is difficult to guess. A comment by Riley offers a clue as to his relationship with Phillips: 'We had respect for each other, but we never did get along too well. I didn't appreciate the lack of promotion, but I appreciated his talent. He knew I had the band that could work with anybody, and he needed us.'[8] Whatever the reason, Phillips saw some kind of potential that made him keep trying for that elusive hit long after he would have given up on any other artist.

For a follow-up single, Riley recorded the weird 'Flyin' Saucer Rock 'n' Roll'. The tune featured Jerry Lee Lewis on piano, during a time when Phillips threw him occasional work as a studio musician, before his own career took off. The single sold around 15,000 copies. Riley tried again with a rockabilly version of 'Red Hot', which Billy 'The Kid' Emerson had recorded for Sun about two years previously. It sold around 37,000 copies.

Apparently, Riley blamed Phillips for the disappointing sales, which were probably due to the limited promotion that so many other Sun artists complained of. When he overheard Phillips cancelling additional orders of 'Red Hot' in favour of Lewis' 'Great Balls of Fire', Riley's temper got the better of him. He went out and got drunk, returning later to trash the studio and slosh wine over Phillips' tape equipment. Phillips corralled Riley in a back room and talked him down from his rage. 'We went back into his little cubby hole and talked 'til sunup,' Riley recalled. 'Sam said, "'Red Hot' ain't got it. We're saving you for something *good*." When I left I felt I was the biggest star on Sun Records.'[9] The good feeling did not last for long. Riley's next single sold only 3,200 copies, eclipsed by the simultaneous release of Lewis' 'Breathless'.

After several attempts at finding chart success elsewhere, Riley returned to Sun at the end of 1958 to find the label scrambling to revive Lewis' career. Riley and his band were put to work as the house band on Lewis' sessions, as well as those of many others. There were three more singles, but with all attention focused on Lewis, there was little hope of getting a hit. Sun and Riley parted ways for good in September 1959. In retrospect, Phillips felt that he might have failed Riley. 'Riley was just a damn good rocker,' he stated, 'but man, he was so damn weird in many ways. He interested the hell out of me, but he was not the easiest person to deal with. When he took a drink he'd become almost a different person. He just never achieved his potential in my studio. I'm sorry I didn't do more with him. I was disappointed we never broke him into the big time. His band was just a rockin' *mother*!'[10]

Albert 'Sonny' Burgess was the last of the rockabillies to arrive at Sun Records. He had become aware of the label in 1955, when he was booked to be the local opening act on an Elvis Presley tour date. Burgess' first audition for Phillips came to nothing; Phillips said that he was looking for a fuller sound. Burgess beefed up his band, renamed them the Pacers, and returned to Memphis on 2 May 1956 for a second try. This time Phillips was impressed, and rushed the nervous group into a recording session that afternoon. The resultant single, 'We Wanna Boogie', sounded like it was recorded in the midst of a drunken bacchanal, but sold about 90,000 copies and charted in several metropolitan markets. None of Burgess' subsequent records sold as well.

The trouble was that what made Burgess' sound unique – the thing that appealed to Phillips originally – also made it difficult to sell. The addition of a trumpet player made his sound different from every other rockabilly band, but also made it difficult to classify. 'Sam Phillips didn't know where to pitch our music,' Burgess explained. 'There was a market for Elvis, because he was a true rockabilly, but not for us. The black stations wouldn't play us, but neither would the white stations, because we weren't what you'd call country.'[11]

Burgess summed up his experience, and that of most of the Sun rockabillies, as follows: 'Once we heard Elvis and Carl Perkins, we knew we had to be where they came from. We were from the same place, we had the same heroes, and played the same music. So we went to see Sam Phillips at Sun. In the studio, Sam would just get behind the board and say, "Play." It didn't have to be technically correct. If you listen to our records, all of us, we made a lot of mistakes. I'm embarrassed by some of them now, to tell you the truth. But if it had a good feeling, he kept it. The one thing that comes through on everything is that Sam had an ear for what sounded good. Thousands of people wanted to be on Sun. People envied us because we were signed with Sam. He only chose about eight of us. And he couldn't even promote us all. He didn't have that kind of money. But what did we know? You reached your peak when you were on a record label. That record had your name on it. It didn't make any difference if it sold.'[12]

Chapter Ten

The Great Contender

ONE MIGHT BE excused for imagining that Sam Phillips' world shifted on its axis the moment that Elvis Presley found his groove during the late night recording session that produced 'That's All Right'. That is hardly the case. Although his money worries had eased, life did not perceptibly change for Phillips overnight. He still had a struggling business to run and a young family that he worked long hours to provide for. As exciting as that moment must have been, it was simply one of many such moments that had come and gone in the course of a recording session since Phillips first opened for business in 1950.

In many ways, however, the period between 1955 and 1960 was the most hectic and fulfilling of Phillips' life. The success of Elvis Presley and the eventual proceeds from the sale of his contract brought Phillips new opportunities and new business ventures. More importantly, Presley's popularity had brought name recognition to Sun Records, and attracted a wave of aspiring artists to the label.

One of those who felt the pull towards Memphis was a hard-drinking, raw-boned country boy named Carl Perkins. The Perkins Brothers Band had been singing and playing in local honky-tonks around Jackson, Tennessee since they were teenagers. When he first heard Elvis sing 'Blue Moon of Kentucky' on the radio, Carl at once recognised the similarity to the music he played: hard driving, energetic, impossible to define. The resemblance was even stronger on the flip side, 'That's All Right (Mama)'. But musical style is where the likeness ended. Perkins was as homely as Presley was pretty. It was unlikely that teenage girls would scream for him like they did for Elvis.

In October 1954, Carl and his two brothers – peacekeeper Jay played rhythm guitar, while volatile Clayton played stand-up bass – packed their instruments and drove to Memphis, banking their futures on getting an audition with Sam Phillips. Perkins had barely made it through the door of Memphis Recording Service before being rejected by Marion Keisker, who flatly stated that Phillips was not looking for new artists. Perkins tried unsuccessfully to engage Keisker in conversation, hoping to win her over. 'I can save you some time,' she said. 'Sam Phillips, the owner, isn't here. And he's not going to listen to you.'¹ With nothing left to say, Perkins politely thanked her and turned for the door.

Back outside, the three brothers were about to accept defeat and drive away when Phillips arrived in his two-tone blue Cadillac. Perkins caught up with Phillips at the door to the studio and pressed him for an audition. Phillips brusquely said he was too busy and tried to brush past. Perkins blocked the door, pleading 'You just don't know what it would mean to me.' But Phillips knew exactly what it would mean to him, and in that instant he also knew he could not turn Perkins away. The two former cotton pickers, sons of impoverished sharecroppers, eyed each other briefly before an annoyed Phillips replied, 'OK, get set up. But I'm busy and can't listen long,' and headed for the control booth.²

Twice Jay attempted to sing one of his original country tunes, and both times Phillips cut him off before the end of the first verse. Phillips had absolutely no interest in anything so traditional. He had left the control booth and was walking away when Carl desperately launched into one of his own tunes, a rollicking country stomper that Phillips, who preferred short song titles, would later name 'Movie Magg'. The brothers joined in and followed Carl's lead, attacking the song with everything they had. Phillips stood by, tapping his foot. When the song was over he shouted, 'Now that's original! That's what we want,' and asked to

Joe Hill Louis (on the right), one of Phillips' earliest acts, *c.* 1950

The Prisonaires rehearse 'Just Walkin' in the Rain', 1953

Phillips sells Elvis to RCA. L–R: Bob Neal, Sam Phillips, Colman Tilly (RCA), Elvis Presley, Col. Parker, November 1955

Two of rock 'n' roll's greatest innovators: Sam Phillips with Elvis, 1955

Johnny Cash and his band recording at Sun Records, 1956

Sam Phillips and Johnny Cash backstage at the Grand Ole Opry, 1956

Sam Phillips awards Carl Perkins a gold record for 'Blue Suede Shoes', May 1956

Marion Keisker in the Sun reception area, 1956

Sam Phillips with the notorious and volatile Jerry Lee Lewis, 1957

Roy Orbison and Sam Phillips, 1960. Balladeer Roy Orbison did not suit Phillips' preferred 'rockabilly' style

A session at
the new Sun
Studio, 1960

Sam Phillips sells Sun Records to Shelby Singleton. L–R: Phillips, Singleton,
Noble Bell, July 1969

Sam Phillips and his sons. L–R: Phillips, Knox Phillips, Jerry Phillips, 1967

L–R: Sam Phillips, B.B. King, Charlie Rich, Jerry Lee Lewis in Memphis, 1987

Sam Phillips in the original Sun Studio, 1959

hear it played again.[3] The second effort was not as good as the first, he told them, but his manner had softened and he was now definitely interested. Phillips told the brothers to work up a few more numbers and come back, but at the moment his time was tied up with Elvis. He also pulled Carl aside to say that it was he, not Jay, who should be the focus of the act. 'You don't sound like anybody else,' Phillips said quietly, 'you may have a chance.'[4]

Phillips was right: Perkins did not sound like the countless similar groups playing in bar-rooms across the South at the time. Neither pure country nor hillbilly, his style borrowed liberally from black music. 'I just speeded up some of the slow blues licks,' he explained, 'that's all. That's what rockabilly music or rock 'n' roll was to begin with: a country man's song with a black man's rhythm.'[5] Phillips also recognised a wealth of potential: '[Carl] was a tremendous honky-tonk picker . . . I was so impressed with the pain and feeling in his country singing, though, that I wanted to see whether this was someone who could revolutionize the country end of the business.'[6]

Writing new songs for Phillips was not a problem for Carl, who had composed many numbers over the years. The trouble lay in the way he worked at the time. None of his songs had titles (he was never good at choosing titles), none were written down, and both the lyrics and the arrangements changed from performance to performance as the mood struck him. What Phillips had seen in the studio resembled the brothers' onstage style: no two performances of a song were ever exactly alike. The brothers picked up on each other's cues, pulling back a little when one decided to launch into a solo, then coming back together and ending with a spontaneous flourish. Carl would regularly set aside the lyric altogether and relate in rhyme the scenes unfolding in the rough honky-tonk crowd before him.

The three brothers competed incessantly for audience attention, making every performance a contest of one-upmanship. Carl and Jay traded singing duties, each in a different style. Jay sang in a traditional country style, sounding very much like rough-hewn *Grand Ole Opry* regular Ernest Tubb. Carl's style was more in the R&B vein, hard driving and rocking. Carl specialised in stinging guitar solos, while Clayton wowed the crowd by riding his bass like a pogo stick as he pounded out the beat.

When the brothers returned to Memphis for their first recording session a few weeks later, Phillips sceptically noted that the band now included drummer W.S. 'Fluke' Holland. Drums were anathema to country bands of the time, but Perkins felt they provided a reinforcing backbeat to the rhythm of his sound. The first number, 'Movie Magg', was captured on the second take. Carl then sang the new song he had brought in, which was dubbed 'Honky Tonk Gal' on the studio log. Phillips liked it well enough to record two takes, but in the end it failed to hold his interest. What he liked about 'Movie Magg' was that it was 'a good, solid country song', but he felt that a country ballad was needed for the B-side.[7] Carl, who had surreptitiously been calming his nerves with intermittent swigs of whiskey, was by now feeling too mellow to argue the point, and the session came to a close.

The ballad came together over the course of several nights, as Carl improvised melody and lyrics onstage during shows. When he sang it to Phillips over the telephone a few days later, Phillips was enthusiastic and wanted to record it right away. To heighten the country sound, Phillips brought in Quentin Claunch on electric guitar, Bill Cantrell on fiddle, and steel guitarist Stan Kesler. Session tapes reveal that Cantrell coached Carl on his delivery between takes in order to bring out the deep emotion heard in the singer's voice. Phillips chose the title 'Turn Around', releasing it as the B-side to 'Movie Magg' on his subsidiary Flip label in February 1955.

To say that Phillips envisioned Carl Perkins as a country version of Elvis Presley is perhaps too simplistic, but not wholly inaccurate. There were obvious differences. Perkins was an accomplished musician and a songwriter, Presley was neither. Still, Phillips recognised a great deal of similarity: Perkins' sound was every bit as rhythm-driven as Presley's, and while he could never compete in the looks department, his onstage gyrations were just as wild, and his vocal sound conveyed a similar intensity of emotion. Phillips felt that two artists so similar, recording at a label as small as his, were likely to cancel each other out on the charts. Instead, he intended to position Perkins towards the country end of the musical spectrum and Presley towards the pop end.

Dewey Phillips, whose eclectic musical tastes cut across all genres, liked 'Turn Around' and gave it airplay in Memphis. The single soon caught on with country stations throughout Tennessee and spread across the South and Southwest, becoming especially popular in Texas. As it began to inch up the local charts, Bob Neal booked Carl as the opening act for two Presley shows. Perkins generated polite applause, as expected, then watched in amazement as Elvis took the stage. Elvis displayed an innate ability to sense the precise moment when the crowd's tension had built to a peak, when the littlest movement would burst the bubble of anticipation and the crowd would erupt in pandemonium.

At Phillips' suggestion, Presley took Perkins to Lansky Brothers, the men's outfitter on Beale Street, to pick out some stage clothes. Phillips felt it was important to give the audience something to look at that was different from what they wore on their own backs. Presley had been picking out his signature Hillbilly Cat clothing at Lansky's for years, and he chose a silky blue shirt and black slacks for Perkins. Carl later claimed credit for the pink and black colour combination, and the side-striped slacks that Elvis favoured at the time, but he was known to have worn these styles before Perkins came on the scene. In any event, Carl was soon emulating Elvis' fashion sense.

Carl would also have liked to record the same rocking music as Elvis. He was a far better musician than Elvis, and had been performing in public for several years prior to Elvis' first Sun Records single. But he was reticent about confronting Phillips.

Instead, he continued to play the country-tinged songs that Phillips wanted to record. At the next session, Carl improvised 'What You're Doin' When You're Cryin'' in a single take as the tape rolled. He followed it up with another improvised song, 'You Can't Make Love to Somebody', which took on a quicker beat. By this time the band was well lubricated with whiskey. They launched into the raucous 'Gone! Gone! Gone!' and nailed it on the second attempt. Despite its similarity to what he was currently recording with Presley, Phillips liked the final song and decided to release it. The result solidified the formula Phillips would use on the majority of Perkins' singles: the pairing of a slow country ballad with an up-tempo rhythmic novelty number.

On this second session Phillips employed some of his low-tech wizardry, facing amplifiers into the corner of the studio and covering them with cardboard boxes. A hole cut in one of the boxes produced a fuzz effect as it rattled. When mic'ed from behind, the sound waves bouncing off the walls created a slight hesitation, and produced the low-level thrum that was a signature of all Sun recordings: what popular Memphis DJ Sleepy-Eyed John, who disliked Phillips, derogatorily referred to as 'sixty-cycle hum'.

Phillips' sessions with Perkins followed a pattern: work up the arrangement in the late afternoon, get comfortable with the lyrics as the evening wore on, then roll the tape once everything came together as midnight approached. Along the way, Perkins lubricated the process with liberal applications of alcohol. Phillips was not averse to joining in, but only after the session had shut down for the night. He appreciated that musicians had their own way of working and let them take their time in finding a groove. When he sensed that the music was beginning to gel, he would start recording, capturing the rawness and spontaneity he craved before repetition gave the songs too much gloss. It was the 'edge' that Phillips looked for in each recording.

On 1 August 1955, along with the release of Elvis' 'Mystery Train'/'I Forgot to Remember to Forget', came Carl's 'Let the

Jukebox Keep on Playing'/'Gone! Gone! Gone!' The country hit Phillips envisioned did not materialise. Radio stations instead chose 'Gone! Gone! Gone!' for airplay – they eventually applied the term 'rockabilly' to describe the sound – and the record entered the regional charts.

It even caught the attention of country singer Webb Pierce, who wanted to record his own version of 'Let the Jukebox Keep on Playing' and 'Turn Around' in exchange for a share of the publishing credit and resulting royalties. Pierce had the popularity to make the songs hits, which could have made a fortune for Carl, even with a reduced share. But he was never given the option. Carl signed his publishing rights over to Phillips' Hi-Lo Music after each recording session, without ever establishing what those rights were. He only knew what Phillips told him, never questioning what he heard. So when Phillips refused to give up a royalty share and the deal with Pierce fell apart, Carl did not understand how much potential revenue the loss had cost him.

To capitalise on their latest releases, Bob Neal booked Presley and Perkins on a string of regional tour dates along with one of his new artists, Johnny Cash. The tour allowed Carl the opportunity to re-establish his acquaintance with Cash, to whom he had previously been introduced by Phillips. It was backstage at one of these dates that Cash related an anecdote from his military days, about a fellow soldier who was aggressively protective of his new blue suede shoes. He suggested that Perkins use the story as the basis of a song. Carl brushed the idea off at the time, saying that he knew nothing about that type of footwear, but the idea stuck with him. A few months later, when he overheard a chance remark about suede shoes, it took root. The song practically wrote itself in a single night, and when he played 'Don't Step on My Blue Swade Shoes' for his wife the following morning, Carl felt sure he had a hit. (It was his wife, Valda, who corrected the spelling from 'swade' to 'suede'.) Carl sang the song over the telephone for Phillips, who was not overly impressed, but suggested shortening the title to 'Blue Suede Shoes'. Though a recording session would have to wait until interest in 'Gone! Gone! Gone!' had begun to wane, Carl was undaunted. He included the song in his stage shows, giving the band a chance to perfect the arrangement. Audience response convinced him that this song would mark a turning point in his career, and he was anxious to get it recorded.

One possible reason for Phillips' lack of enthusiasm was his precarious financial situation. In a January 1955 letter to brother Jud, to whom he still owed money for buying out Jud's share of Sun Records, Phillips repeated his commitment to avoid bankruptcy: 'Anyone less interested in saving face would have given it up long ago, but I intend to pay every dollar the company owes – including you – even while I know there is no possible way to ever get out with a dollar.'[8] Brave words and a noble sentiment, but the reality was that he owed money everywhere – to investors, banks, pressing plants, artists. The total was approximately three times Sun Records' assets. There was no way he could repay the debt.

Sun Records' only viable asset at the time was Elvis Presley, and Phillips' only hope lay in exploiting that asset. In the belief that Presley's success would reverse the label's dismal financial picture and bring Sun Records national recognition, he encouraged Bob Neal to book the singer on as many performance dates as possible. Neal was eager to oblige, but since his influence was merely regional, he signed an agreement with Nashville-based Jamboree Attractions to act as booking agents. Within weeks, Elvis was performing throughout the South- and Midwest, and Phillips was fielding enquiries from major labels with interest in buying out the singer's contract.

Carl Perkins' third recording session finally took place on 19 December. Following the first take of 'Blue Suede Shoes', Phillips suggested a lyric change from 'Go, boy, go!' to 'Go, cat, go!' in order to appeal to a younger audience. Despite the singer's objections, he insisted that the second take was the keeper. Carl wanted to try again, but Phillips was convinced it was a smash hit and excitedly got Dewey Phillips on the phone to tell him so. The more he listened to Phillips' praises, the more Carl began to recognise the magic that had been captured on tape. 'I really believed that it was going to be big,' Phillips recalled. 'I really did, but you never know. Till this day, you don't know. But I knew that I just couldn't miss this one.'[9]

Carl worked up a second song, 'Honey Don't', that he had been toying with since summer. As usual, the lyrics and solos evolved over several takes, of which the third was the strongest. Recordings of 'Sure to Fall' and 'Tennessee' finished the session. Phillips cut the masters and sent them off to have to have both 45 and 78 rpm stamps produced. By the end of the month, Plastic Products had rushed out the first copies of 'Blue Suede Shoes'/'Honey Don't'.

Career wise, the end of 1955 marked a low point for both Phillips and Perkins. This next record had to be a hit. Elvis Presley had just left the label, allowing Phillips to get out from under a crushing load of debt but at the same time depriving him of his biggest moneymaker. Perkins, too, was desperate. The expected royalties from his previous releases had failed to materialise, partly because Phillips was unable to pay them. Between tour bookings, he frequently earned only a couple of dollars a night from his local club gigs, and just that autumn had been reduced to picking cotton in order to keep his family fed.

The single was released on 1 January 1956. Local stations gave airplay to 'Honey Don't', but elsewhere radio response quickly established that 'Blue Suede Shoes' was the potential hit. In Cleveland, Ohio alone there were orders of 25,000 copies. The song topped the local country charts in February, remaining at no. 1 for three months. Within two months of release, 'Blue Suede Shoes' was averaging sales of 20,000 copies a day. It was placed high in the pop charts, even crossing over to the R&B charts in some areas. In the end, the song topped all three charts, making it – in some music historians' minds – the first true rock 'n' roll hit record.

Demand for tour dates quickly escalated the going rate for the Perkins Brothers Band from $100 a night to $250. Bob Neal booked them on an extensive Sun Records package tour with Johnny Cash, who was riding the popularity of his own recent release, 'So Doggone Lonesome'/'Folsom Prison Blues'. Predictably, Perkins was well received throughout the South and Southwest, particularly in Texas, where rockabilly found its first major audience. With orders placed following a series of *Big D Jamboree* broadcasts from the Dallas Sportatorium, Phillips was convinced that he had a million-seller on his hands.

But it was the response from other regions where country music was not in favour that proved the most surprising. The song touched a nerve with American youth from coast to coast. In many places, Perkins generated the same riotous reception that had previously been reserved for Elvis, and his popularity skyrocketed. Phillips must have felt personally vindicated. There was every reason to believe that his newest singer would be just as big a star – if not greater – than the one he had been forced to let go.

'Blue Suede Shoes' entered the national charts in March, on *Billboard*'s Hot 100. Typically for the time, there was soon a spate of cover versions from other artists, all hoping to cash in on the song's popularity. The strongest was an up-tempo rendering by Perkins' former Sun label mate, Elvis Presley. Presley's RCA producer agreed with Phillips to not issue Elvis' version as a single while the original was still on the way up, but included it on a four-song EP and on Elvis' RCA debut album released later that month. Presley was the first to perform the song on network television, pairing it with 'Heartbreak Hotel' on *The Dorsey Brothers Stage Show* on 17 March, just as the original version was breaking out nationally. Perkins was booked to perform 'Blue Suede Shoes' the following week on *The Perry Como Show*. Presley had become a national phenomenon as a result of his appearance on the Dorsey show just a month earlier. Perkins had every expectation of achieving the same level of celebrity.

Phillips squeezed in a recording session a few days prior to 17 March, when Perkins was booked to appear on *Ozark Jubilee*, Red Foley's popular television show broadcast from Springfield, Missouri. With confidence born of a current hit single and a substantial quantity of alcohol, Perkins recorded a number of songs that Phillips planned to release over the coming months. A follow-up single would eventually be needed, and with Perkins so much in demand, scheduling a session would only become more difficult as time went on. The results were mixed. 'All Mama's Children', a songwriting collaboration with Cash, took the same nursery rhyme inspiration that infused several of Perkins' earlier works. 'Boppin' the Blues' was a reworking of an idea supplied by one of Perkins' neighbours. Both referenced 'Blue Suede Shoes', either in lyric or melody. Phillips paired the two for May release.

Phillips rented a limousine and got local DJ Stuart Pinkham to drive the band from Memphis to the *Ozark Jubilee* date in Missouri. Pinkham and the band members shared driving duties on the way to a show booked for 21 March in Norfolk, Virginia, before heading on to New York City for the 24 March television appearance. They never made it.

Chapter Eleven

Go, Cat, Go

IT WAS 23 MARCH before word of the accident reached Sun Records. On the road outside Dover, Delaware, Pinkham had fallen asleep at the wheel and rear-ended a poultry truck with such force that the limousine rolled over four times, careered over the edge of a bridge and landed in a ditch beside a stream. Perkins was thrown unconscious from the car into the water, and would have drowned if drummer W.S. Holland had not pulled him out. Perkins was lucky to survive, suffering concussion, a broken collarbone and multiple lacerations. His already receding hairline was shaved back even further to allow doctors to stitch up the cuts on his head. Phillips had planned to fly up to New York and surprise Perkins by awarding him a gold record on air to commemorate the sales of 500,000 copies of 'Blue Suede Shoes'. Marion Keisker had the duty of notifying band members' relatives, including Perkins' wife, who was eight months pregnant with their third child.

Although Perkins was out of the picture for the immediate future, 'Blue Suede Shoes' continued to climb the charts. Perkins became the first artist to simultaneously hold the no. 1 position on the regional pop, country and R&B charts with the same record. It was only kept off the top of the national charts by Elvis Presley's 'Heartbreak Hotel', which held the no. 1 spot for four weeks; 'Blue Suede Shoes' was at no. 2. Fans had bought over one million copies by the middle of April, making it the first million-seller for both Perkins and Sun Records.

The sale of Presley's contract had narrowly saved Phillips from bankruptcy. Now, just six months later, revenues from Perkins' hit recording made him rich. Phillips' share of the publishing royalties was two cents from every copy sold, eventually amounting to over $30,000 from the two versions of the song. That kind of money went a long way toward replenishing the label's depleted coffers, as well as purchasing Phillips a new house. It also provided the beginnings of Phillips' international dealings, linking Sun Records to licensees in Great Britain and Canada.

Achieving financial success, after all that had led up to it, seems to have brought out another aspect of Phillips' personality. Business dealings with his artists began to conform to the industry norm. Some complained that the terms of their Sun Records contracts were shady, that Phillips had taken advantage of their inexperience to cheat them out of their fair share of royalties. Some even convinced the courts to agree with them. Ethics aside, Phillips' business practices were in line with what other record labels of the time were doing. He was no more ruthless than anyone else – but no less.

As Perkins recuperated, offers of concert dates and television appearances continued to pour in. He was now seen as the nation's number two rock 'n' roll star. Enquiries from powerful Nashville music industry types soon followed. Music publisher Jim Denny, booking agent Oscar Davis and artist manager Dub Allbritton all offered their services. Perkins telephoned Memphis, asking Phillips for advice. Phillips talked him into staying with the representation he already had. It apparently never occurred to Perkins to question the fact the Phillips held a financial interest in that representation.

Phillips, however, did not allow his injured star to rest for long. He summoned Perkins to Memphis on 10 April, directing him to a nearby car dealership, where he presented the surprised singer with the keys to a brand-new, two-tone Cadillac. Never one to waste a gesture, Phillips had arranged for the moment to be captured by a newspaper photographer, and capped the event with a speech. 'I said when I entered the recording business that the first artist to sell one million copies of any record, I would give him a brand-new Cadillac. It looks as if Carl Perkins is that lucky man. We're here this morning to present Carl Perkins with Sun Records' first Cadillac.'[1] Imagine Perkins' dismay when he later found that the cost of the car had been deducted from his royalties.

Phillips also managed to fit in a recording session, which yielded some of the best rockabilly material that Sun Records ever produced. Once again, it was Phillips' choice for the single's B-side, the quintessential rockabilly raver 'Dixie Fried', that received the most airplay. 'Dixie Fried' was different from anything being played on radio at the time, which probably accounts for Phillips' interest in it. Although lyrically superior to 'Blue Suede Shoes', however, its storyline and phrasing is so grounded in rural honky-tonk life that there was no way the single stood a chance in the pop market. More than that, its overtly country character may have been the factor that forever ended Perkins' potential as a pop artist.

Towards the end of April, Perkins was booked to headline the Top Stars of '56, a package tour set to begin in July. The promoter promised an astounding $1,000 a day for performing two songs to close the show. Before the tour began, Phillips arranged for a hairpiece to cover the scars on Perkins' scalp, which improved his looks considerably. Perkins would wear a toupee in public for the remainder of his life.

In the months since leaving Sun Records, the national attention focused on Elvis Presley had intensified. His music and onstage movements were regularly denounced in the press, sometimes on the grounds of moral indecency. But just as often, Elvis was denounced by racist hate groups and individuals, who viewed his music as being 'black' and therefore a corrupting influence on his youthful 'white' audience. These were emotionally charged times in matters of race relations, and it was in the South that the reaction was the most vehement and violent.

As the most visible and popular practitioner of what was increasingly being termed rock 'n' roll music, Elvis became the lightning rod for such charges, but many other artists were attacked on the same grounds. Perkins was one. The references to drinking and fighting in the lyrics of 'Blue Suede Shoes' and 'Dixie Fried' drew the ire of self-appointed moralists, who charged him with contributing to the delinquency of American youth. Some of these 'moralists' went so far as physically attacking artists they viewed as threats to white society. One group attacked and beat pop icon Nat King Cole – whom no one could ever have mistaken for a raucous rock 'n' roller – onstage in Birmingham, Alabama in April 1956.

It was with this attack fresh in his mind that Perkins nervously approached the opening date of the Top Stars of '56 tour in Columbia, South Carolina. This time, however, it was not racial agitators he had to fear, but his own fans. They surged forward as he was introduced, crushing against the front of the stage. Hysteria built during the opening bars of 'Honey Don't', until halfway through, the tour's road manager anxiously signalled to Perkins from offstage. The band ran towards the wings and hid in a dressing room, narrowly escaping the rioting fans that stormed the stage. When Perkins emerged an hour later, he was escorted under police guard to his waiting car, which was covered with messages scratched into the paint by fans. Sickened by the experience, Perkins quit the tour – and the $1,000 per day payout – on the spot. The band quickly loaded up their instruments and drove the vandalised Cadillac back to Tennessee.

Phillips was on the telephone before Perkins had even arrived home, and continued to call every hour that day. His main concern was the potential damage that walking out on the tour might do to Perkins' career. Added to that was the possibility that the tour promoter might sue for breach of contract. None of this was likely to increase record sales. Declining interest had greeted each Perkins record released since 'Blue Suede Shoes'. The follow-up single 'Boppin' the Blues', released in May, reached no. 70 in the pop charts and no. 9 in the country chart. The August release of 'Dixie Fried' was ignored by the pop charts, though it reached no. 10 in the country chart. Neither release made a dent in the R&B chart. While the country radio response to both singles was more than respectable, it was a disappointment after the huge crossover success of 'Blue Suede Shoes'. Perkins would never again have a hit to match it.

At first, Perkins insisted that his departure from the tour was due to the recurrence of a bleeding stomach ulcer. Having never before seen evidence of such an ailment, Phillips refused to accept the excuse. Perkins then cited imminent nervous exhaustion, and produced a note from his doctor stating as much. Finally, after a week of pleading telephone calls, Phillips prevailed. Perkins staved off a threatened lawsuit by agreeing to return to the tour once it moved into the Northern states.

Perkins received his first royalty cheques from Phillips in August, one from Sun Records and the other from Hi-Lo Music. Together, the two cheques totalled about $26,000. While this was more money than Perkins had ever seen, it was far less than the $100,000 he had been led to believe a record as big as 'Blue Suede Shoes' was likely to earn. The accounting that accompanied the cheques was so vague that Perkins could not decipher it, except to note the deduction for the 'gift' Cadillac. Still, he was reluctant to question Phillips about the matter. He blindly regarded Phillips as the authority in business and artistic decisions, and did not want to believe that Phillips would cheat him.

Perkins finally got the opportunity to appear on television that autumn, making up the *Como Show* booking that had been sidelined earlier in the year. By then, however, Elvis 'owned' the airwaves by virtue of his many televised performances, and Perkins seemed to be just another in a string of Presley imitators.

★ ★ ★

Following the sale of Elvis Presley's contract and the success of Perkins' 'Blue Suede Shoes', Phillips' financial situation improved dramatically. But prosperity brought its own problems, one of which was the deterioration of his working relationship with Marion Keisker. No longer dependent on her for emotional support, Phillips began to view her more as a secretary than an assistant. Keisker was hurt, and left Memphis Recording Service in 1955 to work at Phillips' newly acquired radio station, before severing the relationship for good in 1957 to join the air force. Her responsibilities at Sun Records were assumed by a small staff that grew to include general manager Bill Fitzgerald, Phillips' assistant Sally Wilbourn, promotion manager Cecil Scaife and promotional assistant Barbara Barnes.

Starting around 1957, Phillips hired a recording engineer and began to relinquish more of his studio responsibilities. First he handed over the job of rehearsing of new artists and working up their material prior to recording sessions. Eventually, auditioning new talent, vetting demo tapes and operating the control board were passed to staff members.

Despite Sun Records' success, Phillips never bothered to install a sign to identify the label. 'I just felt like if I put up a big sign on this little building or tried to fancy it up, it would look all out of proportion,' he explained to journalist Edwin Howard in 1959. 'There's something about that little Memphis Recording Service sign that just goes with it.' Nor was he the type to supply himself with a big office, or even a desk: 'As for a desk, well, I'm not the kind that runs things by bangin' on a desk, so I didn't figure I needed one. Anyhow, I've got four girls and a man at the three desks and they know how to handle the desk work.' Despite having earned a reported $2 million in the six years since starting up his label, Phillips adamantly maintained the same laid-back atmosphere he had begun with. 'Everyone around here has a smattering of knowledge of the whole business, and I've got no secrets. Our informality is what gives us our hit records. Our artists just get the feeling we're goofing off. As I tell 'em, there's no sense being nervous, because there's nobody else here can do any better.'[2]

★   ★   ★

At the end of 1956 and the beginning of 1957 there were a series of sessions at Sun Records. Phillips intended to get as many songs recorded as possible before Carl Perkins' touring schedule began in the spring. A session on 4 December was Perkins' introduction to Jerry Lee Lewis. The first Sun single by Phillips' current golden boy had been released just days earlier, and he came with an ego that overwhelmed the tiny recording studio.

Brought in by Phillips to play piano for the session, Lewis irritated Perkins right from the start. Possibly Phillips wanted to inject some kick into Perkins' material, possibly he thought a little professional rivalry might stimulate Perkins' performance. If that was the intent, it worked. Perkins pulled out all the stops as the two musicians strove to outdo each other on 'Matchbox', a number he improvised from a half-remembered snatch of lyric. After it was recorded, Phillips called Perkins into the control booth to listen. As the tape played, Phillips raved about how brilliant Lewis' piano playing was. Phillips was always excited about whichever artist was his latest discovery, but it seemed to Perkins that he was particularly intense in his enthusiasm for Lewis.

Johnny Cash stopped by at some point during the session, and was soon joined by Elvis Presley, who was passing through town with a Las Vegas dancer in tow. During a break, Presley sat down at the piano and began fingering a favourite gospel melody. Cash, Perkins and Lewis joined in, with various band members strumming guitar and Presley's date adding harmonies. After several songs, Phillips realised that 'we might never have these people together again', and instructed engineer Jack Clement to begin taping.[3] He called the local newspaper, which sent a photographer. Cash left soon after the pictures were shot, but the tape rolled for almost 70 minutes, capturing Presley, Perkins and Lewis singing a variety of spiritual and secular tunes. The newspaper ran the story the next day, dubbing the group the 'Million Dollar Quartet'.

Two more sessions followed. Phillips chose the country tune 'Your True Love' for Perkins' January 1957 release, burying the stronger rockabilly number 'Matchbox' on the flip side. Though 'Your True Love' reached no. 13 on the country chart and no. 67 on the pop chart, Perkins hated the finished recording. Phillips had mistakenly – or perhaps deliberately – sped up the tape during the mastering process, creating a higher vocal pitch that a 16 February *Billboard* reviewer charitably dubbed 'youthful sounding'. 'Matchbox' proved an even greater disappointment, failing to chart at all.

Although Perkins was still getting solid recognition in the country charts, his real musical strength lay elsewhere. His guitar work alone should have placed him at the forefront of the R&B and pop markets. But he seemed to be caught in the middle at a moment when musical tastes were diverging. He was too country for rock 'n' roll, too hillbilly for country.

For the time being, however, Perkins continued to tour off the lingering popularity of 'Blue Suede Shoes'. Though his pay had slipped into the $500 a day range and other acts were headlining, the crowds still gathered and fans cheered Perkins' driving beat and blistering guitar solos in city after city, night after night.

In August, Phillips received an enquiry about including Perkins and Lewis in a low-budget rock 'n' roll film called *Jamboree* being shot in New York. Phillips welcomed the publicity, Perkins welcomed the $1,000 actor's fee, and Lewis welcomed any opportunity to garner the acclaim he felt was his due. Offered first choice between two tunes, both of which he considered rubbish, Perkins chose 'Glad All Over'. The other number, 'Great Balls of Fire', he left to Jerry Lee.

Phillips delegated production responsibilities for recording 'Glad All Over' to Jack Clement. Released in November to coincide with the film's debut, the single was immediately trampled by the phenomenal response to 'Great Balls of Fire'. Just as he had done with each new member of the Sun stable in turn, Phillips now devoted his effort and praise to Jerry Lee Lewis. Perkins' resentment had been building for nearly a year, and he felt slighted by the attention Phillips paid to his newest star. Unfortunately, the rising of Lewis' star coincided with the decline of Perkins' own. Perkins desperately needed encouragement and support, but all Phillips' attention was focused on building a rival's career. Later in the month, while Perkins and Johnny Cash were touring in California, they were approached by Don Law, head of Columbia Records' country division and one of the most influential music executives in Nashville. Law offered each of them recording contracts, effective when their Sun contracts expired in 1958: Perkins in January and Cash in August. Both artists were eager for a change, and soon agreed.

Phillips inevitably heard about the defection. He called Perkins to confirm the rumour and requested that the artist meet him in Memphis to discuss the matter. Perkins drove his Cadillac through the streets of the city for hours as the two men talked business. Despite Phillips' persuasive arguments for staying with Sun – primarily that no one in Nashville would know what to do with Perkins because none of them understood rockabilly music or appreciated the uniqueness of his talent – Perkins had already made up his mind to leave the label. Late in the day, he left Phillips standing on the sidewalk in front of the Sun studio and drove away.

The split was more than mere jealousy over a rival. Phillips was deeply committed to a single musical vision. But the raw, edgy twang of rockabilly, with its wrong-side-of-the-tracks honky-tonk savour, was quickly being homogenised by teen idols named Buddy and Bobby and Ricky into middle-American, pop-infused rock 'n' roll. Even veteran rockabilly cats like Elvis Presley were jettisoning their musical roots and cultivating a smoother sound. Where did that leave Perkins, a man who really knew nothing else? There was nothing to do but change with the times. Since Phillips would not, Perkins had to make the attempt on his own.

Chapter Twelve

Selling Johnny

WHEN J.R. CASH showed up on the doorstep of Memphis Recording Service late in 1954 (or possibly early 1955), he was a 22-year-old, recently married, former air force sergeant. His day job as a door-to-door appliance salesman took him into some of the poorer neighbourhoods of Memphis, where he first heard and came to love Southern blues music. Previous to that, his upbringing in segregated rural Arkansas had ensured that his sole musical influence had been through the local hillbilly radio stations.

On his discharge from military service in July 1954, Cash headed to Memphis, hoping for a career in music. His elder brother introduced him to three mechanics that worked at the Automobile Sales Company, who had formed a combo to play at small gatherings around town. The four men hit it off almost immediately and began practising together in the evenings after work. While none of them were particularly proficient musicians, they quickly developed a distinctive sound. Intrinsic to that sound was Cash's singular voice. Despite its limited range, Cash's voice already possessed the deep resonance and stark honesty that later became his trademark.

When the group felt prepared to audition, Cash called Phillips, saying that he was a gospel singer. Phillips turned him down, explaining that the market for gospel recordings was too small to warrant producing them. His advice to the aspiring singer was to go sin a little bit and see if it produced some more marketable material. On the second attempt, Cash represented himself as a country singer, which also failed to generate interest: Phillips had a particular dislike for the bland and predictable country tunes he heard coming out of Nashville.

A subsequent conversation with Scotty Moore convinced Cash that he might have better luck if he contacted Phillips in person. Cash began stopping in at the studio on his way to and from the Keegan School of Broadcasting, where he was taking some classes towards becoming a radio announcer. Every day it was a different excuse: either Phillips had not yet arrived, or he was in a meeting or busy in the studio. Finally, Cash went to Memphis Recording Service early one morning and sat outside waiting for Phillips to arrive. He introduced himself when Phillips eventually walked up: 'Mr. Phillips, sir, if you listen to me, you'll be glad you did.'[1]

Impressed by Cash's confidence, Phillips agreed to listen, and invited him into the studio. For the next two or three hours, Cash sang every song he knew, from folk to country to gospel, including a few he had written himself. 'Their material was all religious at that time,' Phillips later explained, 'songs which Cash had composed. I liked them, but I told him that I would not at that time be able to merchandise him as a religious artist and that it would be well if he could secure some other material or write some other songs.'[2] It was the songs written by Cash that most interested Phillips. When Cash sang 'Hey! Porter', Phillips was hooked. He invited Cash to return with his band.

The band consisted of Luther Perkins (a 27-year-old guitar player of limited ability, but a distinctive sound), Marshall Grant (also 27, who had only recently acquired a stand-up bass and was still learning how to play it) and A.W. 'Red' Kernodle (at 37 the most experienced of the group, possessing moderate skill on the steel guitar). The group's simple *boom-chicka-boom* backing sound was less the result of deliberate styling than it was all that the unpolished musicians could manage.

When Cash did return on 22 March 1955, it was with many apologies for his band's ragged musicianship. Phillips recalled, 'I said that he should let me hear what they could do and I would be able to tell whether they had a style I would be able to work with. I was immediately impressed with John's unusual voice. I was also interested in Luther's guitar playing . . . he wasn't super good – but he was different, and that was important.'³ The band members were so nervous that they could barely play. After a faltering recording of 'Wide Open Road' and several fumbling attempts at other numbers, the especially nervous Kernodle abruptly quit the band and left the studio, much to the other players' relief. Through a period of trial and error, the remaining musicians pulled themselves together enough to complete a take of 'Hey! Porter'. Cash, who thought he was still auditioning, was surprised when Phillips announced that he intended to release the recording. Cash recalled, 'Luther Perkins had a little second-hand Sears amplifier with a six-inch speaker. Marshall Grant had a bass that was held together with masking tape. I had a $4.80 guitar that I had brought back from Germany. Phillips had to be a genius to get anything out of that conglomeration.'⁴

The session also produced an early version of 'Folsom Prison Blues'. Phillips did not think it was right for the other side of the single. Instead, he requested a love song, 'a real weeper'.⁵ Having nothing suitable in his repertoire, Cash was instructed to write one. He called Phillips a couple of weeks later with 'You're Gonna Cry, Cry, Cry', and booked a session in May.

Phillips recalled that it was this third session in the studio when he began to record Cash's material seriously. Still, it took 35 takes to get the song right, mostly because Luther struggled with the arrangement. Once a planned guitar break was eliminated, the session proceeded smoothly. Phillips hit on the correct mix from the beginning. He made Cash's haunting baritone the prime focus with the band relegated to keeping time in the background, the whole being fattened with Phillips' signature slapback echo effect. This spare approach was very different from what Nashville was producing at the time, where lead vocals blended into backing instrumentation in a more balanced manner. In Phillips' hands, Cash's recordings stood out from other country releases, just as the unique quality of his voice stood out from the band.

'Cry! Cry! Cry!'/'Hey! Porter', released on 21 June 1955, was credited to Johnny Cash and the Tennessee Two. Phillips had shortened the song's title, as he frequently did, and proposed that 'John' become 'Johnny', because it sounded younger and more rebellious. 'Cry!' entered the local country charts in August, reaching no. 1 in September, and made a brief appearance on the national country charts for one week in November.

Prior to the release of 'Hey! Porter', Cash had performed one-night gigs at theatres, clubs and honky-tonks in small, outlying towns in Tennessee, Arkansas and Mississippi, returning home after each show. His first big concert date, and first performance in Memphis, occurred at the Overton Park Shell on 5 August 1955 as part of the 22-act show put together by Bob Neal and headlined by Elvis Presley. The show marked a turning point in Cash's career. His debut performance before a Memphis audience of 4,000 screaming fans was a triumph, and the press judged him to be an artist of the same calibre as Presley. Afterwards, Neal signed Cash to a management deal and booked him on tours farther afield, including a brief tour through West Texas on which he opened for Carl Perkins and Elvis Presley. From then on, Cash was on the road almost constantly, enduring a seemingly endless round of performing for faceless crowds in nameless towns as he criss-crossed his way through the Southern states. The punishing tour schedule led to his eventual dependence on prescription amphetamines, which he used initially as a way to stay alert on the long overnight car trips between gigs.

Cash and Perkins continued to tour together after Elvis left Sun Records, becoming firm friends. Cash was particularly close to Clayton Perkins, the volatile bass player in the Perkins Brothers Band, who shared his fondness for practical jokes that bordered on outright vandalism. The tedium of life on the road led the two friends to egg each other on, competing to see who could perpe-trate the most outrageous stunt on unsuspecting hoteliers. One time they painted an entire room black because they disliked the peach colour scheme, another time they set loose two hundred baby chicks.

In December, Phillips released 'Folsom Prison Blues'/'So Doggone Lonesome' as Cash's second single. The songs had actually been recorded at the end of July, but he held off releasing them while 'Cry!' was still active in the charts. Although 'Folsom Prison Blues' later came to be regarded as the quintessential Cash composition, it is nearly a direct copy of Gordon Jenkins' 'Crescent City Blues' that had been released in 1954. The single rose quickly in the country charts, keeping pace with Carl Perkins' 'Blue Suede Shoes', but failed to cross over to the pop and R&B charts like Perkins' hit did. Cash made several attempts to break into the emerging rock 'n' roll market, writing songs that were recorded by Sun label mates Warren Smith and Roy Orbison, but his rock 'n' roll lyrics lacked the poetry, honesty and conviction of his country material.

Amazingly, Cash had kept his day job with the Home Equipment Company. His salary was paid as an advance against the commis-sion he would supposedly earn on the sale of domestic appliances to the public, but the commission never materialised – he could not bring himself to pressure people into buying appliances he knew they could not afford. Still, his employer believed in Cash – if only as a musician – and continued to advance his salary. When Cash received his first cheque from Phillips at the end of the year, he gave up his day job and repaid his employer $1,200 out of the $6,000 in royalties he had earned.

Cash reported to a recording session on 2 April 1956 with a song that would change the course of his career. 'I Walk the Line' practically wrote itself in about 20 minutes following an on-tour conversation between Cash and Carl Perkins. The two men, both married and recent fathers, were discussing their lives back home and the temptations of the road when inspiration struck. In the studio, Phillips worked his improvisational magic, weaving strips of paper through the strings of Cash's guitar to imitate the sound of brushes on a snare drum.

The song was initially conceived and recorded as a slow ballad. Phillips thought it dragged, and asked Cash to record a faster version for comparison. It was this version that Phillips released, much to Cash's consternation. His first knowledge of the switch came when he heard the record played on a late night radio programme while driving home from a show. Phillips calmly listened to Cash's insistent request that the current pressing be withdrawn and the original ballad released. He even promised to consider the matter, but he had no intention of doing so. He felt that he had a better understanding of what would sell, and he was proved right. The song became the first of Cash's recordings to cross over into the pop market.

'Get Rhythm'/'I Walk the Line' was released in May 1956 to immediate acclaim, climbing to no. 2 in the country charts and no. 19 in the pop charts. Cash, who had been a regular on the Saturday night *Louisiana Hayride* radio show since January, was invited to join the *Grand Ole Opry* in July. Near the end of the year, 'I Walk the Line' was still charting at no. 3 in the country charts and at no. 88 in the pop charts.

Cash's fourth and fifth Sun singles failed to attract as much attention as the previous three. It may be that his stripped-down sound, once so unique, was now being imitated in Nashville and no longer seemed so different. Or maybe Phillips switched the focus of his attention to other projects once he felt that Cash was sufficiently established. Certainly changes were afoot at the label, suggesting that Phillips was being pulled in multiple directions. It was now that he brought in musician and songwriter Jack Clement as a trainee engineer, adding to a staff that had previously consisted of only a secretary, an office manager, and a part-time engineer who split his hours between the studio and Phillips' radio station.

Phillips assigned Clement to oversee Cash's recording sessions, beginning in July 1957. The outcome, 'Home of the Blues', marked a new direction, with the addition of a piano and a vocal chorus. Phillips was sceptical; the added flourishes helped cover up the inadequacies of Luther Perkins' guitar playing, but they also overwhelmed the minimal instrumentation that had previously showcased Cash's voice. 'Jack was a very creative person,' Phillips stated, 'but he didn't follow the lines of my thinking.'[6] Cash did not care for the finished result, but the single's rise to no. 5 in the country charts and no. 88 in the pop charts seemed to indicate that the new formula was working.

However, there was a major bone of artistic contention brewing between Cash and Phillips. Cash was adamant about wanting to record religious songs. Phillips, who claimed to enjoy gospel music personally, nonetheless refused, insisting that the financial return would fail to cover production costs, let alone turn a profit. From a purely business perspective, a gospel release at this point in Cash's career would only slow down the momentum Phillips was building in the pop arena by diverting record sales. This was the big picture that Cash failed to grasp.

Phillips' continuing refusal rankled Cash to such an extent that when Don Law at Columbia Records wanted to talk about a recording contract, Cash was ready to listen. Phillips was unaware of the planned defection when he released his label's first album in November 1957: *Johnny Cash with His Hot and Blue Guitar*. That same month, following minor throat surgery, Cash returned to the studio to record his next single. Determined to reach the growing teenage market, Jack Clement produced a saccharine story song he had written entitled 'Ballad of a Teenage Queen'. Following the session, recently hired musical director Bill Justis dubbed in a keening soprano and a vocal chorus. Cash hated the result. His offering, 'Big River', although it was the stronger of the two numbers, was relegated to the B-side.

The December release of 'Ballad of a Teenage Queen' was

followed up in April 1958 with a 15-day tour of Canada, where Quality Records, Sun's Canadian licensee, had organised extensive promotion. Entry in the contest to crown a Teenage Queen in each city visited by the tour could be gained only by purchasing the single. The event drove sales much higher than the song's content warranted, pushing it to no. 16 in the Hot 100 chart and – ironically – supplying Cash with his first no. 1 country recording. From then on, Sun Records tried to market Cash as a pop act.

By the early spring of 1958, rumours of Cash's impending departure to Columbia Records had begun to reach Memphis. Cash denied making plans to leave. Phillips was satisfied for a time, but the rumours persisted and eventually he confronted the issue directly. Phillips drove over to Cash's home and angrily demanded that Cash look him in the eye and tell the truth. Cash did so. Asked why he felt the need for deception, Cash replied that it was payback for several occasions when Phillips had been less than truthful with him in the past. Cash might have been referring to the substandard royalty payments that nearly all Sun artists complained about, although in a later statement he said that '[Phillips had] always told me the truth, but I'd been too ignorant to know what it meant.'[7] Marshall Grant was more blunt: 'Sam was stealing us blind.'[8]

For Cash, it was never really about the money, it was about artistic control. Columbia agreed to let him record the religious album that Phillips had refused. But the deal also promised a larger cut of mechanical royalties, which would yield a substantially increased income, as well as the prestige and promotional machinery that only a major label could offer. 'Sun was still more or less a regional label,' Grant continued. 'After Elvis left and we left, it got a lot of recognition nationwide and finally worldwide, but that wasn't the case when we were there.'[9] Phillips had another explanation. Cash, he said, like Carl Perkins, was jealous over the amount of attention being given to Jerry Lee Lewis. Both artists had forgotten the amount of attention he had given them when their careers were first being launched.

Phillips was indignant, but more that that, he was hurt. 'Sam Phillips loved Johnny Cash,' stated Jack Clement. 'He respected him a lot more than the other characters because he was a real gentleman. Sam was always raving about how easy he was to work with. He loved his singing. He would talk about the authority he had in his voice and how people trusted him.'[10] For Phillips, this was not just a business decision, it was a betrayal by a man he considered to be a friend.

Added to this was Phillips' suspicion that long-time friend and associate Bob Neal had also betrayed him. Neal's management company – Stars, Inc. – represented both Cash and Perkins, so it was virtually impossible for Neal not to know of the deal with Columbia. As a professional courtesy, Phillips should have been offered the chance to match any offer from a rival label. That chance was denied him. Neal later claimed that Phillips had been informed, but pleaded poverty when it came to the royalty hike. Phillips responded that he would have paid it, had he known that Columbia's offer was serious. But Neal's connection to Sun Records was irreparably damaged. He soon closed his business, continuing to manage Cash and Perkins from his home.

Choosing to exercise his remaining rights, Phillips sent Cash a formal letter, ordering him into the studio to begin recording the rest of the 65 songs stipulated by his contract. Cash refused, but relented when Jack Clement – whom Phillips had once again assigned to produce the sessions – stated that his job depended on completing the task. A brief battle of wills ensued. Having learned an expensive lesson from the loss of Elvis, Phillips wanted to make sure that his latest moneymaker did not escape without supplying a large backlog of recordings for Sun to release after his departure. Cash, on the other hand, did not want to provide the best of his original compositions for the sessions, since the royalty rate Sun Records paid was significantly lower than the standard rate he would soon receive at Columbia. Clement defused the situation by agreeing to supply the necessary songs, offering Cash approval of the material he recorded.

Cash need not have been concerned. The studio was empty when he arrived on the appointed date in May, except for Clement and a young piano player. Clement proposed a song he had written entitled 'Guess Things Happen That Way'. The piano player, Charlie Rich – who would soon have a successful singing career of his own – supplied 'Story of a Broken Heart', 'You Tell Me' and 'The Ways of a Woman in Love'. 'I did every song that Jack asked me to do,' Cash recalled. 'I really don't think I would have done it for anyone else in the world. I could have played off sick or pulled this or that excuse. Jack said after we got working, "I don't like this any better than you do." I said, "Well, I'm really kind of enjoying it."'[11]

The first single released from these final sessions was 'Guess Things Happen That Way'. It became Cash's biggest Sun hit, shooting to no. 1 on the country charts and no. 11 on the pop charts. Several more sessions followed in the coming weeks, ending in mid-July. Although the quality of the compositions was top notch and subsequent releases performed well commercially, Cash was never happy with the extraneous orchestration and background vocals that Clement employed as embellishments, feeling they diminished his artistry.

At the end of his contract with Phillips, Cash was unhappy on several fronts. In the studio, Phillips noticed no change in the quality of his work, but his abuse of amphetamines on the road had begun to negatively affect his onstage performances and posed a serious threat to his marriage. He had lost weight, his face now appearing gaunt and drawn.

Phillips announced the departure of Johnny Cash from Sun Records in mid-July ads placed in music industry trade papers, which assured readers that the label had enough unissued Cash material on tape to provide regular releases for the next two years.

In fact, Sun issued eleven singles, four EPs and six LPs after Cash's departure on 31 July 1958, the final album being released in November 1964. In the liner notes to one of the albums, Phillips summed up what he felt Cash had accomplished during his stay with the label: 'Almost reluctantly, Johnny evolved a pop-country style in arrangement and instrumentation . . . He caused more of a revolution in pop music than in country music, as was his aim, by being one of the first country and western artists exposed on national "general entertainment" TV shows.'[12] Cash immediately dumped the overdubbed pop trappings once he left Sun Records, which seems to confirm his reluctance to have them thrust upon him. Still, the crossover brought him to the attention of a greater audience than he would have gained had he remained strictly a country act, and no doubt played a role in the later success of his national television programme.

For years afterwards, Cash downplayed his tenure at Sun Records, although by the time he wrote his 1997 autobiography, his attitude towards the experience had mellowed a little. 'My feelings about Sam Phillips are still mixed,' he said. 'I think he was one of those angels who appear in your life, but I'm not sure he treated me properly in a financial sense (I'm not sure he didn't, either). Mainly, though, I'm still annoyed that he never gave me a Cadillac.'[13]

Chapter Thirteen

A Square Peg

ROY ORBISON WAS almost 20 years old, a geology major from the oilfields of Wink, Texas, when he first appeared at the door of Memphis Recording Service in late March 1956. He had performed on local radio since the age of eight, graduating to television in his teens as part of a country dance band called the Wink Westerners. After enrolling at Odessa Junior College, the band was reformed as the Teen Kings, and landed a weekly television spot sponsored by the Pioneer Furniture company on KMID-TV in Midland. Elvis Presley is believed to have appeared as a guest on the show in 1955, to plug a local tour date; Johnny Cash is known to have done the same later in the year. When asked about joining the Sun Records roster, it was Cash who suggested Orbison should contact Sam Phillips directly. Orbison telephoned, saying that Cash had referred him. Phillips hotly replied, 'Johnny Cash doesn't run my record company!' and slammed down the receiver.[1]

Early in March 1956, the Teen Kings recorded a novelty dance number titled 'Ooby Dooby'. Written by a pair of North Texas State frat boys, and musically a near relation to Carl Perkins' 'Blue Suede Shoes', it was released by Je-Wel Records. A Texas record shop owner who knew Orbison called Phillips and played the record over the phone. Despite the throwaway lyrics, Phillips was impressed by Orbison's vocal inflection, and asked the shop owner to send him a copy. Said Phillips later, 'I thought if we got a good cut on it we could get some attention. Even more, I was very impressed with the inflection Roy brought to it. In fact, I think I was more impressed than Roy.'[2]

Orbison and the rest of the Teen Kings drove to Memphis a few weeks later to re-record 'Ooby Dooby' for the Sun label. 'Go! Go! Go!', written by Orbison and the band's drummer, was recorded as the B-side, with the publishing rights assigned to Hi-Lo Music. The band returned to Odessa and waited.

'Ooby Dooby' was released in April 1956. Phillips telephoned in May with the news that the song looked to be a hit in Memphis and the surrounding area. The Teen Kings quickly signed with Bob Neal's Stars, Inc. and went out on the road with Johnny Cash and the Tennessee Two to open for Carl Perkins. As the song gained momentum in the charts, Phillips was able to get the group a national television appearance on the *Ed Sullivan Show* in June. The single managed to reach no. 59 on *Billboard*'s Hot 100 chart, providing the capital for achieving Orbison's long-held dream of owning a Cadillac and a diamond ring before reaching his twenty-first birthday.

Unlike Presley or even Cash, Orbison was an accomplished guitarist. 'I don't think people know how good a guitar player Roy was,' Phillips later recalled. 'He also had the best ear for a beat of anybody I recorded, outside of Jerry Lee Lewis . . . His timing would amaze me.' Orbison enjoyed studio work, and sat in as a session player for other Sun artists. '[Roy] just hated to lay his guitar down,' Phillips continued. 'He was either writing or developing a beat. He was totally preoccupied with making records.'[3]

Orbison was constantly writing songs, both on and off the road, but that did not help him much when it was time to choose material for his next recording session. 'Rockhouse' by fellow Sun artist Harold Jenkins – who would later change his name to Conway Twitty when he moved to Nashville and became a country music legend – was chosen for the A-side. Johnny Cash supplied 'You're My Baby', originally titled 'Little Wooly Booger', for the B-side. The former was wrong for Orbison, the latter was just plain bad. Why Phillips chose either of them is mystifying.

In Orbison's case, Phillips' ability to recognise and develop talent failed him. He repeatedly attempted to cast Orbison as a rockabilly artist, releasing a string of poor quality novelty numbers that were patently wrong for his voice. To his credit, Orbison tried hard to fill the role, but it is obvious that his heart was not in it. He described his sound as being 'more or less a mixture of pop and country'.[4]

In fairness, Phillips was spread thin at the time: record sales had recently slipped for both Carl Perkins and Johnny Cash, and Phillips was working to get them back into the charts. He was also developing a large roster of new artists. Perhaps he was simply unable to invest the attention in Orbison that he might otherwise have done. For whatever reason, the combination of Phillips and Orbison never clicked. It was a relationship of missed opportunity.

Some have suggested that Phillips did not know what to do with Orbison's talent, but it may be that he honestly thought he did. Given Orbison's proficiency on the guitar and the success of his first single, it seems natural that Phillips would position him as a rockabilly artist. It had worked for Carl Perkins, who was also a gifted guitar player. And like Perkins, Orbison was no matinee idol. Perhaps Phillips steered Orbison away from ballads because he did not feel that the singer could successfully sell himself as a romantic balladeer, or perhaps that was simply a direction Phillips had no interest in pursuing. Orbison complained that Phillips would pull out old blues and R&B recordings and tell him, 'Sing just like that.'[5] Having had little exposure to such music, Orbison was at a loss to understand what Phillips meant. As usual, Phillips sought a raw and unpolished sound, preferring spontaneous intensity over technical perfection. Unfortunately, Orbison sought the exact opposite: purity and precision.

The failure of Orbison's second record may have softened Phillips' resolve a bit. The third single offered up two pop ballads, 'Sweet and Easy to Love' and 'Devil Doll'. The latter hints at the dark side of love, a theme that Orbison would explore in his later work. The session got off to a bad start. Already smarting from being relegated to secondary status when Phillips credited their records to 'Roy Orbison and the Teen Kings', the band members took offence when Orbison brought in a vocal group to perform on 'Devil Doll' without consulting them. Tempers flared, and Phillips removed Orbison to the coffee shop next door – third booth by the window was his usual spot – in an attempt to defuse the situation. He gave the singer a brief pep talk – Orbison did not need the band anyway, he said, they were not the only musicians in town. They returned to the studio to find that the Teen Kings had packed up their instruments in a huff and quit, leaving the distraught Orbison in the lurch. Phillips called in a few of the local players he sometimes used and the session went on. 'Really,' he recalled, 'it was nothing more than their being extremely young.'[6]

The experiment of the third single fizzled out and when Phillips called Orbison back into the studio, it marked a return to novelty numbers. Sun musical director Bill Justis provided the rock 'n' roll fluff 'Chicken Hearted', which was backed by Jack Clement's equally insipid 'I Like Love'. Orbison hated the songs, but complied. The single's release in December 1957 predictably marked the last of his recordings for Sun Records. Much later, Orbison put forward a reason for his frustration – he had felt Phillips was out of touch: 'The industry just outgrew him overnight and he didn't know it.'[7]

Orbison did see some success at Sun after his first single – as a songwriter. 'So Long I'm Gone', recorded by Warren Smith, made a brief appearance on *Billboard*'s Hot 100 chart in 1957. 'Down the Line', Jerry Lee Lewis' reworking of 'Go! Go! Go!', climbed to the top of the charts as the flip side of 'Breathless' in 1958. 'You Tell Me', recorded by Johnny Cash before leaving the label, was released in 1959. Orbison returned to the studio several times after he had stopped recording for the label to supervise the recording of his songs by other Sun artists.

In fact it was Orbison's songwriting that eventually brought an end to his affiliation with Sun Records. He had written a song about his wife, a tormented small-town beauty who looked like a young Elizabeth Taylor, and who would provide the basis for many of his future tortured ballads. 'Claudette' was pitched to the Everly Brothers, who made it a two-sided hit with 'All I Have to Do Is Dream'. Phillips laid claim to the publishing rights to 'Claudette', based on the fact that Orbison's Sun contract was still in effect. A deal was finally struck, releasing Orbison from the contract in return for giving Phillips all of the publishing rights to his Sun Records material.

It appears that the publishing rights to 'Claudette' may have been assigned elsewhere, in breach of the Sun contract. Johnny Cash remembered being present when Phillips confronted Orbison over the matter: '[Phillips] got Roy on the phone and really let him have it. "Why, you little so-and-so; you can't sing! I had to cram the microphone down your throat just to pick you up, your voice is so weak!" Roy just laughed at him. He thought that was pretty funny.'[8]

For many years, Orbison distanced himself from his Sun recordings. Decades would pass before he would perform 'Ooby Dooby' or 'Down the Line' in his stage show. Phillips later recognised his mistake in trying to force Orbison into the wrong mould. 'I really have to take the blame for not bringing Roy to fruition,' he stated. 'It's still my regret that I didn't do more promotion [for him].'[9]

Chapter Fourteen

Two Sides of the Same Coin

E ACH OF THE major artists who began their careers at Memphis Recording Service was tormented in some way, whether thanks to alcohol, drugs or personal tragedy. None, however, was more tortured – or more self-sabotaging – than Jerry Lee Lewis. In a telling snatch of conversation caught on tape during a recording session, Lewis can be heard arguing theology with an astonished Sam Phillips. The discourse leaves little doubt that Lewis believed he was beset by the devil – that he was living in defiance of God and heaven, and was subject to eternal damnation for playing the devil's music. He obviously felt tormented by his situation, but it is difficult to be sure whether he relished the prospect or feared it.

As Phillips would discover, internal conflict was a recurring theme with Lewis. 'Hell, Jerry Lee and I got in the damnedest religious argument in the middle of a session,' he recalled. 'A lot of things like that came up.' Still, more than any other artist he worked with, Phillips recognised in Lewis a kindred spirit that he was quick to defend. 'Hey, everybody's got their own damn personality, and they should have their individuality. Any time anyone tries to destroy that in you, you better watch out.'[1]

Jerry Lee Lewis left Ferriday, Louisiana late in 1956, intent on duplicating the success of Elvis Presley in Memphis. When he arrived, Lewis was 21 years old, twice married, a divinity school dropout, possessing a degree of self-confident bravado that bordered on offensive. He carried himself like a man destined for greatness, or for a great fall.

Phillips was out of town when Lewis presented himself at Memphis Recording Service in autumn 1956 to request an audition. By way of introduction, he boldly stated that he played piano the way Chet Atkins played guitar. Jack Clement, who was working in the studio control room with Roy Orbison at the time, decided that this was something he needed to hear. Lewis played a variety of country songs. Though Clement felt they were passé, he was impressed enough to tape a few for Phillips to listen to when he returned.

The initial tape must have sparked some interest, because Clement scheduled a complete audition session for 14 November, while Phillips was still out of town. A group of session players were rounded up to provide backing for Lewis' rendition of 'Crazy Arms', currently a hit for country singer Ray Price. The result impressed Phillips, who had been toying with the idea of expanding rockabilly beyond its guitar-driven beginnings. 'Where the hell did this man come from?' he exclaimed on hearing the session tape. Between the chords and frills lay a spiritual element he could relate to. 'Just get him in here as fast as you can.'²

Lewis returned with an original jug band boogie he called 'End of the Road', which became the flip side of the single when Phillips released 'Crazy Arms' in December. The record was a risk – Price's version was still in the charts – but Phillips was anxious to put his experiment to the test. He made an acetate of 'Crazy Arms' and took it to a local radio station for airplay. Hundreds of listeners called in with favourable responses, encouraging him to proceed with the release. The single's sales figures were good, but not great. Still, Phillips was excited about his new protégé.

He put Lewis to work in the studio, playing on sessions for Johnny Cash, Carl Perkins and Billy Riley. Lewis toured Canada in April 1957 as the opening act to Cash and Perkins. It was on this trip that he is said to have developed his flamboyant onstage style. 'John and I told him,' Perkins recalled, '"Turn around so they can see you; make a fuss." So the next night he carried on, stood up, kicked the stool back, and a new Jerry Lee was born.'[3]

Lewis was frequently in the studio during 1957, both on his own sessions and those of others. Boxes of outtake tapes attest to the wide range of musical styles he was capable of playing, as well as his ability to effortlessly adapt material to whatever it was that Phillips wanted to hear. The number of tapes still in existence suggests that Phillips liked what he heard. It was standard practice for Phillips to turn on the tape machine and let it roll, waiting for the magic moment to be captured. What he liked, he kept; what he did not like got recorded over. Brief snippets of unreleased songs by many of Sun's major artists exist at the ends of reused tapes, tantalising music historians with lost potential masterpieces, as well as the evidence of how songs evolved in the studio. The fact that so many of Lewis' outtakes survive attests to the value Phillips placed on them.

The tape was rolling at a session in February 1957 when Lewis launched into a song he sometimes played at club dates. As he often did, Lewis forgot the lyrics halfway into the number. He inserted a spoken break that he used in such cases, enabling him to vamp while he caught his place, then pounded his way back to the finish. The resulting 'Whole Lotta Shakin' Going On' was implicitly sexual, made so by the lascivious delivery of the lyrics rather than by the words themselves. Phillips recognised the genius, but was doubtful how it would be received by the audience. He released it in March as the flip side to 'It'll Be Me', a song written by Jack Clement in which he had more faith.

By the time Lewis returned from the Canadian tour at the beginning of May, it was obvious that 'Whole Lotta Shakin' Going On' was the hit. Pushed by Dewey Phillips, the song had topped the local charts. Entering the national country charts in the middle of June, it reached no. 70 in *Billboard*'s Hot 100 at the end of the month despite being banned in many areas for its suggestive content.

Jud Phillips had recently returned to the label to help with promotion. Sensing that the moment was ripe, he embarked on a risky scheme to introduce Lewis to a national audience. He managed to get Lewis booked on to NBC television's popular *Steve Allen Show*, increasing production to ensure that every US retail outlet had copies of the single before the broadcast. If Lewis flopped, the label stood to take a huge financial loss.

If the audience's reaction was in question before the 28 July broadcast, there was no doubt afterwards: Lewis was an unqualified hit. With arms flailing and fingers pounding out the notes, he tore through the number like a man possessed, whipping up a fervour seldom witnessed outside of a fundamentalist revival meeting. Near the end of the number he kicked the piano stool back across the stage, and finished the performance standing up, all the while his gaze fixed menacingly on the camera. The single, which had stalled near the bottom of the Top 30 prior to the broadcast, climbed to no. 1 in the country and R&B charts, and no. 2 in the pop charts.

On the heels of his television debut, Lewis was a last-minute addition to *Jamboree*. Carl Perkins' decision not to record 'Great Balls of Fire' inadvertently gave Lewis his next big hit. An inkling of how bad the original demo tapes must have sounded can be gained from the fact that Lewis – who typically nailed a recording in two or three takes – devoted two full days to working up the song.

No one was more aware of the importance of this next release than Phillips, who turned his full attention to getting it right. 'Jerry is an informal person and the conditions had to be right,' Phillips explained. 'You had to have a good song, of course, but atmosphere is nearly everything else . . . With great artists, almost fifty percent of something good they might do happens because of an almost instant reaction to what is taking place around them.'⁴ The result speaks for itself. Recorded in August and released in the middle of November to coincide with the debut of the film, 'Great Balls of Fire' topped most national charts in December.

Just a year after the release of his first single, Lewis was being widely touted as the successor to Elvis Presley. Certainly Lewis was the most exciting performer to hit the scene since Presley. At the end of 1957, Pte. Presley became the property of the US Army, and he would remain so for almost another year. For Lewis, the future appeared limitless.

At this point in their careers, most Sun artists celebrated their success with the purchase of a splashy new Cadillac or a diamond ring. Not so Lewis; he celebrated with a marriage to wife number three. In a Christmas ceremony kept secret even from most of their own family members, Jerry Lee Lewis wed Myra Gale Brown – his 13-year-old cousin. Phillips had advised Lewis against the marriage, but could not dissuade him. When Lewis told Elvis Presley what he was planning to do, Presley thought he was joking. Once convinced that he was serious, Presley reputedly said, 'God bless you, Jerry Lee. You just saved my career.'[5]

As 1958 began, Phillips was occupied with the daunting task of finding a song that could follow 'Great Balls of Fire'. Each of its co-writers, Otis Blackwell and Jack Hammer, provided numbers and in the end 'Breathless' was selected for February release. Jud Phillips came through with another marketing brainwave: a promotional tie-in between Sun Records, the *Dick Clark Show* and the show's network sponsor. Lewis performed the song on national television on 8 March, after which Clark invited viewers to get their own autographed copy of the single, in exchange for 50 cents and five of the sponsor's chewing gum wrappers. The Sun Records staff mailed out 38,000 copies of 'Breathless' during the promotion.

Lewis did not stick around to autograph records; that was done with a rubber stamp. Instead, he filmed a cameo appearance in *High School Confidential*, an otherwise abysmal rock 'n' roll exploitation flick, performing the title song on a piano that was perched on the back of a flatbed truck. Phillips released it, backed by 'Fools Like Me', the pop-flavoured country ballad he chose for the flip side, at the beginning of April.

★　★　★

In 1959, the *New York Post* revealed the details of Sun Records' involvement with Dick Clark in the promotion of 'Breathless' as part of its reporting on alleged instances of payola. Long a standard practice and an open secret within the recording industry, payola was the payment of cash or gifts to influential disc jockeys and television show hosts, in return for airplay of a given record. While unethical, payola was not then illegal. Phillips was called to the nation's capital to testify before the Federal Communication Commission regarding his role in the case.

In the proceedings, Phillips stated that the promotion did not constitute payola because 'Breathless' was already a hit record. 'There was no question of [Clark] plugging the record,' Phillips testified. 'He would have had to play it anyhow, because it was already high on the charts. The record was selling big and didn't need any help.' He went on to explain how the deal was structured, and detailed the costs involved. Overall, the promotion had distributed approximately 38,000 records and generated about $16,000. After expenses totalling slightly less than $11,000, both Clark and Sun Records had split the difference and walked away with about $2,700 each. Phillips ended his testimony with the avowal that 'I want payola cleaned up as much as anyone. There wasn't any payola involved here. I want to bring the guilty to justice, but let's not condemn the whole music business in the process.'[6] The hearings soon degenerated into an attack on rock 'n' roll music, which was made the scapegoat for a variety of social ills, both real and imagined. The end result was that DJs could no longer choose which records they played, but were dictated to by station programme directors. The days when a DJ like Dewey Phillips could make a hit out of a record he believed in were over.

Sam Phillips was quickly exonerated, but many others suffered as a result of the FCC's findings. 'I was never a part of any damn payola or that bullshit,' Phillips later stated. 'In fact, I testified against it. People got tarred on that.'[7] Clark walked away with a slap on the wrist and returned to Philadelphia to resume his career. Not everyone was so lucky. One of those whose career never recovered was popular DJ and promoter Alan Freed, the man reputed to have first applied the name 'rock 'n' roll' to the music. His refusal to cooperate in the hearings got him fined on two counts of accepting payola, after which he was virtually blackballed within the industry. He spent the rest of his life fighting off the Internal Revenue Service on the charge of income tax evasion, dying in 1965.

★ ★ ★

When 'Breathless' hit the shops, Lewis was well into an Alan Freed package tour that lasted until 10 May. Annoyed at having to take second place to headliner Chuck Berry, Lewis pulled out all the stops on stage, causing riots at nearly every venue along the way. At the end of one performance, he reputedly poured lighter fluid over the piano and set a match to it, hollering to the stage crew as he stomped away from the blaze, 'I'd like to see any son of a bitch follow that!'[8] Phillips rushed an album and three EPs into production to capitalise on the success of the engagements. For the moment, there was every reason to believe that Lewis stood poised to supplant Presley as the king of rock 'n' roll.

Two weeks after the Freed tour ended, Lewis took his career international with a 37-date tour in England. He also made the mistake of taking along his child bride. An offhand remark by one of his entourage made the British press curious about his new wife's age. Lewis claimed she was 15. When the truth came out, the scandal was headline news and was even discussed in Parliament. Although

Myra was of legal age in the state where the marriage took place, her extreme youth – coupled with the whiff of incest implied in their close family connection – made Lewis a target for public outrage. Even worse was the next revelation: that he had somehow neglected to finalise his divorce from wife number two before embarking on his current marriage. Lewis was jeered from the stage, and was ejected from the tour after only three concerts.

Lewis returned to America dumbfounded by what had occurred. He simply could not understand what all the fuss was about. Within days, he saw his career evaporate before his uncomprehending eyes. He was banned from the radio. High profile bookings were cancelled. Record sales died, including the album and three EPs just released, causing Phillips a substantial financial loss. 'It was a stupid damn thing,' Phillips recalled. 'I think Jerry's innocence then, and his trying to be open and friendly and engaging with the press, backfired. They scalped him . . . So many people wanted to point a finger of scorn at rockers and say, "We told you so; rockers are no good."'9

At first, Phillips tried to defuse the situation with satirical humour. He rushed out a single that used clips from Lewis' past recordings to answer questions posed by a mock reporter. 'We think it's a cute record,' Phillips stated in the press. 'It makes light of the whole British episode, which is the way we think the whole thing should be treated.'10 But he had misjudged the controversy, and 'The Return of Jerry Lee' was ignored by radio. A more serious attempt at a *mea culpa* was concocted by Phillips and Sun Records press officer Barbara Barnes, and published at the end of June in the trade papers. The humble and heartfelt apology, ostensibly written by Lewis, had no appreciable effect. There was nothing left to do but lay low and wait for the furore to die down.

★　★　★

In many ways, 1958 was not a good year for Phillips. Carl Perkins and Johnny Cash had parted ways with Sun Records early in the year and Lewis' career was wedged firmly in the toilet before the summer was over. Jud Phillips left in August to start up his own label, although he continued as Lewis' personal agent into the late 1970s. If Lewis had continued his climb to stardom instead of self-destructing, most likely he would have soon left Sun too, just like the label's other big names. As things stood, Lewis was going nowhere any time in the foreseeable future: no other label would touch him.

For Lewis at least, 1959 and 1960 were no better. His live performances remained as popular as ever, but the fees he now earned were a fraction of what they had once been. As 1961 approached, Lewis was still unheard on the radio, record sales had slowed to a trickle, and a dispute with the musicians' union over $10,000 in unpaid dues barred him from performing on stage in the United States. The series of career disappointments began to take its toll on Lewis. The egotistical braggart of the pre-scandal years was slowly becoming mean and bitter. Phillips, however, never stopped believing in Lewis' potential. Despite stagnant sales, he released nine Lewis singles between the summer of 1958 and the end of 1960.

When, in keeping with the old saw, 'If you can't beat 'em, join 'em', Phillips opened a recording studio in Nashville at the beginning of 1961, Lewis was the first artist to record there. The 9 February session yielded his version of the two-year-old Ray Charles standard 'What'd I Say'. Released at the end of February 1961, the song broke into the Hot 100, climbing to no. 30 in May. Phillips felt encouraged enough to assemble a second album for release.

In response to this reversal of fortune, he shifted direction, emphasising an R&B influence on Lewis' subsequent releases. But it was not enough. Of the next five singles, only the July 1962 cover of the Chuck Berry classic 'Sweet Little Sixteen' managed to make a fleeting appearance on the Hot 100 chart. It was the last original-release Sun Records single to do so.

Although nearly forgotten by the American music scene, Lewis became a huge hit in Europe. His return to England in May 1962 was extremely well received, as was his tour the following year. The marked disparity between the reception abroad and at home prompted Lewis to reconsider his connection to Sun Records, which was set to expire on 6 September 1963. With the backing of Memphis businessman Frank Casone, Lewis tested the interest of major labels. Phillips made a stab at retaining his artist, but the planned third album went unreleased when Lewis announced that he was signing with Mercury Records. Phillips got Lewis into the studio for a final session on 23 August. Sun released only one of the numbers, and that not until 1965. Lewis finally dragged his career back on track in the late 1960s. Nashville reinvented him as a country artist with a string of hit recordings that spanned the next decade.

Lewis viewed himself as a rock 'n' roll evangelist, out to shake up the musical establishment. He saw Phillips as a partner in that endeavour, characterising their relationship as one of shared insanity. 'Sam? He's a crazy son of a bitch,' he said of his former mentor. 'He's nutty as a fox squirrel. He's just like me. He ain't got no sense. Me and him and Jack Clement, birds of a feather flock together. It took all of us to get together to really screw up the world.'[11]

But that explanation hardly accounts for why Phillips willingly backed Lewis to the exclusion of his other artists. No doubt Phillips was impressed with Lewis' musical ability and star potential, and deservedly so. Lewis might easily have overshadowed Elvis Presley and changed the course of musical history. But it all fell apart at the critical moment, and Phillips held on long after it was evident that that moment had passed. So, the question remains.

Obviously, Phillips' attachment to Lewis was more complex than Lewis believed. Certainly they shared similar backgrounds, similar influences, and held similar views about their personal destinies. However, the two men were less kindred spirits than opposite sides of the same coin. Lewis was spontaneous where Phillips was methodical. Phillips was contemplative where Lewis was impulsive. Lewis was reckless where Phillips practised restraint. Right down the line, Lewis made a lifestyle out of being irresponsible, whereas Phillips had shouldered responsibility from a very early age. True, Phillips took risks throughout his career, but they were calculated and carefully considered. If only a little, he must have envied Lewis' ability to indulge in life without regard to the consequences, must have wanted a piece of Lewis' life for himself. Letting Lewis go meant letting go of freedom desired but unfulfilled, and Phillips was not yet ready to let go.

Chapter Fifteen

Last Hurrah

WHEN THE HIT singles of Elvis Presley, Carl Perkins and the host of rockabilly artists that followed brought recognition to the Sun Records name, Sam Phillips grew concerned that the label might become so identified with rock 'n' roll that it would lose its credibility in the wider music market. In response, he inaugurated the Phillips International label in 1957, to present a more sophisticated alternative to Sun's rough-edged image. The new label featured the Phillips name spanning the globe, and claimed offices in New York and Hollywood in addition to Memphis. Although the first releases were rockabilly and rock 'n' roll, press releases proclaimed the intention to enter the pop and jazz markets,

The Phillips International label never really achieved its purpose, but it did produce three creditable hit singles in its initial three years of operation. The first of these came at the end of 1957: the appropriately named saxophone instrumental 'Raunchy', written and performed by Sun Records' in-house arranger Bill Justis. The single sold around three million copies.

The label's second hit was a fluke, a beat arrangement of the 1951 Nat King Cole pop standard 'Mona Lisa', recorded in 1958 by 16-year-old piano player Carl Mann. Phillips hated the finished version and refused to release it. Conway Twitty successfully revived the original slow version later in the year, finally convincing the still reluctant Phillips that he might be missing out on a hit. Mann's version was released in 1959 and eventually reached no. 25 in the *Billboard* charts, though it sparked threats of legal action from the outraged holder of the publishing rights. Phillips tried to continue the momentum by releasing a succession of Mann's beat covers of classic pop and Broadway tunes. Each sold progressively fewer copies, and by 1962, when Mann's final Phillips International single was released, he was a washed-up 19-year-old alcoholic.

The final and most successful hit of the three was written and performed by a young artist named Charlie Rich. In comparison to the poverty that had plagued the childhoods of Phillips and most of his label's artists, Rich grew up in relatively comfortable circumstances in Arkansas. He exhibited an affinity for both the piano and blues music at an early age. After a stint in the air force, he divided his time between farming in Oklahoma and playing weekend club and bar-room gigs in Memphis.

Rich made demo tapes of some of his original compositions, which he played for Sun Records music director Bill Justis. Justis immediately recognised that Rich was a talented musician – perhaps too talented – but his noticeable jazz inflections lacked commercial appeal. He recalls 'taking [Rich] into the stockroom at Sun Records and giving him a whole bunch of [records that had been returned]. I told him to take them home and come back when he'd got that bad.'[1]

Rich was a sophisticated songwriter and musician, and it took several tries before he was able to dumb down his output to the level of commerciality Justis thought necessary. In the end, Phillips liked what he heard and took Rich on as a staff writer and occasional session pianist in 1957. 'There was not one human being I know who was more talented than Charlie,' Phillips recalled. 'When I met him I was just blown away by the guy.'[2] In between session work for Sun's leading artists, Rich found time to write 'Break Up' for Jerry Lee Lewis, 'The Ways of a Woman in Love' for Johnny Cash and 'I'm Comin' Home' for Carl Mann.

It appeared that Rich's big break had arrived in 1958. Two of his songs were selected for the follow-up single to the Jerry Lee Lewis hit 'High School Confidential', but the opportunity evaporated when Lewis' career abruptly imploded in scandal. Although Rich was satisfied with his duties behind the scenes at Sun, the economic necessity of supporting a wife and three small children spurred him to consider making his own records. 'Whirlwind'/'Philadelphia Baby' was recorded on 17 August 1958 and released on the Phillips International label. Sales were sufficient to warrant a follow-up recording session in February 1959 that yielded a second single.

The big break postponed in 1958 finally came to fruition in January 1960 with the release of 'Lonely Weekends'. The song became a hit, reaching no. 22 on the Hot 100 chart, and earned Rich a summons to New York for an appearance on *American Bandstand*. The obligatory post-performance interview with Dick Clark was a nightmare for him. Although he possessed a pleasant singing voice and was handsome in a way that prompted comparison to Elvis Presley, Rich was shy almost to the point of paralysis. The role of teen idol sat uneasily on him: his hair was prematurely going grey and he hated the constant touring that took him away from his family. His anxiety was often soothed with alcohol.

Rich was signed to the standard three-year contract on the strength of his success with 'Lonely Weekends'. Phillips' approach to recording him was to stay out of the way and let him play whatever he wanted, trusting that a review of the session tapes the following day would reveal something good enough to release. 'I don't think I ever recorded anyone who was better as a singer, writer, and player,' said Phillips of Rich. 'It is all so effortless, the way he moves from rock to country to blues to jazz.'³

But like so many of the Sun artists, Rich was unable to find an appropriate follow-up to his first hit record. Although he went on to release a number of brilliant records, their themes were generally beyond the scope of the market Phillips catered to. 'If I had my way, I would have spent more time with Charlie, because he needed that,' Phillips explained. 'I'm just sorry I didn't cut some marvelous thing on him – it damn sure wasn't his fault. I didn't do him justice; there's no question about that.'[4] More than any other artist that passed through Phillips' door and later went on to find success elsewhere, Rich is the one that most needed a collaborator to bring out his best work. It was Rich's misfortune that his tenure on the artist roster coincided with a period of major changes in Phillips' personal and professional life. With Phillips' energies occupied elsewhere, Rich was largely lost in the shuffle, despite the obvious regard that Phillips had for his talents.

Ironically, his most successful work for Phillips may have occurred in the studio, where Rich felt most comfortable: in the piano playing heard on other artists' records, and in the songs he wrote for other artists to sing. On hearing one such number, 'Don't Put No Headstone on My Grave', Phillips was impressed enough to say, 'Hell, even *I* could sing that song and make it a hit.'[5]

With his contract about to expire in 1963, Rich was ready for a change. He signed with RCA's Groove label, prompting a lawsuit from Phillips, who claimed that Rich had verbally stated his intention to remain at Sun. RCA suspended their contract with Rich until the matter was resolved. Rich retaliated with a counter suit against Phillips, alleging breach of contract. Tempers cooled a little over the course of the following month and Phillips finally relented, freeing Rich to move on.

At just about the same time that Rich was leaving Sun Records behind, the Phillips International label was reaching the end of its run. Beginning in 1960, Phillips had dabbled in the LP market with the release of eight albums in a range of musical styles But Phillips had a fundamental dislike for the long-play format and it was a half-hearted effort. Lacking promotional and advertising backing, as well as the support of Phillips himself, the venture was doomed from the start. He shut the label down in 1963, ostensibly because its name was easily confused with a subsidiary label belonging to Mercury Records.

Ten years later, Charlie Rich finally found the fame that had eluded him for so long. Under the direction of producer Billy Sherrill, he racked up a string of hits in Nashville with his signature 'countrypolitan' blending of country and jazz. Reminiscing about the many artists who had passed through his studio, Phillips once commented that 'They were all so different in so many different ways, but all so alike in so many others.' But in his mind, one artist stood out as being particularly easy to work with. For a man who admitted to few regrets, the fact that, after so many years, he still felt that he had let that one artist down is significant. 'I'd say the easiest person, probably, was one of the sweetest, most talented human beings on the face of God's earth, and I feel I did not do with him what I should have, because of constraints of time. And that's Charlie Rich.' Phillips thought that Rich had it all: talent, writing ability, a unique piano style. 'Of course, Billy Sherrill, who worked at my Nashville studio, he recorded some fabulous country stuff on him. But I wouldn't have cut country on him. His heart was in the blues field. But he could do anything. He was the most unassuming human being, but so dedicated and so damn talented.'[6]

Part III

The Father of Rock 'n' Roll

Chapter Sixteen

The Slow Decline

THE NATURE OF Sam Phillips' involvement with Sun Records had changed within a few years of starting up the label. As early as 1954, he started handing over artist development to his production staff. By 1958, he had delegated out much of the studio and marketing responsibilities to others, diluting his personal imprint on the signature Sun sound. Now, by the end of the decade, his involvement with the label appeared to be largely as a figurehead; his workload consisted merely of approving cuts for release and setting the release dates. During the years between 1958 and 1960, much about Phillips' life – both professionally and personally – was in a state of change.

In retrospect, the beginning of the end of Sun Records can be traced to the middle of 1958 and Jerry Lee Lewis' spectacular career immolation. Afterwards the label went into a slow decline marked only by occasional resuscitation. The hits were few and after 1960, they ceased altogether. The period from 1960 to 1969 was one of experimentation, as the label tried to establish a new presence in the changing music market. During this time, Sun Records' unofficial house band included some of the city's finest musicians: Ace Cannon, Steve Cropper, Al Jackson, Roland Janes, Booker T. Jones and Scotty Moore. Yet, despite the outstanding talents of these backing musicians, the label's artists failed to find an audience.

There are many reasons – some have already been discussed – but the one thing that stands out as one listens to the recordings made after 1960 is the general level of mediocrity that the label's roster of talent exhibits. Memphis in 1952 had been a hotbed of raw talent to which an independent label owner like Phillips found ready access. That situation did not last long. The major labels soon recognised the sales potential of the type of music Phillips produced, and began scooping up the finest talent. Phillips was still able to find unique voices, but none had the ability to compete nationally.

Perhaps most significantly, Phillips was no longer the only producer willing to record black artists. Many labels now specialised in black music and, more importantly, attracted the best talent. 'Joe Coughi, a good friend of mine, had started Hi Records,' Phillips recalled, 'and it wasn't long after that until Jim Stewart started Stax. They devoted themselves almost exclusively to black music, and that was fantastic, because that's what I wanted.'[1] Still, there appears to be a tone of resignation to his response: an acceptance of a situation not wholly of his own choice: 'At the same time, I would have loved to have recorded more blacks. But you take a guy with no money and a limited amount of help in every way, and he just has to do the best he can. It was more than I could do.'[2]

Phillips had successfully opened the door to black artists, but in doing so he had made his own label redundant in that musical arena. He did not, as has sometimes been charged, abandon black artists after finding Elvis. He continued to release singles by several black artists during and after Presley's tenure at Sun Records. But as additional avenues opened up for the exposure of black artists, Phillips seems to have lost the evangelical zeal for the cause.

Long-awaited financial success had brought new opportunities and allowed him to indulge new interests. Phillips was in the process of building an empire that eventually included multiple recording studios, several radio stations, music publishing companies and additional record labels, all of which made demands on his time. His shrewd early investment in the Holiday Inn motel chain had netted him a small fortune. The hectic work rate he had once endured was no longer necessary.

In addition music had changed dramatically since the label's first hits, and changed in ways that Phillips had little personal interest in following. The raw sound that he favoured was no longer in style and had given way to heavily produced recordings that processed the spontaneity out of songs. Phillips could still produce the hell out of a true rock 'n' roll tune, as he would later prove, but he felt little affinity for the predictable pop influence that prevailed at the time. The more he tried to diversify in order to keep up with the changing music scene, the more he lost focus on the sound that had established Sun Records to begin with. Roy Orbison's terse assessment had some validity: 'The industry just outgrew him overnight and he didn't know it.'[3]

Along with changes in the sound, came changes in the way that sound was disseminated to the public. As the record business evolved, albums took on greater importance. Singles were increasingly seen simply as expensive promotional offspring used to encourage sales of the parent album. Phillips was one of the few holdouts who never fully embraced the album format. 'Albums weren't selling that much,' he maintained – an arguable point – 'but beyond that, I was always very cautious about not putting out a lot of product on my artists simply to ensure a certain level of income. I think that opportunity has always been abused by the major record companies. You only have to look at some of the crap they put out on Elvis Presley, with no regard for the man's great abilities.'[4]

Lastly, Phillips' personal life was also in a state of flux. He separated from his wife of 18 years to live with his former Sun Records assistant Sally Wilbourn, a relationship that would continue for the rest of his life.

Along with all of these changes came an anticipated change of address. By 1958, Sun Records had already outgrown its home at Memphis Recording Service. The desks of label staff crowded the reception area, the control room was too small to accommodate necessary new equipment, and the studio could no longer contain the increasing numbers of musicians that recording sessions demanded. Phillips addressed the situation by purchasing another property at 639 Madison Avenue, just a few blocks from the original studio.

The building had previously housed a muffler shop and a bakery. Phillips had it gutted and carried out a complete renovation that included two spacious recording studios on the ground floor, staff offices and a tape vault on the second level, with accounting, publishing, and executive offices occupying the upper level. The finished facility was ready for occupancy in 1960, by which time the original Sun Records location was bursting at the seams.

Ironically, the flashy new building was the architectural equivalent of the pop-influenced rock 'n' roll music Phillips despised: high on style but low on substance. While the label staff were thrilled with their sleek, modern new surroundings, artists found them disquieting. Promotion manager Cecil Scaife observed that 'it was awful hard to create there. 706 Union had a terrific atmosphere, a creative atmosphere. There was a naturalness about it. You felt *up* when you walked in. The new studio had a sterile atmosphere – it was like a doctor's office.'⁵ From the modern sculpture at the building's entrance to the interior's mosaic tile wall panels and stylized space age motifs, the décor seemed better suited to an airport terminal than a recording studio. Technical problems abounded, particularly in the area of acoustics, which even an expensive retrofit of retractable baffles failed to solve completely.

The new facility was Phillips' personal project. That he got it wrong seems out of character, and leads to inevitable questions about his mindset at the time. By his own admission, he was willing to let the details go in favour of the overall effect, as many of his recordings demonstrate. He may have taken the same approach to the design and construction of his new studio. That the result was conducive to business rather than artistry is less easily explained, and is at odds with the emphasis he placed on putting his artists at ease. Possibly this time his instincts simply failed him. Equally, the result may have been an indication of a diminshing interest in the recording business. Whatever the case, Phillips' sons Knox and Jerry began taking over more and more of the producing work that had once been their father's exclusive domain.

★   ★   ★

Questions had been raised since 1956 concerning royalties owed to Carl Perkins from Hi-Lo Music. Perkins himself had always dismissed those questions, believing that Sam Phillips would not intentionally cheat him. Then, around 1961, Perkins signed with another publishing company and first learned the percentage he should have been paid. His illusions were shattered. From Broadcast Music International (BMI), the agency responsible for collecting and dispersing royalties accruing from the use of songwriters' material, Perkins learned that Phillips had been paid more than $60,000 in royalties from 'Blue Suede Shoes' in 1956. Fifty per cent of that should have been paid by Phillips to Perkins, yet he received less than $15,000. Perkins also learned that there was nothing he could legally do to collect the money owed him, as the three-year period for contesting payments had expired.

Perkins later appeared at Phillips' office to confront him about the matter, and about the fact that royalties should be paid out twice a year, rather than once-yearly as Hi-Lo had been doing. Heated words were exchanged. Phillips even allegedly threatened Perkins with a pistol that he was known to keep in a desk drawer, although neither Perkins nor Dewey Phillips, who witnessed the altercation, actually saw the gun. The encounter ended quickly thereafter, with Phillips shouting his intent to withhold all future royalties. Perkins did not receive another royalty payment until the end of 1967, when he was sent a final cheque for $12,000.

The ongoing dispute was to turn into a lawsuit in January 1975, dragging on until a court ruling in August 1978. While it could not be proved that Phillips had committed fraud, Perkins was awarded a little over $36,000 in back royalties, though the statute of limitations prevented recovery of the full amount. Threatened with further legal action, Phillips agreed to pay a small cash settlement and to assign control of the publishing rights to Perkins' Sun recordings back to the artist.

★   ★   ★

As soon as Phillips' new Memphis facility was operational, he turned his attention to opening a similar studio in Nashville. Phillips leased offices for his music publishing company there in a former Masonic lodge on Seventh Avenue. When a studio housed in the same building came up for sale, Phillips bought it and hired former co-owner Billy Sherrill to stay on as engineer. 'I thought Nashville could be a good center not only for country music, but for the range of music we were recording,' Phillips explained. 'I was also trying to bring a new kind of influence into the business there.'[6]

In contrast to the hard surfaces of the new Memphis facility, and the resulting acoustic problems and cold sound quality, the Nashville studio's wood surfaces produced a warm sound similar to that of the original Memphis Recording Service. The studio opened for business in February 1961 with the Jerry Lee Lewis session that produced his comeback single 'What'd I Say'. Charlie Rich recorded 'Who Will the Next Fool Be' two days later.

The music being produced in Nashville at the time was worlds away from the spare, economical sound that Phillips had developed. Think of the orchestral strings and vocal choruses that Owen Bradley employed to back Patsy Cline, or that Fred Foster used with Roy Orbison. Billy Sherrill took the same approach. 'He had a feeling for the way things were changing, and a tendency to arrange things more than would have been my way,' said Phillips.[7] As much as Phillips appreciated Sherrill's abilities, the difference in their approaches to producing was an ongoing source of frustration. 'I was never able to make myself have the confidence in other people,' Phillips stated. 'I knew they were talented people, and Billy Sherrill proved that, but it just didn't come out the way it could have. We tried to bring in something of a new concept there, but I just didn't stay with it personally long enough to usher it in fully. And there was just so much opposition from the people in Nashville.'[8]

For all its apparent down-home quaintness and good old boy socialising, Nashville's Music Row is a corporate world dominated by the major record labels and the musicians' union. Phillips eschewed conventional rules and prided himself on being a thorn in the side of the establishment. Given the disparity of attitudes, there were bound to be problems. Part of the opposition Phillips referred to came in response to the way that he preferred to work: he ignored the clock. In fact, the clock that hung on the wall of the Memphis Recording Service studio was broken and permanently set at 5.30. Phillips allowed his artists all the studio time they needed to work up and record their songs, with sessions sometimes lasting from one evening to the following morning. Nashville musicians worked according to strict union guidelines: the American Federation of Musicians stipulated scale pay for four songs to be recorded in a standard three-hour session, with overtime pay for anything beyond that. Phillips tried to get around this practice by bringing in Memphis musicians, but only managed to further irritate the union.

Unable to make the studio financially viable and unwilling to compromise, Phillips finally sold it to Fred Foster of Monument Records in 1964. 'I don't think Sam really wanted to sell,' Foster explained. 'He loved to negotiate and he wanted a big negotiating scene – and that's what we had. It lasted three days and two nights. I was a zombie by the time we closed the deal.'[9] Shortly afterwards, the building's owner tore it down, forcing Foster out. The demolition of his former studio marked the end of Phillips' presence in Nashville, and foreshadowed the final stages of his involvement in the recording business in Memphis.

Chapter Seventeen

Sunset

S **AM PHILLIPS PRODUCED** his final Sun Records session in November 1966, at his Madison Avenue facility in Memphis. The artist was a Johnny Cash soundalike named Dane Stinit, who had captured Phillips' attention during a custom recording session that January. Sun issued only two more singles after that, ending production in January 1968.

The scattershot nature of Sun's releases in the mid to late 1960s seems to indicate a loss of identity and purpose, as if the company had lost its primary driving force. To anyone who might have paused to reflect on Sun's waning position in the recording industry, it must have appeared that the label was struggling to find a new direction.

An indication of the extent to which Phillips himself had lost direction can be found in what seems, at least in retrospect, a foolhardy and ill-advised business venture. Whether the deal was originally entered into seriously, or as a demonstration of courtesy toward a respected friend and business colleague, is not known. Beyond its dubious value as a promotional tool, the scheme appears to have had little else to offer.

Despite flagging personal interest in the recording business, Phillips briefly flirted with the notion of forming a new record label in partnership with Holiday Inn founder and longtime business associate Kemmons Wilson. 'Kemmons and I had some conversations,' Phillips remembered, 'and he was very much interested in expanding the Holiday Inn operation. They were beginning to put bands into piano bars in Holiday Inns all across the country and he had the idea of setting up a label that could promote those bands. They had also just bought the Trailways bus line and Kemmons thought he could sell records in racks at bus terminals to all the people passing through and killing time.'[1]

An agreement was reached in March 1968, naming Sam Phillips president of Holiday Inn Records, with brother Jud recruited as national sales and promotions manager and son Knox as an in-house producer. Sam, however, had second thoughts, and begged off before the label became operational. The enterprise collapsed soon afterwards.

★ ★ ★

As the decade wound down, the Sam Phillips Studios on Madison Avenue became only marginally the headquarters of Sun Records, but gained new recognition as a custom recording studio. Other record labels sprang up in the void – American, Hi, Sonic and Stax among them – to become the new purveyors of the city's signature sound. Many of the men who ran these labels, and the musicians who played on their records, had been employed by Phillips at Sun Records just a few years before. But that now seemed like a very long time ago.

The decline of the label's influence seemed to match the decline of Phillips' interest in the business. 'The basic reason that Sun did not become a major label,' he stated, 'was that I preferred to invest my time in other things. I didn't want to hook up with a major corporation because I knew I couldn't do the job the way I wanted to do it as part of a big company – even though I had several offers.'[2]

Issues that had always plagued the independent labels – promotion and distribution – became even more problematic as rock 'n' roll evolved from rebellious outsider to mainstream corporate product. Many independent labels, weary of having their best talent poached by the major labels, either exited the business altogether or sold out to the corporate heavyweights. A man like Phillips was unlikely to find the latter option appealing. 'I could see what was coming,' he explained, 'and I wanted no part of it. It is not my way to work for somebody.'[3]

Phillips had been fielding buyout offers from the majors for several years. A production deal offered by Mercury in 1962 looked promising enough that Phillips halted new releases mid-year, but the deal fell through within a few months. CBS/Columbia made repeated offers in an attempt to stop Phillips cutting into their market with his releases of old Johnny Cash masters. A similar attempt was made to obtain the Jerry Lee Lewis masters once his career was reborn in the country market, but the deal failed due to Phillips' reluctance to sell off his catalogue piecemeal. There had always been some reason for Phillips to decline the offers. By 1969, however, those reasons no longer seemed meaningful.

Shelby Singleton had originally approached Phillips in 1962, representing Mercury Records in their buyout offer. He was back in 1969, having achieved enough personal business success in the meantime to broker the purchase on his own behalf. Singleton reported that negotiations hinged on the stipulation that all future label product would be released under the Sun Records name.

Phillips and Singleton finalised the sale of Sun in July 1969. The exact amount that changed hands remains unknown, but is believed to be about $1 million. Phillips walked away with a percentage of the newly named Sun International Corporation, full retention of publishing rights, the Sam Phillips Studios, and a promise that sons Knox and Jerry would continue as independent producers for Sun International.

In retrospect, it seems nearly impossible to believe that Phillips could have dismembered Sun Records so bloodlessly. But it must be remembered that the label was no longer a viable financial concern. It was more of an expensive hobby that had ceased to hold its owner's interest. Sun's place in the history of music was as yet unacknowledged. Phillips valued his creative product enough to ensure its survival, but he no longer cared about the operation that had produced it. The sale enabled him to offload superfluous assets that had artistic merit but little current commercial value. Singleton must have thought otherwise. He almost immediately undertook a massive programme to reissue the masters, both domestically on the Sun label and through licensees abroad. Long forgotten recordings by Johnny Cash, Roy Orbison and Jerry Lee Lewis were once again made available. More significantly, previously unreleased tracks were mined from the Sun vault, particularly in the case of Lewis, which did much to establish an early body of work for performers who had later gone on to achieve their success with other labels.

Chapter Eighteen

Resurrection

PHILLIPS BEGAN 1970 with the celebration of his 47th birthday, poised to embark on a new phase of life. He had largely ceased to work in the studio some years earlier, and the sale of Sun Records formally closed the door on the recording phase of his life. Judicious investments, not only in the Holiday Inn motel chain but in tracts of land with mineral rights and radio stations in Tennessee and Alabama, had made him a wealthy man. Phillips settled into a comfortable but not ostentatious life. He did not, however, retire. 'I'll never retire,' he once famously said. 'If I did, I'd just be using up someone else's oxygen.'[1] For Phillips, letting go of Sun Records simply freed up more time and energy to oversee his other business interests.

It is difficult to know what, if anything, Phillips thought about his career path in 1970. Did he look back on the two decades he had spent in the recording industry and his contribution to the development of modern music, or was his vision directed solely to the future? At the time no one else had any real sense of what he had accomplished, and no one seems to have asked the question of him later on. Probably he himself had not yet begun to think in terms of historical significance or of framing his legacy. Never a particularly sentimental man, Phillips likely viewed the entire Sun Records episode as simply one in a string of business ventures, the only difference being that this one had run its course. There had been some exciting moments while it lasted, but now it was over and life went on.

Life was not destined to remain quiet for long. Shelby Singleton's repackaging and reissuing of the Sun masters sparked a growing interest in early rock 'n' roll music in the mid to late 1970s, particularly among European listeners. Phillips had initially been opposed to Singleton's reissue programme. A decade afterwards he voiced his concern : 'The way the material has been handled, it truly amazes me that it hasn't been killed. It was not my way to repackage every damn thing every other week or month, because the recordings had too much meaning for the people who were buying the product. In the long run, though, I don't think the reissues have cheapened the image as much as I feared they would.'[2] Ironically, far from demeaning his legacy – as Phillips feared they might – the mass reissue of Sun recordings were eventually to result in his canonisation as the founder of rock 'n' roll.

The Sun reissues were well received, particularly abroad, where the raw, sparse sound coincided with newly emerging music trends. European music historians were among the first to appreciate the significance of these early recordings, and set out to place them in the context of the genesis of rock 'n' roll. They discovered that rock 'n' roll's Big Bang had occurred in the Memphis Recording Service studio under the direction of Sam Phillips. Their findings were written up in books and in music publications, which helped introduce Phillips and Sun to a new generation of listeners.

Not all Sun Records alumni were pleased. With the exception of Carl Perkins and Jerry Lee Lewis, Sun's major stars had gone on to do their best work after leaving the label, and were embarrassed by the renewed interest in their Sun recordings. Responses to interview questions often hinted at unresolved bitterness over their departure from the label, or downplayed Phillips' influence and ability. Yet, in the end, even they admitted a grudging admiration for what their former producer had accomplished.

Phillips really resurfaced in the news in August 1977, in connection with the funeral of Elvis Presley and what followed in its wake. Presley's unexpected death provoked the first serious look at his musical legacy and a new examination of his early career.

When historians and reporters went looking for information, Phillips – unlike Elvis – was still around to comment.

Phillips was deeply saddened by Presley's death. The affection and respect that he still felt for Elvis was obvious in his recollections of the discovery and recording of his label's first star. As the story unfolded in print, it became apparent that had it not been for Phillips' almost prescient ability to sense potential talent, the world would likely never have heard of Elvis Presley. Moreover, the stories related about early recording sessions led to a better understanding and appreciation of Phillips' critical role in the formation of Presley's unique sound. Although he would forever be known as the man who sold Presley's contract, Phillips finally received equal credit for being the man who discovered and moulded Elvis in the first place.

Although he did not grant many interviews, reporters invariably found Phillips charming and gracious, with definite opinions. His intense personality combined a mitigating dash of self-deprecation with a strong conviction of the purpose and value of his life's work. Many interviewers later commented that Phillips did not appear to have changed much physically over the years, retaining the same hypnotic gaze, exhortative voice and luxuriant head of hair as in his youth.

★　★　★

After selling Sun, Phillips largely resisted enticements to return to the recording console. He did make the occasional exception to assist his sons, both of whom were now reputable producers in their own right. In 1978, Knox and Jerry Phillips produced the sessions for John Prine's seminal *Pink Cadillac* album at Sam Phillips Recording Service. A song titled 'Saigon' was posing problems. 'It was a great song,' remembered Knox, 'but we were doing it at like a hundred eighty miles per hour. I thought that was the right way to do it.'[3] Unhappy with the result, Knox consulted his father.

Phillips agreed to lend a hand, despite having not produced a recording session in over a decade.

'Sam says, "I want you to slow down that song and draaaaag it out,"' recalled session engineer Richard Rosebrough. 'The way he used this word "drag" was the whole thing. "I want you to drag it out like you're dragging it across the street so you can find out what's on the other side." It was all in Sam Phillips' control, totally.'[4]

Phillips decided that he wanted some echo on the guitar that introduced the song. 'They had live echo chambers then,' Rosebrough explained. 'He put one hand on the echo-send and the other on the echo-return and cranked it up. You could hear the speaker disintegrate. You could see sparks down the hall. Everyone went, "No. No! NO!" sort of automatically reaching for the board. It turned out to be the most magical song on the album . . . That was Sam Phillips. Sam knows something we don't know.'[5]

'It took doing a session with Sam Phillips to make me believe,' said Rosebrough. 'There was a magic that man had in his finger-tips. There was magic in that man's eyes, they saw forty feet right through you. The words that came out of that man's mouth were bizarre. I had heard this story that when he cut the Yardbirds, he told the bass player to "whip that guitar like a mule's peter." Well, now I believe he said it.'[6]

Many people have tried to explain Phillips' gift, but none as accurately – or as colourfully – as the man himself: 'Producing?' he once said. 'I don't know anything about producing records. But if you want to make some rock and roll music, I can reach down and pull it out of your asshole.'[7]

Chapter Nineteen

Recognition

I N SEPTEMBER 1985, four former Sun Records artists gathered in Memphis to commemorate the impromptu 1955 recording session of the so-called Million Dollar Quartet. Billed as a 'Rock & Roll Homecoming', the Mercury sessions featured performances by Carl Perkins, Johnny Cash, Jerry Lee Lewis and Roy Orbison (substituting for the late Elvis Presley). The four days of sessions (two at the original Sun Records studio on Union Street and two at the American Studio on Thomas Street) were plagued by technical problems, illness, egos and varying degrees of substance abuse.

At one point, Lewis did a handstand, which dislodged pills of all descriptions from his pockets and sent them skittering across the floor. Cash, who had overcome a well publicised amphetamine addiction, estimated there were enough pills on the floor to get everyone arrested, and mused that it was just like old times. Orbison, who had had his own pharmacological issues and was currently battling the flu, wisely retreated to his trailer. Perkins, whose drug of choice was alcohol, was just happy to be reunited with old friends.

Phillips was on hand to witness the proceedings and was co-opted to sing with the backing chorus on the session's final song. Despite the potential and the media hype engendered by the reunion of such legendary talents, the resultant *Class of '55* album proved to be a mixed bag, with none of the performances living up to expectations.

However, in one respect the episode was a resounding success. A group interview was conducted in conjunction with the sessions.

Phillips contributed his reminiscences, and along with the other participants, in 1986 he received a Grammy Award in the Spoken Word category for *Interviews from the Class of '55 Recording Sessions*. The film footage of the interview was later reworked as a television special. *Coming Home: A Rockin' Reunion*, hosted by Dick Clark, was broadcast on 10 August 1989.

There was another Grammy award for Phillips in 1986. His Sun recording of Carl Perkins' 'Blue Suede Shoes' was recognised with a Grammy Hall of Fame Award, which 'honor[s] recordings of lasting qualitative or historical significance'[1] It was the first of eight Phillips recordings that would eventually receive the honour.

In 1986 the Rock and Roll Hall of Fame was also inaugurated. Among the legends inducted at the awards ceremony that first year were former Sun Records artists Elvis Presley and Jerry Lee Lewis. Two non-performers were also honoured: Sam Phillips, the man who had invented rock 'n' roll, and Alan Freed, the man who gave the music its name. Commenting on himself and the artists he recorded, Phillips said: 'We're all crazy. But it's a type of insanity that borders on genius. I really feel that. To be as free as you have to be for any kind of music, you almost have to be in another dimension. And to do the broad expanse of rock and roll takes an element of mind expansion that people less creative would term insanity.'[2]

Phillips' particular brand of mind expansion (or perhaps insanity) was on display a few months later when he appeared as a guest on the *David Letterman Show*. Letterman struggled to get the interview going, eventually giving up as Phillips drifted in and out of coherency. He then tried to engage his guest's attention with a series of vintage photographs depicting Phillips with some of his former Sun Records stars. Phillips would not cooperate. Finally – much to the host's apparent relief – Phillips was hustled offstage by studio bandleader Paul Shaffer,. The episode left some viewers wondering if Phillips had indulged too freely in booze or pills just prior to his appearance. But it was classic Phillips, demonstrating the man's larger-than-life persona and take-no-prisoners style.

Phillips returned to the Rock and Roll Hall of Fame in 1987 for the induction of Carl Perkins and Roy Orbison. Unaware of the past rancour between the two men, the Hall of Fame committee had mistakenly asked Phillips to introduce Perkins. Phillips delivered a speech so lengthy and rambling that, in Perkins' words, 'he got a standing ovation just for quittin'.'[3]

★ ★ ★

There is a noticeable difference in tone between the interviews Phillips granted in the years immediately following the death of Elvis Presley and those following the Rock and Roll Hall of Fame honours a decade later. Sometimes irascible but always passionate, in the earlier interviews Phillips displays an impressive command of expletives and a freewheeling tendency to wander off into a stream of conscious tangents. Later on, he became more careful of the image he projected, and began to cultivate a thoughtful style more in keeping with his growing role as elder statesman of rock 'n' roll. Perhaps this reflected a personal reassessment of his life's accomplishments that ran parallel to his increasing public recognition.

In any event, that recognition continued to multiply in 1991 when the Recording Academy granted Phillips its prestigious Grammy Trustees Award, in acknowledgement of his 'significant contribution to the field of recording'. In 1998 five more of his recordings were honoured with Grammy Hall of Fame Awards: 'Great Balls of Fire' (Jerry Lee Lewis), 'I Walk the Line' (Johnny Cash), 'Raunchy' (Bill Justis), 'Rocket 88' (Jackie Brenston for Chess Records) and 'That's All Right' (Elvis Presley). 'Whole Lotta Shakin' Going On' (Jerry Lee Lewis) in 1999 and 'Folsom Prison Blues' (Johnny Cash) in 2001 later received similar honours.[4]

Attention abated for a few years, but resumed in 1998 when

Phillips was inducted into the Blues Foundation Hall of Fame. This honour probably meant more to him than any other. In recalling the early days of his recording career – days of strict racial segregation, when most Memphians reviled him for consorting with black musicians – Phillips described his reasoning for recording black artists: 'I just did not feel that the gutbucket Southern Blues that was here was being displayed as something that we should not only not be ashamed of, but [that] was the real-life essence. I wasn't out to change the world or anything like that; I was out for these people to be heard.'[5]

At the time, the only blues music being committed to shellac was a watered-down version geared to white audiences. 'I knew that there had to be something far beyond just the things that we were hearing,' Phillips explained. 'I wasn't trying to make any great statement other than the fact that you don't just hear this and not give it some kind of an exposure. We had very limited facilities to do the things we wanted to do, but we had the courage to try. And that is what I am proudest of, far and away. I'm prouder of beginning this project, of giving these people the emotional opportunity with their music, than I am of any hit record I ever had or of any single artist, be it black or white.'[6]

The following year, after many accolades for his work as a record producer, Phillips was finally acknowledged for his pioneering efforts in radio broadcasting. 1999 marked the 44th anniversary of Phillips' first radio station, which was recognised by National Public Radio in its broadcast of a two-part documentary entitled 'WHER – 1000 Beautiful Watts', part of NPR's *Lost and Found Sound* series. Sam and announcer (and former wife) Becky Phillips were among those interviewed. Fourteen WHER alumni joined him in September for a reunion held at the Peabody Hotel in Memphis, in conjunction with the annual Public Radio Program Directors conference. For many, it was the first time they had seen each other since working together at WHER.

Phillips was off to New York City in October for a ceremony at the Museum of Television and Radio, where he was honoured for his contribution to radio broadcasting, specifically in connection with WHER. In his acceptance speech, Phillips downplayed his efforts, stating, 'I wasn't trying to revolutionize the world.'[7] It was an honest assessment: nearly all of Phillips' most meaningful accomplishments were incidental to what he was trying to achieve at the time. In this instance, Phillips was a businessman responding to a void he sensed in the marketplace, rather than a conscious feminist out to break down traditional gender barriers. That he helped topple some of those barriers could be dismissed as coincidence, if not for the fact that Phillips repeatedly proved to be a unifying force in his endeavours. This has to speak to the man's basic values and overall purpose, whether or not the outcome was the result of conscious intent.

The question of intent was explored as the century neared its end, as historians began to look at the man behind the accomplishments. In honour of 50 years in the recording business, Phillips' life and career were documented in a two-hour instalment of the *Biography* cable television series. The world premiere of 'Sam Phillips: The Man Who Invented Rock and Roll' took place on 8 June 2000 at the Orpheum Theatre in Memphis. Called to the stage prior to the showing, Phillips was named Prime Minister of Memphis Music, just about the only honour not previously bestowed on him by the city. In his acceptance speech, Phillips stated, 'I have given my life to trying to make people understand each other,' and paid tribute to the community for helping him do it. The documentary was broadcast on 18 June 2000 on the Arts and Entertainment Network.

A second two-hour television documentary entitled 'Good Rockin' Tonight: The Legacy of Sun Records' aired on the Public Broadcasting System on 28 November 2001 as part of the *American Masters* series. The programme paid homage to both Phillips and the wealth of talented artists who passed through the doors of his studio, and featured tribute performances by Jimmy Page, Robert

Plant, Paul McCartney and Matchbox 20, among others. An album was planned in conjunction, for release on London/Sire Records.

Considering Phillips' oft-professed distaste for Nashville-style country music, the news that he was about to have yet another honour bestowed on him must have come as a surprise. On 7 November 2001, the Country Music Association inducted Phillips into the Country Music Hall of Fame, naming him 'One of the most important non-performers in American music'.[8] This made Phillips the only individual to be honoured by the Rock and Roll Hall of Fame, the Blues Foundation Hall of Fame and the Country Music Hall of Fame.

During the induction ceremony, Phillips was commended by the CMA for his role in shaping modern music through his influence on some of the greatest artists of the twentieth century. Summing up the ability that allowed him to recognise talent that others did not see, Phillips said, 'I have one real gift and that is to look another person in the eye and be able to tell if he has anything to contribute, and if he does, I have the additional gift to free him from whatever is restraining him.'[9]

★ ★ ★

Having passed through another cycle of honours and media attention, Phillips re-entered a period outside the public eye. He was occasionally drafted as a guest speaker at local college campuses, where he regaled transfixed students with tales of his life in the music business. He attended rockabilly revival festivals in the United States and abroad, where audience and performers alike were surprised to spot him in the crowd. He was quick to offer encouragement to struggling young performers, and was always gracious to music aficionados eager to speak to him.

Photographs taken at the time make it appear that Phillips had not aged a day in the preceding two decades. He spoke extensively to reporter Eric P. Olsen in 2001 about his long and varied career and his thoughts about his place in music history. Olsen gave a vivid description of the legendary figure: 'At seventy-eight, Phillips is by any standard a remarkable specimen. With a piercing gaze, a head of brown hair, and a full beard without a trace of gray, Phillips looks every bit the patriarch of postwar American music . . . Phillips combines the magnetism of a rock star with the courtliness of a patrician southern planter. (Asked how it is he looks so young, Phillips characteristically explained, "I chase women every day, but I don't know what the hell to do with them when I catch them.") Phillips speaks in a gloriously unreconstructed southern drawl, and with a conviction about his lifework that has not diminished over the decades . . . and the warmth of his responses was a testimony to the passion he still feels not just toward music but toward the recognition due the artistically disenfranchised.'[10]

In a September 2002 interview with Keith Phipps, Phillips summed up his musical legacy as the founder of rock 'n' roll: 'It was one of those things where what we did, in my opinion, started the vibration of certain people out of certain categories into a cross-section of different genres of music that started rock 'n' roll. And I truly believe that. I don't give a damn about the credit, myself. I was out there traveling 60 or 70,000 miles a year, in addition to working until I had a damn nervous breakdown and everything else. I mean, that was no cost to pay to do something I really think has formed a base for some of the best damn opportunities for people to get to know each other around this world. I'm glad I was a little part of it, and I give credit to every person I've ever worked with, whether I had a hit on them or not.'[11]

★　★　★

Samuel Cornelius Phillips died at his home in Memphis on Wednesday, 30 July 2003, just one year shy of the fiftieth anniversary of the birth of rock 'n' roll. His body was taken by ambulance to St Francis Hospital, where he was pronounced dead at a little after 7 pm. He was 80 years old. A lifelong smoker, Phillips' health had been in decline for most of the previous year, and he had been in and out of hospital. The cause of death was listed as respiratory failure, as a result of complications from heart disease and emphysema. A memorial service was held in Memphis at the Cannon Center for the Performing Arts on 7 August. His body was interred at Memorial Park Cemetery.

The day after Phillips' death, a prescheduled ceremony was held in Washington DC to recognise the official designation of the original Sun studio as a National Historic Landmark. (A simultaneous event scheduled to take place in Memphis had to be postponed due to bad weather.) Phillips had retained ownership of the Sun studio location when he moved his operation to its new facility in 1960. The Union Street space was leased to a variety of businesses over the years, but was empty when it was used for the *Class of '55* sessions. Phillips sold the property in 1987, but helped to restore it and reopen it as a tourist attraction and working custom recording studio.

Eulogies to Phillips' musical legacy appeared in news publications over the following weeks, in which he was generally credited for his paternity in the genesis of rock 'n' roll. However, most articles did little more than repeat the oft-told story of the discovery of Elvis Presley, and quote the sale price of his recording contract. Some writers followed up by listing the range of extraordinary talents that Phillips had discovered and produced at the Sun studio. A few went further to pay tribute to his efforts in breaking down the colour barrier in recording black artists, and for making those recordings accessible to a white audience. Most of the articles concluded with mention of the major honours Phillips had received in recognition of his life's work.

What these eulogies almost universally failed to convey was a sense of the profound emotional impact that Phillips' recordings had on listeners at the time of their original release, and that they continued to have on new audiences. That outpouring came in a less public manner, through messages posted on various Internet tribute sites. Most of the individuals who offered their condolences admitted to having never personally met Sam Phillips, yet they felt a strong connection to him through the music that he produced. They spoke of the joy those recordings had given them, and often linked a particular song to an especially memorable event in their lives.

More than the many honours and impressive achievements, Phillips' true legacy was this rare ability to touch hearts and change attitudes. In an interview published two years prior to his death, Phillips offered his personal assessment of his own life's work, which concentrated on the unifying nature of the music he helped create, both blues and rock 'n' roll: 'There is music and there is everything else,' he observed. 'Music has done more to bring glad news and to bring nations and peoples into an understanding of each other than anything else. I don't care what anybody says. All the diplomacies in the world can't hold a candle to that one damn common denominator called music.'[12]

A year later and in failing health, Phillips looked back on his life, satisfied with the way it had all turned out: 'I can't think of too many damn things that I would have done differently,' he told an interviewer. 'And I don't mean that I did everything right: I made more mistakes, I guarantee you, than I didn't . . . Hey, I don't believe I'd change a whole hell of a lot.'[13]

Epilogue

ALTHOUGH SAM PHILLIPS' marriage broke up in 1960, he remained on amicable terms with his wife and maintained close relationships with his two sons. An inkling of Phillips' parenting style can be gained from an anecdote about his younger son, who at one time performed professionally as 'DeLayne Phillips: The World's Most Perfectly Formed Midget Wrestler'.

In 1950s Memphis, Sputnik Monroe was to professional wrestling what Sam Phillips was to rock 'n' roll. Both were entrepreneurs who had created new forms of entertainment that attracted youthful audiences by drawing on the tension between races. Phillips combined black and white musical influences; Monroe combined blacks and whites in the same audience. Monroe was so popular that he could accomplish this feat in a region where mixed audiences were still largely forbidden by law. Inevitably, the two men came to know each other.

One of the most ardent members of the Sputnik Monroe Fan Club was Phillips' younger son, Jerry. Although small for his age, the athletic 12-year-old was determined to follow his hero into a career in professional wrestling. Inspired by Jerry's passion, Monroe created a new opening act for his own main event exhibitions: midget wrestling. He recruited Fabulous Frankie Thumb, an actual midget, and Jerry – newly re-christened 'DeLayne' – as his first contenders, and began their training.

The scheme relied heavily on the fact that Jerry was clearly a child and not a midget. Monroe counted on the audience working themselves into a screaming frenzy denouncing the fraud, and instructed Jerry on how best to provoke a response. 'The announcer would say, "He doesn't have short legs, his arms appear normal . . ." that sort of talk,' Jerry recalled. 'If I had been twenty-five and the size of a midget, it might have been believable, but I was obviously a kid, twelve or thirteen. They'd have me walk through the crowd, chewing a big cigar, taunting the people. Sputnik had taught me pretty good how to pull my pants down and tell 'em to kiss my ass. The audience knew I wasn't real and I just made 'em madder.'[1] It was every kid's dream: being paid $100 a night to smart-mouth a crowd of adults who couldn't do anything about it.

With the elder Phillips' blessings, Monroe set up exhibition matches around the Memphis area. Additional midget combatants were located and tag teams formed. Jerry loved the act and was soon accompanying Monroe to local bars and nightclubs; there, with a cigar clenched in his prepubescent teeth, Monroe lifted him up and set him on the bar. 'The bartender would say, "How old is that guy?"' Jerry remembered. 'And Sputnik would say, "He's twenty-one. He's with me." Who's going to argue with Sputnik Monroe? Anywhere that he went, he was king.'[2]

The fun lasted for a couple of years, until about 1962. While performing in a small town in Arkansas, a crazed fan attacked Jerry with a knife and tried to stab him. Jerry was unharmed, but when his parents found out, his professional wrestling career suffered an early and abrupt retirement.

★ ★ ★

In honour of their father's contribution to modern music, Knox and Jerry Phillips hosted a week-long Sam Phillips Music Celebration in January 2006. The event was held in Phillips' hometown of Florence, Alabama, and kicked off with the dedication of the Official Sam Phillips Cancellation Stamp at the Florence, Alabama Post Office on 4 January. The A&E Biography presentation 'Sam Phillips: The Man Who Invented Rock and Roll' was screened at the Marriott Shoals Hotel that evening. Festivities culminated on the 7th with an evening concert headlined by former Sun Records artist Jerry Lee Lewis.

Also on the bill that night was rockabilly guitarist Eric Heatherly, whom Phillips had seen perform at a Memphis nightclub in 1995. Greeting the performer after his set, Phillips had offered the young musician some advice that effectively summed up his own attitude towards life: 'Don't let the world change what you're doing, because they'll try it. Just do what you believe, always stand true to it, and it'll find a way.'³

Picture Credits

Notes

Where necessary, original punctuation of quotes has been standardised for clarity.

Introduction
1 Keith Phipps, 'Sam Phillips', theonionavclub.com (2002)

PART I: I FOLLOWED MUSIC

1 David Gates, 'Transition: Sam Phillips', *Newsweek* (11 August 2003), p. 10

1 Hard Times, Sweet Sounds
1 Phipps, 'Sam Phillips'
2 Colin Escott with Martin Hawkins, *Good Rockin' Tonight: Sun Records and the Birth of Rock 'n' Roll*, St Martins Press (1991), p. 9
3 Escott, *Good Rockin' Tonight*, p. 9
4 Escott, *Good Rockin' Tonight*, p. 9
5 Alex Halberstadt, 'Sam Phillips: The Sun King', salon.com (2001)
6 Phipps, 'Sam Phillips'
7 Escott, *Good Rockin' Tonight*, p. 10
8 Phipps, 'Sam Phillips'
9 Phipps, 'Sam Phillips'
10 Eric Olsen, 'Founding Father: Sam Phillips and the Birth of Rock and Roll', worldandi.com (May 2001)
11 Olsen, 'Founding Father: Sam Phillips and the Birth of Rock and Roll'
12 Olsen, 'Founding Father: Sam Phillips and the Birth of Rock and Roll'

13 Escott, *Good Rockin' Tonight*, p. 10
14 Olsen, 'Founding Father: Sam Phillips and the Birth of Rock and Roll'
15 Phipps, 'Sam Phillips'
16 Phipps, 'Sam Phillips'
17 Phipps, 'Sam Phillips'
18 Phipps, 'Sam Phillips'
19 Escott, *Good Rockin' Tonight*, p. 10

2 On the Air

1 Phipps, 'Sam Phillips'
2 Peter Guralnick, *Last Train to Memphis: The Rise of Elvis Presley*, Little Brown & Co. (1994), p. 59
3 Halberstadt, 'Sam Phillips: The Sun King'
4 Escott, *Good Rockin' Tonight*, pp. 9–10
5 Escott, *Good Rockin' Tonight*, p. 10
6 Olsen, 'Founding Father: Sam Phillips and the Birth of Rock and Roll'
7 Olsen, 'Founding Father: Sam Phillips and the Birth of Rock and Roll'
8 Halberstadt, 'Sam Phillips: The Sun King'
9 Jim Cogan and William Clark, *Temples of Sound: Inside the Great Recording Studios*, Chronicle Books (2003), p. 86
10 'Sam Phillips', Blues Foundation Hall of Fame, www.blues.org (1998)
11 Escott, *Good Rockin' Tonight*, p. 10
12 Escott, *Good Rockin' Tonight*, p. 11

3 We Record Anything – Anywhere – Anytime

1 Olsen, 'Founding Father: Sam Phillips and the Birth of Rock and Roll'
2 Phipps, 'Sam Phillips'
3 Cogan, *Temples of Sound*, p. 87
4 Cogan, *Temples of Sound*, p. 87
5 Guralnick, *Last Train to Memphis*, p. 61
6 Guralnick, *Last Train to Memphis*, pp. 61–2
7 Guralnick, *Last Train to Memphis*, p. 61

8 Cogan, *Temples of Sound*, p. 87

9 Escott, *Good Rockin' Tonight*, pp. 18–19

10 Phipps, 'Sam Phillips'

11 Halberstadt, 'Sam Phillips: The Sun King'

12 Larry Nager, *Memphis Beat: The Lives and Times of America's Musical Crossroads*, St. Martins Press (1998), p. 138

13 Nager, *Memphis Beat*, p. 137

14 Escott, *Good Rockin' Tonight*, p. 14

15 Escott, *Good Rockin' Tonight*, p. 14

16 Escott, *Good Rockin' Tonight*, p. 15

17 Cogan, *Temples of Sound*, p. 90

18 Craig Morrison, *Go Cat Go! Rockabilly Music and Its Makers*, University of Illinois Press (1996), pp. 22–3

19 Escott, *Good Rockin' Tonight*, p. 14

4 The Hottest Thing in the Country

1 Escott, *Good Rockin' Tonight*, p. 19

2 Phil Galo, 'Sam Phillips: The Father of Rock 'n' Roll', *Variety* (4 August 2003), p. 45

3 Escott, *Good Rockin' Tonight*, p. 5

4 William McKeen, *Rock and Roll Is Here to Stay*, W.W. Norton & Co. (2000), p. 131

5 Escott, *Good Rockin' Tonight*, p. 20

6 Halberstadt, 'Sam Phillips: The Sun King'

7 Halberstadt, 'Sam Phillips: The Sun King'

8 Halberstadt, 'Sam Phillips: The Sun King'

9 Guralnick, *Last Train to Memphis*, p. 131

10 Escott, *Good Rockin' Tonight*, p. 156

11 Guralnick, *Last Train to Memphis*, p. 131

12 Cogan, *Temples of Sound*, p. 87

13 Olsen, 'Founding Father: Sam Phillips and the Birth of Rock and Roll'

14 Johnny Cash, *Cash: An Autobiography*, HarperCollins (1997), p. 80

15 Cash, *Cash: An Autobiography*, p. 80

16 Guralnick, *Last Train to Memphis*, p. 133

17 Escott, *Good Rockin' Tonight*, p. 156

18 Guralnick, *Last Train to Memphis*, p. 131

19 Escott, *Good Rockin' Tonight*, p. 156

20 Halberstadt, 'Sam Phillips: The Sun King'

21 Carl Perkins with David McGee, *Go, Cat, Go! The Life and Times of Carl Perkins*, Hyperion (1996), p. 118

22 Cash, *Cash: An Autobiography*, pp. 79–80

23 Escott, Colin, *Good Rockin' Tonight*, St. Martins Press (1991) p. 187

24 Olsen, 'Founding Father: Sam Phillips and the Birth of Rock and Roll'

25 Guralnick, *Last Train to Memphis*, p. 132

26 Guralnick, *Last Train to Memphis*, p. 133

27 Cogan, *Temples of Sound*, p. 94

28 Cogan, *Temples of Sound*, p. 91

29 Cogan, *Temples of Sound*, p. 87

30 National Public Radio, *Morning Edition*, 'Sam Phillips', www.npr.org (28 November 2001)

31 Cash, *Cash: An Autobiography*, p. 80

32 Guralnick, *Last Train to Memphis*, p. 131

33 Perkins, *Go, Cat, Go!*, p. 118

34 Anthony DeCurtis and James Henke, *Rolling Stone Illustrated History of Rock & Roll: The Definitive History of the Most Important Artists and Their Music*, Random House (1992), p. 276

35 DeCurtis, *Rolling Stone Illustrated History of Rock & Roll*, p. 153

36 Cash, *Cash: An Autobiography*, pp. 80–1

37 Guralnick, *Last Train to Memphis*, p. 133

38 Phipps, 'Sam Phillips'

39 Phipps, 'Sam Phillips'

5 Pursuing the Dream

1 Phipps, 'Sam Phillips'

2 Escott, *Good Rockin' Tonight*, p. 24

3 Phipps, 'Sam Phillips'

4 Cohodas, Nadine, *Spinning Blues Into Gold: The Chess Brothers and the Legendary Chess Records*, St Martins Press (2000), p. 58

5 Cohodas, *Spinning Blues Into Gold*, p. 58

6 Escott, *Good Rockin' Tonight*, p. 30

7 Cohodas, *Spinning Blues Into Gold*, p. 63

8 Escott, *Good Rockin' Tonight*, p. 32
9 Cogan, *Temples of Sound*, p. 88
10 Escott, *Good Rockin' Tonight*, p. 32
11 Escott, *Good Rockin' Tonight*, p. 32
12 Cohodas, *Spinning Blues Into Gold*, p. 65
13 Nager, *Memphis Beat*, p. 136
14 Cohodas, *Spinning Blues Into Gold*, p. 63
15 Escott, *Good Rockin' Tonight*, p. 31
16 Phipps, 'Sam Phillips'
17 Halberstadt, 'Sam Phillips: The Sun King'

6 A New Day

1 Escott, *Good Rockin' Tonight*, p. 35
2 McKeen, *Rock and Roll Is Here to Stay*, p. 103
3 McKeen, *Rock and Roll Is Here to Stay*, p. 103
4 Phipps, 'Sam Phillips'
5 Escott, *Good Rockin' Tonight*, p. 38
6 Escott, *Good Rockin' Tonight*, p. 40
7 McKeen, *Rock and Roll Is Here to Stay*, p. 103
8 Escott, *Good Rockin' Tonight*, p. 42
9 Escott, *Good Rockin' Tonight*, p. 60
10 Escott, *Good Rockin' Tonight*, p. 47
11 Escott, *Good Rockin' Tonight*, p. 57
12 Halberstadt, 'Sam Phillips: The Sun King'
13 Phipps, 'Sam Phillips'
14 Phipps, 'Sam Phillips'

PART II: THE RISING

7 Starlight

1 Guralnick, *Last Train to Memphis*, p. 63
2 Nager, *Memphis Beat*, p. 152
3 Francis Davis, 'The Million Dollar Quartet', *Atlantic Monthly* (October 1994) p. 108
4 Escott, *Good Rockin' Tonight*, p. 60
5 Olsen, 'Founding Father: Sam Phillips and the Birth of Rock and Roll'

6 Wayne Hicks, 'A Talk With the Man Who Found Elvis', *Denver Business Journal* (16 June 2000), p. 37A

7 Hicks, 'A Talk With the Man Who Found Elvis', p. 37A

8 Hicks, 'A Talk With the Man Who Found Elvis', p. 37A

9 Hicks, 'A Talk With the Man Who Found Elvis', p. 37A

10 Associated Press, 'Sam Phillips Dies', *Hollywood Reporter* (31 July 2003), p. 31

11 McKeen, *Rock and Roll Is Here to Stay*, p. 130

12 Olsen, 'Founding Father: Sam Phillips and the Birth of Rock and Roll'

13 Olsen, 'Founding Father: Sam Phillips and the Birth of Rock and Roll'

14 Escott, *Good Rockin' Tonight*, p. 63

15 McKeen, *Rock and Roll Is Here to Stay*, p. 129

16 Mark Steyn, 'The Man Who Invented Elvis', *Atlantic Monthly* (October 2003), p. 44

17 Escott, *Good Rockin' Tonight*, p. 64

18 Galo, 'Sam Phillips: The Father of Rock 'n' Roll' p. 45

19 Olsen, 'Founding Father: Sam Phillips and the Birth of Rock and Roll'

20 Nager, *Memphis Beat*, p. 140

21 Escott, *Good Rockin' Tonight*, p. 64

22 Guralnick, *Last Train to Memphis*, p. 101

23 Olsen, 'Founding Father: Sam Phillips and the Birth of Rock and Roll'

24 Escott, *Good Rockin' Tonight*, p. 64

25 Hicks, 'A Talk With the Man Who Found Elvis', p. 37A

26 Hicks, 'A Talk With the Man Who Found Elvis', p. 37A

27 Associated Press, 'Sam Phillips Dies', p. 31

28 Guralnick, *Last Train to Memphis*, p. 110

29 Escott, *Good Rockin' Tonight*, p. 67

30 Phipps, 'Sam Phillips'

31 Editors of Rolling Stone, *The Rolling Stone Interviews: Talking with the Legends of Rock & Roll 1967–1980*, St Martins Press (1981), p. 29

32 Hank Davis, 'Barbara Pittman', www.rockabillyhall.com (1989)

33 Peter Doggett, *Are You Ready for the Country: Elvis, Dylan, Parsons*

and the Roots of Country Rock, Penguin Books (2001), p. 202

34 Doggett, *Are You Ready for the Country*, p. 202

8 Sold Out

1 Guralnick, *Last Train to Memphis*, p. 205

2 Hicks, 'A Talk With the Man Who Found Elvis', p. 37A

3 Guralnick, *Last Train to Memphis*, p. 209

4 Halberstadt, 'Sam Phillips: The Sun King'

5 Olsen, 'Founding Father: Sam Phillips and the Birth of Rock and Roll'

6 Halberstadt, 'Sam Phillips: The Sun King'

7 Halberstadt, 'Sam Phillips: The Sun King'

8 Olsen, 'Founding Father: Sam Phillips and the Birth of Rock and Roll'

9 National Public Radio, *All Things Considered*, 'WHER – 1000 Beautiful Watts', www.npr.org (29 October 1999)

10 Halberstadt, 'Sam Phillips: The Sun King'

11 *All Things Considered*, 'WHER – 1000 Beautiful Watts'

12 Cogan, *Temples of Sound*, p. 93

13 Doggett, *Are You Ready for the Country*, p. 216

14 James Dickerson, *Goin' Back to Memphis: A Century of Blues, Rock 'n' Roll, and Glorious Soul*, Schirmer Books (1996), p. 99

15 Alanna Nash, 'The Kingmaker: Sam Phillips 1923–2003', *Entertainment Weekly* (15 August 2003), p. 16

16 Hicks, 'A Talk With the Man Who Found Elvis', p. 37A

9 A Different Country

1 Escott, *Good Rockin' Tonight*, p. 119

2 Escott, *Good Rockin' Tonight*, p. 121

3 Escott, *Good Rockin' Tonight*, p. 123

4 Doggett, *Are You Ready for the Country*, p. 260

5 Escott, *Good Rockin' Tonight*, p. 170

6 Morrison, *Go Cat Go!*, p. 74

7 Escott, *Good Rockin' Tonight*, p. 184

8 Escott, *Good Rockin' Tonight*, p. 177

9 Escott, *Good Rockin' Tonight*, p. 176

10 Escott, *Good Rockin' Tonight*, p. 177

11 Doggett, *Are You Ready for the Country*, p. 255

12 Doggett, *Are You Ready for the Country*, pp. 252–3

10 The Great Contender

1 Perkins, *Go, Cat, Go!*, p. 88

2 Perkins, *Go, Cat, Go!*, p. 88

3 Perkins, *Go, Cat, Go!*, p. 90

4 Perkins, *Go, Cat, Go!*, p. 90

5 Escott, *Good Rockin' Tonight*, pp. 127–8

6 Escott, *Good Rockin' Tonight*, pp. 129–30

7 Perkins, *Go, Cat, Go!*, p. 96

8 Perkins, *Go, Cat, Go!*, p. 138

9 Cogan, *Temples of Sound*, p. 93

11 Go, Cat, Go

1 Perkins, *Go, Cat, Go!*, p. 192

2 Escott, *Good Rockin' Tonight*, p. 158

3 Perkins, *Go, Cat, Go!*, p. 227

12 Selling Johnny

1 Cash, *Cash: An Autobiography*, p. 75

2 Escott, *Good Rockin' Tonight*, p. 98

3 Escott, *Good Rockin' Tonight*, p. 98

4 Editors of Rolling Stone, *The Rolling Stone Interviews*, p. 275

5 Cash, *Cash: An Autobiography*, p. 76

6 Doggett, *Are You Ready for the Country*, p. 255

7 Cash, *Cash: An Autobiography*, p. 85

8 Steve Turner, *The Man Called Cash: The Life, Love and Faith of an American Legend*, W Publishing Group (2004), p. 79

9 Turner, *The Man Called Cash*, p. 79

10 Turner, *The Man Called Cash*, p. 78

11 Dickerson, *Goin' Back to Memphis*, p. 110

12 Doggett, *Are You Ready for the Country*, p. 257

13 Turner, *The Man Called Cash*, p. 78

13 A Square Peg

1 Escott, *Good Rockin' Tonight*, p. 148
2 Escott, *Good Rockin' Tonight*, p. 148
3 Escott, *Good Rockin' Tonight*, p. 149
4 Editors of Rolling Stone, *The Rolling Stone Interviews*, p. 154
5 Editors of Rolling Stone, *The Rolling Stone Interviews*, p. 153
6 Escott, *Good Rockin' Tonight*, p. 150
7 Editors of Rolling Stone, *The Rolling Stone Interviews*, p. 154
8 Cash, *Cash: An Autobiography*, p. 85
9 Escott, *Good Rockin' Tonight*, p. 151

14 Two Sides of the Same Coin

1 Phipps, 'Sam Phillips'
2 Escott, *Good Rockin' Tonight*, p. 192
3 Editors of Rolling Stone, *The Rolling Stone Interviews*, p. 76
4 Escott, *Good Rockin' Tonight*, p. 207
5 Dickerson, *Goin' Back to Memphis*, p. 109
6 Escott, *Good Rockin' Tonight*, p. 228
7 Phipps, 'Sam Phillips'
8 Editors of Rolling Stone, *The Rolling Stone Interviews*, p. 76
9 Escott, *Good Rockin' Tonight*, p. 202
10 Doggett, *Are You Ready for the Country*, p. 265
11 Doggett, *Are You Ready for the Country*, p. 258

15 Last Hurrah

1 Escott, *Good Rockin' Tonight*, p. 215
2 Halberstadt, 'Sam Phillips: The Sun King'
3 Escott, *Good Rockin' Tonight*, p. 214
4 Halberstadt, 'Sam Phillips: The Sun King'
5 Escott, *Good Rockin' Tonight*, p. 218
6 Phipps, 'Sam Phillips'

PART III: THE FATHER OF ROCK 'N' ROLL

16 The Slow Decline

1 Phipps, 'Sam Phillips'

2 Phipps, 'Sam Phillips'

3 DeCurtis, *Rolling Stone Illustrated History of Rock & Roll*, p. 153

4 Escott, *Good Rockin' Tonight*, p. 234

5 Escott, *Good Rockin' Tonight*, p. 224

6 Escott, *Good Rockin' Tonight*, p. 225

7 Escott, *Good Rockin' Tonight*, p. 225

8 Escott, *Good Rockin' Tonight*, p. 226

9 Escott, *Good Rockin' Tonight*, p. 226

17 Sunset

1 Escott, *Good Rockin' Tonight*, p. 234

2 Escott, *Good Rockin' Tonight*, p. 232

3 Escott, *Good Rockin' Tonight*, p. 232

18 Resurrection

1 'Sam Phillips', *Guitar Player* (November 2003), p. 23

2 Escott, *Good Rockin' Tonight*, p. 240

3 Gordon, Robert, *It Came From Memphis*, Pocket Books (1995), p. 257

4 Gordon, *It Came From Memphis*, p. 257

5 Gordon, *It Came From Memphis*, p. 257

6 Gordon, *It Came From Memphis*, p. 257

7 Gordon, *It Came From Memphis*, p. 258

19 Recognition

1 The Recording Academy: Awards, 'Sam Phillips', www.grammy.com

2 Rock and Roll Hall of Fame + Museum: Inductees, 'Sam Phillips', www.rockhall.com

3 Perkins, *Go, Cat, Go!*, p. 362

4 The Recording Academy: Awards, 'Sam Phillips'

5 Blues Foundation Hall of Fame, 'Sam Phillips', www.blues.org (1998)

6 Blues Foundation Hall of Fame, 'Sam Phillips'

7 Olsen, 'Founding Father: Sam Phillips and the Birth of Rock and Roll'

8 Country Music Hall of Fame and Museum: Inductees, 'Sam Phillips', www.countrymusichalloffame.com

9 Greg Halberstam, 'Sam Phillips', as quoted at www.countrymusichalloffame.com

10 Olsen, 'Founding Father: Sam Phillips and the Birth of Rock and Roll'

11 Phipps, 'Sam Phillips'

12 Olsen, 'Founding Father: Sam Phillips and the Birth of Rock and Roll'

13 Phipps, 'Sam Phillips'

Epilogue

1 Gordon, *It Came From Memphis*, p. 36

2 Gordon, *It Came From Memphis*, p. 36

3 Nash, 'The King Maker', p. 16

Discography

CHESS RECORDS: PRODUCED BY SAM PHILLIPS

1458 Jackie Brenston & The Delta Cats: Rocket 88/Come Back Where You Belong (1951)

1459 Ike Turner & His Kings Of Rhythm: Heartbroken And Worried/I'm Lonesome, Baby (1951)

1465 Lou Sargent: Ridin' The Boogie/She Really Treats Me Wrong (1951)

1466 Rufus Thomas: Night Walkin' Blues/Why Did You Dee Gee (1951)

1469 Jackie Brenston & The Delta Cats: In My Real Gone Rocket/Tuckered Out (1951)

1472 Jackie Brenston & The Delta Cats: Juiced (vocal: Billy Love)/Independent Woman (1951)

1475 Harmonica Frank: Swamp Root/Goin' Away Walkin' (1951)

1475 Harmonica Frank: Swamp Root/Step It Up And Go (1951)

1479 Howlin' Wolf: Moanin' At Midnight/How Many More Years (1951)

1487 Roscoe Gordon: Booted/I Love You Till The Day I Die (vocal: Bobby Bland) (1951)

1489 Robert Bland: Letter From A Trench In Korea/Crying (1951) (piano: Roscoe Gordon)

1492 Rufus Thomas: No More Doggin' Around/Crazy 'Bout You, Baby (1952)

1493 L.J. Thomas: Sam's Drag/Baby, Take A Chance With Me (1952)

1494 Harmonica Frank: Howlin' Tomcat/She's Done Moved (1952)

1495 Bob Price: How Can It Be/Sticks & Stones (1952)

1496 Jackie Brenston (with Edna McRaney): Hi-Ho Baby/Leo Louse (1952)

1497 Howlin' Wolf: Wolf Is At Your Door/Howlin' Wolf Boogie (1952)

1502 The Brewsteraires: Where Shall I Be/Wings For My Soul (1952)

1504 Dr Ross: Country Clown/Doctor Ross Boogie (1952)

1508 Billy 'Red' Love: Love Drop Top/You're Gonna Try (1952)

1510 Howlin' Wolf: Getting Old & Grey/Mister Highway Man (1952)

1515 Howlin' Wolf: Saddle My Pony/Worried All The Time (1952)

1516 Billy 'Red' Love: Just Plain Poor/My Teddy Bear Baby (1952)

1517 Rufus Thomas: Juanita/Decorate The Counter (1952) (piano: possibly Roscoe Gordon)

1528 Howlin' Wolf: Oh, Red!/My Last Affair (1952)

1529 Walter Horton: Walter's Boogie/West Winds Are Blowing (unreleased)

1532 Jackie Brenston & The Delta Cats: Blues Got Me Again/Starvation (1953)

RPM/Modern Records discography: www.bsnpubs.com/modern/modernstory.html

SAM PHILLIPS DISCOGRAPHY

Phillips label: single

9001 Joe Hill Louis: Gotta Let You Go/

9002 Boogie In The Park (Aug. 1950) *sides had separate issue numbers*

Sun Records: singles

174 Jackie Boy and Little Walter: Blues In My Condition/Sellin' My Whiskey (unissued)

175 Johnny London, Alto Wizard: Drivin' Slow/Flat Tire (April 1952)

176 Walter Bradford and the Big City Four: Dreary Nights/Nuthin' But The Blues (April 1952)

177 Gay Garth: Got My Application, Baby/Handy Jackson: Trouble (Will Bring You Down) (Jan. 1953)

178 Joe Hill Louis: We All Gotta Go Sometime/She May Be Yours (But She Comes To See Me Sometimes) (Jan. 1953)

179 Willie Nix, The Memphis Blues Boy: Baker Shop Boogie/Seems Like A Million Years (Jan. 1953)

180 Jimmy & Walter (Jimmy DeBarry & Walter Horton): Easy/Before Long (March 1953)

181 Rufus 'Hound Dog' Thomas Jr: Bear Cat (The Answer To 'Hound Dog')/Walkin' In The Rain (March 1953)

182   Dusty Brooks and His Tones: Heaven Or Fire (vocal: Juanita Brown)/Tears And Wine (vocal: Juanita Brown & Joe Alexander) (March 1953)

183   D.A. Hunt: Lonesome Ol' Jail/Greyhound Blues (June 1953)

184   Big Memphis Marainey, Onzie Horne Combo: Call Me Anything, But Call Me/Baby No, No! (June 1953)

185   Jimmy DeBerry: Take A Little Chance/Time Has Made A Change (June 1953)

186   The Prisonaires: Baby Please/Just Walkin' In The Rain (July 1953)

187   Little Junior's Blue Flames: Feelin' Good/Fussin' And Fightin' (Blues) (8 July 1953)

188   Rufus Thomas, Jr: Tiger Man (King Of The Jungle)/Save That Money (8 July 1953)

189   The Prisonaires, Confined To Tennessee State Penitentiary, Nashville: My God Is Real/Softly And Tenderly (8 July 1953)

190   Ripley Cotton Choppers: Silver Bells/Blues Waltz (Sep. 1953)

191   The Prisonaires, Confined To Tennessee State Penitentiary, Nashville: A Prisoner's Prayer/I Know (1 Nov. 1953)

192   Little Junior's Blue Flames: Mystery Train/Love My Baby (1 Nov. 1953)

193   Doctor Ross: Come Back Baby/Chicago Breakdown (24 Dec. 1953)

194   Little Milton: Beggin' My Baby/Somebody Told Me (24 Dec. 1953)

195   Billy 'The Kid' Emerson: No Teasing Around/If Lovin' Is Believing (20 Feb. 1954)

196   Hot Shot Love: Wolf Call Boogie/Harmonica Jam (20 Feb. 1954)

197   Earl Peterson, Michigan's Singing Cowboy: Boogie Blues/In The Dark (20 Feb. 1954)

198   Howard Seratt: Troublesome Waters/I Must Be Saved (20 Feb. 1954)

199   James Cotton: My Baby/Straighten Up, Baby (15 April 1954)

200   Little Milton: If You Love Me/Alone And Blue (15 April 1954)

201   Hardrock Gunter: Gonna Dance All Night/Fallen Angel (1 May 1954)

202   Doug Poindexter and the Starlite Wranglers: Now She Cares No More For Me/My Kind Of Carrying On (1 May 1954)

203   Billy 'The Kid' Emerson: I'm Not Going Home/The Woodchuck (1 May 1954)

204 Raymond Hill: Bourbon Street Jump/The Snuggle (1 May 1954)

205 Harmonica Frank: The Great Medical Menagerist/Rockin' Chair Daddy (1 July 1954)

206 James Cotton: Cotton Crop Blues/Hold Me In Your Arms (1 July 1954)

207 The Prisonaires, Recorded In The Tennessee State Prison, Nashville, Tenn.: There Is Love In You/What'll You Do Next (1 July 1954)

208 Buddy Cunningham, Cliff Parman's Orchestra: Right Or Wrong/Why Do I Cry (15 July 1954)

209 Elvis Presley, Scotty and Bill: That's All Right/Blue Moon Of Kentucky (19 July 1954)

210 Elvis Presley, Scotty and Bill: Good Rockin' Tonight/I Don't Care If The Sun Don't Shine (22 Sep. 1954)

211 Malcolm Yelvington, Star Rhythm Boys: Drinkin' Wine Spo-Dee-O-Dee/Just Rolling Along (10 Nov. 1954)

212 Doctor Ross: The Boogie Disease/Juke Box Boogie (10 Nov. 1954)

213 The Jones Brothers: Look To Jesus/Every Night (8 Jan. 1955)

214 Billy 'The Kid' Emerson: Move Baby Move/When It Rains It Pours (8 Jan. 1955)

215 Elvis Presley, Scotty and Bill: Milkcow Blues Boogie/You're A Heartbreaker (8 Jan. 1955)

216 Slim Rhodes: Don't Believe (vocal: Brad Suggs)/Uncertain Love (vocal: Dusty & Dot) (1 April 1955)

217 Elvis Presley, Scotty and Bill: I'm Left, You're Right, She's Gone/Baby Let's Play House (25 April 1955)

218 Sammy Lewis, Willie Johnson Combo: I Feel So Worried/So Long Baby Goodbye (25 April 1955)

219 Billy 'The Kid' Emerson: Red Hot/No Greater Love (21 June 1955)

220 Little Milton: Homesick For My Baby/Lookin' For My Baby (21 June 1955)

221 Johnny Cash, Tennessee Two: Cry! Cry! Cry!/Hey, Porter! (21 June, 1955)

222 Five Tinos: Don't Do That!/Sitting By My Window (21 June 1955)

223 Elvis Presley, Scotty and Bill: Mystery Train/I Forgot To Remember To Forget (1 Aug. 1955)

224 Carl Perkins: Let The Jukebox Keep On Playing/Gone, Gone, Gone (1 Aug. 1955)

225 Slim Rhodes: The House Of Sin (vocal: Dusty & Dot)/Are You Ashamed Of Me? (vocal: Brad Suggs) (1 Aug. 1955)

226 Eddie Snow: Ain't That Right/Bring Your Love Back Home To Me (1 Aug. 1955)

227 Rosco Gordon: Just Love Me Baby/Weeping Blues (Sep. 1955) *also Flip 227*

228 Smokey Joe: The Signifying Monkey/Listen To Me Baby (15 Sep. 1955) *also Flip 228*

229 Maggie Sue Wimberly: Daydreams Come True/How Long (Dec. 1955)

230 The Miller Sisters: There's No Right Way To Do Me Wrong/You Can Tell Me (15 Jan. 1956)

231 Charlie Feathers: Defrost Your Heart/A Wedding Gown Of White (Dec. 1955) *also Flip 231*

232 Johnny Cash, Tennessee Two: So Doggone Lonesome/Folsom Prison Blues (15 Dec. 1955)

233 Billy 'The Kid' Emerson: Little Fine Healthy Thing/Something For Nothing (15 Jan. 1956)

234 Carl Perkins: Blue Suede Shoes/Honey, Don't! (Dec. 1955)

235 Carl Perkins: Sure To Fall/Tennessee (unissued)

236 Jimmy Haggett: No More, No More/They Call Our Love A Sin (Dec. 1955)

237 Rosco Gordon: The Chicken (Dance With You)/Love For You Baby (1956) *also Flip 237*

238 Slim Rhodes: Gonna Romp And Stomp (vocal: Dusty & Dot)/Bad Girl (vocal: Brad Suggs) (April 1956)

239 Warren Smith: Rock 'n' Roll Ruby/I'd Rather Be Safe Than Sorry (April 1956)

240 Jack Earls and the Jimbos: Slow Down/A Fool For Lovin' You (April 1956)

241 Johnny Cash, Tennessee Two: Get Rhythm/I Walk The Line (April 1956)

242 Roy Orbison, Teen Kings: Ooby Dooby/Go! Go! Go! (May 1956)

243 Carl Perkins: Boppin' The Blues/All Mama's Children (May 1956)

244 Jean Chapel: Welcome To The Club/I Won't Be Rockin' Tonight (June 1956) *leased to RCA*

245 Billy Riley: Trouble Bound/Rock With Me Baby (May 1956)

246 Malcolm Yelvington: Rockin' With My Baby/It's Me Baby (3 Aug. 1956)

247 Sonny Burgess: Red Headed Woman/We Wanna Boogie (3 Aug. 1956)

248 The Rhythm Rockers: Fiddle Bop (vocal: Buddy Durham)/Jukebox, Help Me Find My Baby (vocal: Hardrock Gunter) (3 Aug. 1956)

249 Carl Perkins: I'm Sorry I'm Not Sorry/Dixie Fried (3 Aug. 1956)

250 Warren Smith: Black Jack David/Ubangi Stomp (24 Sep. 1956)

251 Roy Orbison, Teen Kings: You're My Baby/Rockhouse (24 Sep. 1956)

252 Kenneth Parchman: Love Crazy Baby/I Feel Like Rockin' (unissued)

253 Barbara Pittman: I Need A Man/No Matter Who's To Blame (24 Sep. 1956)

254 Ray Harris: Where'd You Stay Last Night/Come On Little Mama (24 Sep. 1956)

255 Miller Sisters: Ten Cats Down/Finders Keepers (3 Aug. 1956)

256 Slim Rhodes, vocal: Sandy Brooks: Take And Give/Do What I Do (21 Nov. 1956)

257 Rosco Gordon: Shoobie Oobie/Cheese And Crackers (21 Nov. 1956)

258 Johnny Cash, Tennessee Two: Train Of Love/There You Go (21 Nov. 1956)

259 Jerry Lee Lewis: Crazy Arms/End Of The Road (1 Dec. 1956)

260 Billy Riley and His Little Green Men: Flyin' Saucer Rock & Roll/I Want You Baby (23 Jan. 1957)

261 Carl Perkins: Matchbox/Your True Love (23 Jan. 1957)

262 Ernie Chaffin: Feelin' Low/Lonesome For My Baby (23 Jan. 1957)

263 Sonny Burgess: Ain't Got A Thing/Restless (24 Jan. 1957)

264 Glenn Honeycutt: I'll Be Around/I'll Wait Forever (24 Jan. 1957)

265 Roy Orbison and The Roses: Sweet And Easy To Love/Devil Doll (24 Jan. 1957)

266 Johnny Cash, Tennessee Two: Don't Make Me Go/Next In Line (15 March 1957)

267 Jerry Lee Lewis: It'll Be Me/Whole Lot Of Shakin' Going On (15 March 1957)

268 Warren Smith: So Long I'm Gone/Miss Froggie (15 April 1957)

269 Wade & Dick, The College Kids (Wade Moore & Dick Penner): Bop Bop Baby/Don't Need Your Lovin' Baby (15 April 1957)

270 Jimmy Williams: Please Don't Cry Over Me/That Depends On You (14 Sep. 1957)

271 Rudi Richardson: Fools Hall Of Fame/Why Should I Cry (15 April 1957)

272 Ray Harris: Greenback Dollar, Watch And Chain/Foolish Heart (June 1957)

273 Mack Self: Every Day/Easy To Love (June 1957)

274 Carl Perkins: Forever Yours/That's Right (15 Aug. 1957)

275 Ernie Chaffin: I'm Lonesome/Laughin' And Jokin' (15 Aug. 1957)

276 Edwin Bruce: Rock Boppin' Baby/More Than Yesterday (15 Aug. 1957)

277 Billy Riley and His Little Green Men: Red Hot/Pearly Lee (14 Sep. 1957)

278 Tommy Blake, Rhythm Rebels: Lordy Hoody/Flat Foot Sam (14 Sep. 1957)

279 Johnny Cash and the Tennessee Two: Home Of The Blues/Give My Love To Rose (14 Sep. 1957)

280 Dickey Lee and the Collegiates: Memories Never Grow Old/Good Lovin' (12 Oct. 1957)

281 Jerry Lee Lewis and His Pumping Piano: You Win Again/Great Balls Of Fire (3 Nov. 1957)

282 Dick Penner: Your Honey Love/Cindy Lou (3 Nov. 1957)

283 Johnny Cash and the Tennessee Two: Ballad Of A Teenage Queen/Big River (Dec. 1957)

284 Roy Orbison: Chicken-Hearted/I Like Love (Dec. 1957)

285 Sonny Burgess: My Bucket's Got A Hole In It/Sweet Misery (Dec. 1957)

286 Warren Smith: I've Got Love If You Want It/I Fell In Love (Dec. 1957)

287 Carl Perkins, The Rockin' Guitar Man: Glad All Over/Lend Me Your Comb (vocal: Carl and Jay) (Dec. 1957)

288 Jerry Lee Lewis and His Pumping Piano: Down The Line/Breathless (Feb. 1958)

289 Billy Riley and His Little Green Men: Baby Please Don't Go/Wouldn't You Know (Feb. 1958)

290 Rudy Grayzell: Judy/I Think Of You (9 April 1958)

291 Jack Clement: Ten Years/Your Lover Boy (9 April 1958)

292 Edwin Bruce: Sweet Woman/Part Of My Life (9 April 1958)

293 The Sunrays: Love Is A Stranger/The Lonely Hours (9 April 1958)

294 Magel Priesman: I Feel So Blue/Memories Of You (9 April 1958)

295 Johnny Cash and the Tennessee Two: Guess Things Happen That Way/Come In Stranger (9 April 1958)

296 Jerry Lee Lewis and His Pumping Piano: High School Confidential/Fools Like Me (9 April 1958)

297 Dickey Lee and the Collegiates: Fool, Fool, Fool/Dreamy Nights (9 April 1958)

298 Ray Smith: So Young/Right Behind You Baby (9 April 1958)

299 Gene Simmons: Drinkin' Wine/I Done Told You (9 April 1958)

300 Tommy Blake: Sweetie Pie/I Dig You Baby (June 1958)

301 Narration by George & Louis: The Return Of Jerry Lee/Jerry Lee Lewis: Lewis Boogie (June 1958)

302 Johnny Cash and the Tennessee Two: The Ways Of A Woman In Love/You're The Nearest Thing To Heaven (May 1958)

303 Jerry Lee Lewis and His Pumping Piano: Break-Up/I'll Make It All Up To You (10 Aug. 1958)

304 Sonny Burgess: Itchy/Thunderbird (10 Aug. 1958)

305 Rosco Gordon: Sally Jo/Torro (20 Sep. 1958)

306 Jimmy Isle: I've Been Waiting/Diamond Ring (25 Oct. 1958)

307 Ernie Chaffin: (Nothing Can Change) My Love For You/Born To Lose (15 Oct. 1958)

308 Ray Smith: Why, Why, Why/You Made A Hit (25 Oct. 1958)

309 Johnny Cash and the Tennessee Two: I Just Thought You'd Like To Know/It's Just About Time (12 Nov. 1958)

310 Vernon Taylor: Breeze/Today Is A Blue Day (12 Nov. 1958)

311 Jack Clement: The Black Haired Man/Wrong (20 Nov. 1958)

312 Jerry Lee Lewis and His Pumping Piano: It Hurt Me So/ I'll Sail My Ship Alone (20 Nov. 1958)

313   Billy Riley: No Name Girl/Down By The Riverside (1 Feb. 1959)

314   Warren Smith: Goodbye Mr. Love/Sweet, Sweet Girl (15 Feb. 1959)

315   Onie Wheeler: Jump Right Out Of This Jukebox/Tell 'Em Off (15 Feb. 1959)

316   Johnny Cash and the Tennessee Two: Thanks A Lot/Luther Played The Boogie (15 Feb. 1959)

317   Jerry Lee Lewis and His Pumping Piano: Lovin' Up A Storm/Big Blon' Baby (15 Feb. 1959)

318   Jimmy Isle: Time Will Tell/Without A Love (23 March 1959)

319   Ray Smith: Sail Away/Rockin' Bandit (23 March 1959)

320   Ernie Chaffin: Don't Ever Leave Me/Miracle Of You (27 April 1959)

321   Johnny Cash and the Tennessee Two: I Forgot To Remember To Forget/Katy Too (2 June 1959)

322   Bill Riley: One More Time/Got The Water Boilin' Baby (2 June 1959)

323   Alton & Jimmy (Alton Lott & Jimmy Harrell): Have Faith In My Love/No More Crying The Blues (2 June 1959)

324   Jerry Lee Lewis and His Pumping Piano: Let's Talk About Us/The Ballad Of Billy Jo (15 June 1959)

325   Vernon Taylor: Sweet And Easy To Love/Mystery Train (16 July 1959)

326   Jerry McGill and the Topcoats: I Wanna Make Sweet Love/Lovestruck (11 Aug. 1959)

327   Johnny Powers: With Your Love, With Your Kiss/Be Mine, All Mine (15 Sep. 1959)

328   Sherry Crane: Willie Willie/Winnie The Parakeet (11 Aug. 1959)

329   Will Mercer: You're Just My Kind/Ballad Of St. Marks (15 Sep. 1959)

330   Jerry Lee Lewis and His Pumping Piano: Little Queenie/I Could Never Be Ashamed Of You (15 Sep. 1959)

331   Johnny Cash and the Tennessee Two: You Tell Me/Goodbye Little Darlin' (15 Sep. 1959)

332   Jimmy Isle: What A Life/Together (15 Sep. 1959)

333   Ray B. Anthony: Alice Blue Gown/St. Louis Blues (25 Oct. 1959)

334   Johnny Cash, Tennessee Two and the Gene Lowery Singers: Straight A's In Love/I Love You Because (31 Dec. 1959)

335   Tracy Pendarvis and the Swampers: A Thousand Guitars/Is It Too Late? (Jan. 1960)

336 Mack Owen: Walkin' And Talkin'/Somebody Just Like You (Jan. 1960)

337 Jerry Lee Lewis and His Pumping Piano: Old Black Joe (with the Gene Lowery Singers)/Baby Baby Bye Bye (March 1960)

338 Paul Richy with the Gene Lowery Singers: The Legend Of The Big Steeple/Broken Hearted Willie (8 March 1960)

339 Rayburn Anthony: Who's Gonna Shoe Your Pretty Little Feet (with the Gene Lowery Singers)/There's No Tomorrow (30 March 1960)

340 Bill Johnson with the Gene Lowery Singers: Bobaloo/Bad Times Ahead (30 March 1960)

341 Sonny Wilson with the Gene Lowery Singers: The Great Pretender/I'm Gonna Take A Walk (1 Aug. 1960)

342 Bobbie Jean, Ernie Barton Orchestra: Cheaters Never Win/You Burned The Bridges (7 July 1960)

343 Johnny Cash and the Tennessee Two: The Story Of Broken Heart/Down The Street To 301 (14 July 1960)

344 Jerry Lee Lewis and His Pumping Piano: John Henry/Hang Up My Rock And Roll Shoes (1 Aug. 1960)

345 Tracy Pendarvis: South Bound Line/Is It Me (15 Aug. 1960)

346 Bill Strength with the Gene Lowery Singers: Guess I'd Better Go/Senorita (12 Sep. 1960)

347 Johnny Cash and the Tennessee Two: Port Of Lonely Hearts/Mean Eyed Cat (Oct. 1960)

348 Lance Roberts with the Gene Lowery Singers: The Good Guy Always Wins/The Time Is Right (Oct. 1960)

349 Tony Rossini: I Gotta Know (Where I Stand)/Is It Too Late (To Say I'm Sorry) (with the Gene Lowery Singers) (14 Nov. 1960)

350 The Rockin' Stockings: Yulesville, U.S.A./Rockin' Old Lang Syne (14 Nov. 1960) *also Sun 1960*

351 Ira Jay II (Ira Jay Lichterman): You Don't Love Me/More Than Anything (In The World) (14 Nov. 1960)

352 Jerry Lee Lewis: When I Get Paid/Love Made A Fool Of Me (14 Nov. 1960)

353 Roy Orbison: Sweet And Easy To Love/Devil Doll (25 Nov. 1960) *reissue of Sun 265*

354 Bobby Sheridan (Charlie Rich): Sad News (with the Gene Lowery Singers)/Red Man (10 Dec. 1960)

355 Johnny Cash and the Tennessee Two: Oh Lonesome Me (with the Gene Lowery Singers/Life Goes On (10 Dec. 1960)

356 Jerry Lee Lewis and His Pumping Piano: What'd I Say/Livin' Lovin' Wreck (27 Feb. 1961)

357 (unissued)

358 George Klein: U.T. Party, Part I/U.T. Party, Part II (10 March 1961)

359 Tracy Pendarvis: Belle Of The Suwannee/Eternally (25 April 1961)

360 Wade Cagle and the Escorts: Groovey Train/Highland Rock (25 April 1961)

361 Anita Wood: I'll Wait Forever/I Can't Show How I Feel (25 June 1961)

362 Harold Dorman: I'll Stick By You/There They Go (21 May 1961)

363 Johnny Cash and the Tennessee Two: Sugartime/My Treasurer [misprint of 'My Treasure'] (21 May 1961)

364 Jerry Lee Lewis and His Pumping Piano: Cold, Cold Heart/It Won't Happen With Me (26 May 1961)

365 Shirley Sisk: I Forgot To Remember To Forget/Other Side (Aug. 1961)

366 Tony Rossini: Well I Ask Ya/Darlena (Aug. 1961)

367 Jerry Lee Lewis and His Pumping Piano: Save The Last Dance For Me/As Long As I Live (1 Sep. 1961)

368 Don Hosea: Since I Met You/Uh Huh Unh (9 Oct. 1961)

369 Bobby Wood: Everybody's Searching/Human Emotions (9 Oct. 1961) *probably unissued*

370 Harold Dorman: Uncle Jonah's Place/Just One Step (7 Nov. 1961)

371 Jerry Lee Lewis and His Pumping Piano: Money/Bonnie B (21 Nov. 1961)

372 Ray Smith: Travelin' Salesman/I Won't Miss You ('Til You Go) (21 Nov. 1961)

373 Rayburn Anthony: How Well I Know/Big Dream (19 Jan. 1962)

374 Jerry Lee Lewis and His Pumping Piano: I've Been Twistin'/Ramblin' Rose (19 Jan. 1962)

375 Ray Smith: Candy Doll/Hey, Boss Man (Twist) (9 Feb. 1962)

376 Johnny Cash and the Tennessee Two: Blue Train/Born To Lose (27 April 1962)

377 Harold Dorman: In The Beginning/Wait Til' Saturday Night (4 April 1962)

378 Tony Rossini: (Meet Me) After School/Just Around The Corner (4 April 1962)

379 Jerry Lee Lewis and His Pumping Piano: Sweet Little Sixteen/How's My Ex Treating You (7 July 1962)

380 Tony Rossini and The Chippers: You Make It Sound So Easy/New Girl In Town (10 July 1962)

381 The Four Upsetters: Midnight Soiree/Crazy Arms (5 Nov. 1962)

382 Jerry Lee Lewis: Good Golly Miss Molly/I Can't Trust Me (In Your Arms) (5 Nov. 1962)

383 Johnny Cash: (unissued)

384 Jerry Lee Lewis and His Pumping Piano: Teenage Letter/Jerry Lee Lewis with Linda Gail Lewis: Seasons Of My Heart (April 1963)

385 Linda Gail Lewis: Nothin' Shakin' (But The Leaves On The Trees)/Sittin' And Thinkin' (unissued)

386 The Four Upsetters: Surfin' Calliope/Wabash Cannon Ball (15 July 1963)

387 Tony Rossini: Nobody/Moved To Kansas City (15 July 1963)

388 The Teenangels: Ain't Gonna Let You (Break My Heart)/Tell Me My Love promotional copies only

389 Billy Adams: Betty And Dupree/Got My Mojo Workin' (1 Jan. 1964)

390 Bill Yates and His T-Birds: Don't Step On My Dog/Stop, Wait And Listen (1 May 1964)

391 Billy Adams: Trouble In Mind (with Jesse Carter)/Lookin' For Mary Ann (1 May 1964)

392 Johnny Cash and the Tennessee Two: Wide Open Road/Belshazar (1 May 1964)

393 Smokey Joe: The Signifying Monkey/Listen To Me Baby (1 May 1964)

394 Billy Adams: Reconsider Baby/Ruby Jane (Sep. 1964)

395 Randy and the Radiants: Peek-A-Boo/Mountain High (Jan. 1965)

396 Jerry Lee Lewis: Carry Me Back To Old Virginia/I Know What It Means (15 March 1965)

397 Gorgeous Bill: Carleen/Too Late To Right My Wrong (15 March 1965)

398 Randy and the Radiants: My Way Of Thinking/Truth From My Eyes (25 Nov. 1965)

399 Bill Yates: Big Big World/I Dropped My M&M's (1 Feb. 1966)

400 The Jesters: Cadillac Man/My Babe (1 Feb. 1966)

401 Billy Adams: Open The Door Richard/Rock Me Baby (1 Feb. 1966)

402 Dane Stinit: Don't Knock What You Don't Understand/Always On The Go (May 1966)

403 David Houston: Sherry's Lips/Miss Brown (10 Oct. 1966) *also Phillips International 3583*

404 The Climates: No You For Me/Breaking Up Again (Feb. 1967)

405 Dane Stinit: Sweet Country Girl/That Muddy Ole River (Near Memphis, Tennessee) (Feb. 1967)

406 Brother James Anderson: I'm Gonna Move In The Room With The Lord/I'm Tired, My Soul Needs Resting (Feb. 1967) *'Gospel Series'*

407 Load of Mischief: Back In My Arms Again/I'm A Lover (Jan. 1968)

503 Charlie Feathers: I've Been Deceived/Peepin' Eyes (April 1955) *also Flip 503*

504 The Miller Sisters: Someday You Will Pay/You Didn't Think I Would (April 1955) *also Flip 504*

1960 The Rockin' Stockings (feat. Billy Riley): Yulesville U.S.A./Rockin' Old Lang Syne (Nov. 1960) *also Sun 350*

Sun Records compilations: EPs

EPA 101 Johnny Cash (unissued)
EPA 102 Johnny Cash (unissued)
EPA 103 Johnny Cash (unissued)
EPA 104 Jerry Lee Lewis (unissued)
EPA 105 Jerry Lee Lewis (unissued)
EPA 106 Jerry Lee Lewis (unissued)
EPA 107 Jerry Lee Lewis: *The Great Ball Of Fire* (1957)
EPA 108 Jerry Lee Lewis: *Jerry Lee Lewis* (1) (1958)
EPA 109 Jerry Lee Lewis: *Jerry Lee Lewis* (2) (1958)
EPA 110 Jerry Lee Lewis: *Jerry Lee Lewis* (3) (1958)
EPA 111 Johnny Cash: *Sings Hank Williams* (1960)
EPA 112 Johnny Cash: *Country Boy* (1960/61)

EPA 113 Johnny Cash: *I Walk The Line* (1960/61)

EPA 114 Johnny Cash: *His Top Hits* (1960/61)

EPA 115 Carl Perkins: *Blue Suede Shoes* (1961)

EPA 116 Johnny Cash: *Home Of The Blues* (1961?)

EPA 117 Johnny Cash: *So Doggone Lonesome* (1961?)

Sun Records: LPs

LP 1220 *Johnny Cash With His Hot & Blue Guitar* (Oct. 1957)

LP 1225 *Dance Album Of Carl Perkins* (1957) reissued as *Teenbeat – The Best Of . . .* (1961)

LP 1230 *Jerry Lee Lewis* (1958)

LP 1235 *Johnny Cash Sings The Songs That Made Him Famous* (Nov. 1958)

LP 1240 Johnny Cash: *Greatest* (Oct. 1959)

LP 1245 *Johnny Cash Sings Hank Williams And Other Favorite Tunes* (Sep. 1960)

LP 1250 – Various Artists (Lewis, Cash, Perkins, Mann. Rich, Justis): *Million Sellers* (1961) reissued as *Sun's Gold Hits, Volume I*

LP 1255 *Now Here's Johnny Cash* (Oct. 1961)

LP 1260 *Roy Orbison At The Rockhouse* (1961)

LP 1265 *Jerry Lee's Greatest* (1961)

LP 1270 *All Aboard The Blue Train With Johnny Cash* (Nov. 1962)

LP 1275 *Original Sun Sound Of Johnny Cash* (Nov. 1964)

Flip: singles

501 Carl Perkins: Movie Magg/Turn Around (Feb. 1955)

502 Bill Taylor, Clyde Leoppard's Snearly Ranch Boys: Lonely Sweetheart/Bill Taylor and Smokey Jo, Clyde Leoppard's Snearly Ranch Boys: Split Personality (Feb. 1955)

503 Charlie Feathers: I've Been Deceived/Peepin' Eyes (April 1955) *also Sun 503*

504 Miller Sisters: Someday You Will Pay /You Didn't Think I Would (April 1955) *also Sun 504*

227 Rosco Gordon: Just Love Me Baby/Weeping Blues (Sep. 1955) *also Sun 227*

237 Rosco Gordon: The Chicken (Dance With You)/Love For You, Baby (Dec. 1955) *also Sun 237*

Phillips International: singles

3516 Buddy Blake: You Pass Me By/Please Convince Me (Sep. 1957)

3517 Hayden Thompson: Love My Baby/One Broken Heart (Sep. 1957)

3518 Barbara Pittman: Two Young Fools In Love/I'm Getting Better All The Time (Sep. 1957)

3519 Bill Justis and His Orchestra: Raunchy/The Midnite Man (vocal: Roger Fakes & the Spinners) (Sep. 1957)

3520 Johnny Carroll: That's the Way I Love/I'll Wait (Sep. 1957)

3521 Cliff Thomas, Ed & Barbara (Thomas): Treat Me Right/I'm On My Way Home (Jan. 1958)

3522 Bill Justis and His Orchestra: College Man/The Stranger (vocal: the Spinners) (Feb. 1958)

3523 Wayne Powers: My Love Song/Point Of View (March 1958)

3524 Bill Pinky and the Turks, Bill Justis Orchestra: After The Hop/Sally's Got A Sister (March 1958)

3525 Bill Justis and His Orchestra: Wild Rice/Scroungie (March 1958)

3526 Carl McVoy: You Are My Sunshine/Tootsie (June 1958) *originally Hi Records 2001*

3527 Barbara Pittman with the Bill Justis Orchestra: Cold, Cold Heart/Everlasting Love (June 1958)

3528 Ernie Barton: Stairway Of Nowhere/Raining The Blues (June 1958)

3529 Bill Justis Orchestra: Cattywampus/Summer Holiday (June 1958)

3530 Lee Mitchell, the Curley Mooney Trio: The Frog/A Little Blue Bird Told Me (1958)

3531 Cliff Thomas, Ed & Barbara: Sorry I Lied/Leave It To Me (Sep. 1958)

3532 Charlie Rich: Whirlwind/Philadelphia Baby (Oct. 1958)

3533 Mickey Milan, the Bill Justis Orchestra with the Montclairs: Somehow Without You/Mickey Milan, the Bill Justis Orchestra: The Picture (with Chorus) (Sep. 1958)

3534 Ken Cook: Crazy Baby/I Was A Fool (Oct. 1958)

3535 Bill Justis and His Orchestra: Bop Train/String Of Pearls – Cha Hot Cha (Oct. 1958)

3536 Clement Travelers: The Minstrel Show/Three Little Guitars (Feb. 1959)

3537 Jimmy Demopoulos: Hopeless Love/If I Had My Way (Feb. 1959)

3538 Cliff Thomas, Ed & Barbara: I'm The Only One/Tide Wind (March 1959)

3539 Carl Mann: Mona Lisa/Foolish One (March 1959)

3540 Edwin Howard: Forty-'Leven Times/More Pretty Girls Than One (April 1959)

3541 Ernie Barton: Open The Door, Richard/Shut Your Mouth (probably unissued)

3542 Charlie Rich: Rebound/Big Man (June 1959)

3543 Bobbie and the Boys: To Tell The Truth/These Silly Blues (June 1959)

3544 Bill Justis and His Orchestra: Flea Circus/Cloud Nine (July 1959)

3545 Brad Suggs: 706 Union/Low Outside (Sep. 1959)

3546 Carl Mann: Rockin' Love/Pretend (Sep. 1959)

3547 Memphis Bells (featuring Shirley Sisk): The Midnite Whistle/Snow Job (Oct. 1959)

3548 Mack Self: Mad At You/Willie Brown (Oct. 1959)

3549 Brad Suggs Orchestra & Chorus: I Walk The Line/Ooh Wee (Oct. 1959)

3550 Carl Mann: Some Enchanted Evening/I Can't Forget (with the Gene Lowery Chorus) (Dec. 1959)

3551 Sonny Burgess: Sadie's Back In Town/A Kiss Goodnite (Jan. 1960)

3552 Charlie Rich: Lonely Weekends (with the Gene Lowery Chorus)/Everything I Do Is Wrong (Jan. 1960)

3553 Barbara Pittman with the Gene Lowery Singers: The Eleventh Commandment/Handsome Man (April 1960)

3554 Brad Suggs: Cloudy/Partly Cloudy (April 1960)

3555 Carl Mann: South Of The Border (with the Gene Lowery Singers)/I'm Comin' Home (May 1960)

3556 Don Hinton: Jo-Ann (with the Gene Lowery Singers)/Honey Bee (May 1960)

3557 Jeb Stuart with the Gene Lowery Singers: Sunny Side Of The Street/Take A Chance (June 1960)

3558 Eddie Bush with the Gene Lowery Singers: Baby I Don't Care/Vanished (June 1960)

3559 The Hawk (Jerry Lee Lewis): In The Mood/I Get The Blues When It Rains (Aug. 1960)

3560 Charlie Rich with the Gene Lowery Singers: Schooldays/Gonna Be Waitin' (May 1960)

3561 Danny Stewart: Somewhere Along The Line/I'll Change My Ways (Aug. 1960)

3562 Charlie Rich: On My Knees/Stay (Sep. 1960)

3563 Brad Suggs Orchestra and Chorus: My Gypsy/Sam's Tune (Oct. 1960)

3564 Carl Mann: Wayward Wind/Born To Be Bad (Oct. 1960)

3565 Jimmy Louis: Your Fool/Gone And Left Me Blues (Nov. 1960) *originally Nita Records 128*

3566 Charlie Rich: Who Will The Next Fool Be/Caught In The Middle (Feb. 1961)

3567 Jeb Stuart: Dream/Coming Down With The Blues (April 1961)

3568 Nelson Ray: You're Everything/You've Come Home (April 1961)

3569 Carl Mann: If I Could Change You/I Ain't Got No Home (July 1961)

3570 Jean Dee: My Greatest Hurt/Nothing Down (99 Years To Pay) (July 1961)

3571 Brad Suggs Orchestra and Chorus: Elephant Walk/Like, Catchin' Up (Nov. 1961)

3572 Charlie Rich: Just A Little Bit Sweet/It's Too Late (Sep. 1961)

3573 Mikki Wilcox: I Know What It Means/Willing And Waiting (Sep. 1961)

3574 Freddie North: Don't Make Me Cry/Someday She'll Come Along (Oct. 1961)

3575 Jeb Stuart: Betcha Gonna Like It/Little Miss Love (Feb. 1962)

3576 Charlie Rich: Easy Money/Midnight Blues (April 1962)

3577 Thomas Wayne: I've Got It Made/The Quiet Look (April 1962)

3578 Frank Frost: Crawlback/Jelly Roll King (June 1962)

3579 Carl Mann: When I Grow Too Old To Dream/Mountain Dew (June 1962)

3580 Jeb Stuart and the Chippers: I Ain't Never/In Love Again (June 1962)

3581 David Wilkins: Thanks A Lot/There's Something About You (June 1962)

3582 Charlie Rich: Sittin' And Thinkin'/Finally Found Out (Oct. 1962)

3583 David Houston: Sherry's Lips/Miss Brown (1963)
3584 Charlie Rich: There's Another Place I Can't Go/I Need Your Love (1963)
3585 Jeanne Newman: The Boy I Met Today/Thanks A Lot (1963)
3586 The Quintones: Times Sho' G'tting' Ruff/Softie (1963)

Phillips International: LPs

PLP 1950 – *Cloud Nine – Far Out Tunes By Bill Justis and His Orchestra* (1959)
PLP 1955 Graham Forbes and the Trio: *The Martini Set* (1960)
PLP 1960 Carl Mann: *Like Mann!* (1960)
PLP 1965 *Chuck Foster At Hotel Peabody, Overlooking Old Man River* (1960)
PLP 1970 *Lonely Weekends With Charlie Rich* (1960)
PLP 1975 Frank Frost with the Night Hawks: *Hey! Boss Man* (1962)
PLP 1980 *Eddie Bond Sings Greatest Country Gospel Hits* (1962)
PLP 1985 *Rhythm Blues Party With Frank Ballard and the Phillips Reynolds Band* (1962)

SOURCES

Escott, Colin and Hawkins, Martin, *Sun Records: The Discography* (1987)

Hoppula, Pete, www.wangdangdula.com

Leadbitter, Mike and Slaven, Neil, *Blues Records 1943 to 1970, Volume One* (1987)

Leadbitter, Mike, Fancourt, Leslie and Pelletier, Paul, *Blues Records 1943 to 1970, Volume Two* (1994)

Neely, Tim, *Goldmine Price Guide To 45 Rpm Records* (2003)

Neely, Tim, *Goldmine Standard Catalog Of Rhythm & Blues Records* (2002)

Bibliography

Associated Press, 'Sam Phillips Dies', *Hollywood Reporter*, 31 July 2003, p. 31

Balfour, Victoria, 'Surviving Marriage to the Killer', *People Weekly*, 10 July 1989, p. 48

Cannon, Bob, 'Great Balls of Fire!', *Entertainment Weekly*, 20 May 1994, p. 76

Cantor, Louis, *Dewey and Elvis: The Life and Times of a Rock 'n' Roll DJ*, University of Illinois Press, 2005

Cash, Johnny, *Cash: An Autobiography*, HarperCollins, 1997

Clark, Rick, 'Phillips Family Sees Select-O-Hits Endure, Prosper', *Billboard*, 1 February 1997, p. 51

Cocks, Jay, 'Jerry Lee Lewis: The Sun Years', *Time*, 14 March 1983, p. 98

Cogan, Jim and Clark, William, *Temples of Sound: Inside the Great Recording Studios*, Chronicle Books, 2003

Cohodas, Nadine, *Spinning Blues Into Gold: The Chess Brothers and the Legendary Chess Records*, St Martins Press, 2000

Collum, Danny Duncan, 'Keeping It Real', *Sojourners*, February 2004, p. 40

Crouch, Kevin and Tanja, *The Gospel According to Elvis*, Bobcat Books, 2007

Dansby, Andrew, 'Rock Legend Sam Phillips Dies', *Rolling Stone*, 31 July 2003

Davis, Francis, 'The Million Dollar Quartet', *Atlantic Monthly*, October 1994, p. 108

Davis, Hank, 'Barbara Pittman', Rockabilly Hall of Fame, rockabillyhall.com, 1989

DeCurtis, Anthony, 'Is Rock 'n' Roll a White Man's Game?', *Time*, 29 April 1996, p. 78

DeCurtis, Anthony, 'Sam Phillips 1923–2003', *Rolling Stone*, 4 September 2003, p. 75

DeCurtis, Anthony and Henke, James, *Rolling Stone Illustrated History of Rock & Roll: The Definitive History of the Most Important Artists and Their Music*, Random House, 1992

Dickerson, James, *Goin' Back to Memphis: A Century of Blues, Rock 'n' Roll, and Glorious Soul*, Schirmer Books, 1996

Doggett, Peter, *Are You Ready for the Country: Elvis, Dylan, Parsons and the Roots of Country Rock*, Penguin Books, 2001

Dougherty, Steve, 'Present at the Creation', *People Weekly*, 13 October 1997

Dougherty, Steve, 'Blue Suede Schubert', *People Weekly*, 2 February 1998, p. 73

Editors of Rolling Stone, *The Rolling Stone Interviews: Talking with the Legends of Rock & Roll 1967–1980*, St Martins Press, 1981

Escott, Colin with Hawkins, Martin, *Good Rockin' Tonight: Sun Records and the Birth of Rock 'n' Roll*, St Martins Press, 1991

Floyd, John, *Sun Records: An Oral History*, Avon Books, 1998

Galo, Phil, 'Music titan Sam Phillips, first to record Elvis, dies', *Daily Variety*, 1 August 2003, p. 2

Galo, Phil, 'Sam Phillips: The Father of Rock 'n' Roll', *Variety*, 4 August 2003, p. 45

Gates, David, 'Transition: Sam Phillips', *Newsweek*, 11 August 2003, p. 10

Gieske, Tony, 'Legacy of Sun Records', *Hollywood Reporter*, 28 November 2001, p. 7

Gordon, Robert, *It Came From Memphis*, Pocket Books, 1995

Gore, Joe, 'Carl Perkins: 1932–1998', *Guitar Player*, May 1998, p. 31

Greg, Craig and John, 'Fond Farewells', *EQ*, 1 October 2003, p. 12

Guralnick, Peter, *Last Train to Memphis: The Rise of Elvis Presley*, Little Brown & Co., 1994

Guralnick, Peter, *Careless Love: The Unmaking of Elvis Presley*, Little Brown & Co., 1999

Halberstadt, Alex, 'Sam Phillips: The Sun King', salon.com, 2001

Hawkins, Martin, *A Shot in the Dark: The Making of Records in Nashville 1945–1955*, Vanderbilt University Press, 2005

Hay, Carla, 'Sun Records Founder', *Billboard*, 7 October 2000, p. 86

Hicks, Wayne, 'A Talk With the Man Who Found Elvis', *Denver Business Journal*, 16 June 2000, p. 37A

Jerome, Jim, 'Bard of the Lonely', *People Weekly*, 19 December 1988, p. 60

Kaye, Elizabeth, 'The Memphis Blues Again', *Rolling Stone*, 21 November 1985, p. 75

Kaye, Elizabeth, 'The Rolling Stone Interview: Sam Phillips', *Rolling Stone*, 13 February 1986, p. 53

Leslie, Jimmy, 'Good Rockin' Tonight: The Legacy of Sun Records', *Gig*, 1 February 2003, p. 14

'The Man Who Made a King: An Interview With Sam Phillips', *Business Perspectives*, Summer 2002, p. 20

McGee, David, 'The Million Dollar Quartet', *Smithsonian*, November 2001, p. 84

McKeen, William, *Rock And Roll Is Here To Stay: An Anthology*, W.W. Norton & Co., 2000

Morris, Chris and Flippo, Chett, 'Charlie Rich', *Billboard*, 5 August 1995, p. 10

Morris, Chris and Newman, Melinda, 'Sun Records Founder Sam Phillips, 80, Dies', *Billboard*, 9 August 2003, p. 8

Morrison, Craig, *Go Cat Go! Rockabilly Music and Its Makers*, University of Illinois Press, 1996

Nager, Larry, *Memphis Beat: The Lives and Times of America's Musical Crossroads*, St Martins Press, 1998

Nash, Alanna, *The Colonel: The Extraordinary Story of Colonel Tom Parker and Elvis Presley*, Simon & Schuster, 2003

Nash, Alanna, 'The Kingmaker: Sam Phillips 1923–2003', *Entertainment Weekly*, 15 August 2003, p. 16

Olsen, Eric P., 'Founding Father: Sam Phillips and the Birth of Rock and Roll', *World and I*, May 2001, p. 76

Palmer, Robert, *Rock & Roll: An Unruly History*, Harmony Books, 1995

Perkins, Carl and McGee, David, *Go, Cat, Go! The Life and Times of Carl Perkins*, Hyperion, 1996

Phipps, Keith, 'Sam Phillips', theonionavclub.com, 2002

Pond, Steve, 'Roy Orbison: 1936–1988', *Rolling Stone*, 26 January 1989, p. 22

Pond, Steve, 'Roy Orbison', *Rolling Stone*, 15 October 1992, p. 135

Ramzy, Austin, 'Milestones', *Time International*, 11 August 2003, p. 11

Robertshaw, Nicky, *Memphis*, The Globe Pequot Press, 2002

'Sam Phillips', *Guitar Player*, November 2003, p. 23

Seidenberg, Robert, 'Great Balls of Ire: Jerry Lee Lewis', *Entertainment Weekly*, 9 June 1995, p. 30

Stark, John, 'Coming Home: A Rockin' Reunion', *People Weekly*, 14 August 1989, p. 13

Steyn, Mark, 'The Man Who Invented Elvis: Sam Phillips (1923–2003)', *Atlantic Monthly*, October 2003, p. 44

Stuessy, Joe and Lipscomb, Scott, *Rock & Roll: Its History and Stylistic Development*, Prentice Hall, 1999

Sumrall, Harry, *Pioneers of Rock and Roll*, Billboard Books, 1994

'Sun Records Studio', *Sing Out!*, Winter 2004, pp. 9, 198

Turner, Steve, *The Man Called Cash: The Life, Love and Faith of an American Legend*, W Publishing Group, 2004

Young, Charles M., 'The Killer Reloaded', *Rolling Stone*, 19 October 2006, p. 114

Zimmerman, Peter Coats, *Tennessee Music: Its People and Places*, Backbeat Books, 1998

WEBSITES

Blues Foundation, www.blues.org

Country Music Hall of Fame and Museum, www.countrymusichalloffame.com

National Public Radio, www.npr.org

Rock and Roll Hall of Fame + Museum, www.rockhall.com

Rockabilly Hall of Fame, www.rockabilly.com

The Recording Academy, www.grammy.com

Index